Charades

Adrienne McGlinchey and the Donegal Gardaí

Charades

Adrienne McGlinchey and the Donegal Gardaí

Karen McGlinchey

Gill & Macmillan

Gill & Macmillan Ltd
Hume Avenue, Park West, Dublin 12
with associated companies throughout the world
www.gillmacmillan.ie
© Karen McGlinchey 2005
0 7171 3925 5
Design and print origination by Carole Lynch
Printed by Nørhaven Paperback A/S, Denmark

This book is typeset in Goudy 10.5 on 14.5pt.

*The paper used in this book comes from the wood pulp of
managed forests. For every tree felled, at least one tree
is planted, thereby renewing natural resources.*

A CIP catalogue record for this book is available
from the British Library.

1 3 5 4 2

The author and publishers wish to thank the Tribunal of Enquiry
into complaints concerning some Gardaí in the Donegal Division
— the Morris Tribunal — for permission to reproduce various
extracts from the transcripts of evidence.

Dedicated to Mum

Contents

❖

Acknowledgments

The mark of a true friend is one who shares the tough times as much as the good times. This book is dedicated to Liz, our mother, but more than that she is our friend and no one could love more or be prouder than Adrienne or I to have such a friend. Special friends need a special mention because of their support in our pursuit of the truth. Eleanor for always being there. The weeks and months became bearable because of Friday nights with Deirdre and Gerry. The texts from Jacqueline, which amused us and kept us sane. The constant prayers and cards from Daisy, Noelle, Madeline, Frank, Carmel and wee Dolores. The many people who met Adrienne, giving words of encouragement, who sent letters, cards and floral bouquets. A special mention to the Gallagher family and in particular Alfie who understood.

Brian Gallagher, of Gallagher Shatter & Co., our family solicitor for more years than I care to remember. The time and work which Brian devoted in his determination to vindicate Adrienne can only be truly appreciated by our family. The dedication of his staff, especially Emer, is also acknowledged. We are grateful to Anne, who initially came to the Tribunal, then subsequently Will, Kyle and Dylan who are all much wiser people. Bill Shipsey SC for his plain-talking advice to Adrienne. Paul Murray was without doubt the finest barrister at the Tribunal, who fought for his clients with dogged determination and who along with Brian will be forever our friends. Natasha, who Paul is lucky to be married to, and who typed the hundreds of pages, sacrificing family holidays and events on our behalf.

Adrienne and I decided in 2002 to try and put together her story, as it had never been told. Writing this has been a learning curve. Books take time to write. While Fergal Tobin may not have recognised the same award-winning qualities in my writing as I did, we are forever grateful to him for his advice and encouragement, and to Gill & Macmillan for publishing this book.

I knew I had arrived when I told someone to check with my agent. Faith O'Grady kept me on track when I thought everyone else had fallen off.

Those who listen to Vincent Browne will be familiar with the reports from Gerard Cunningham, a freelance journalist who has covered the Tribunal from day one. A special thanks to him for his reporting of the Tribunal, but especially as my source of facts without whose invaluable assistance it would have been impossible to give an accurate record of the events surrounding the charade that took place. To the staff of the Morris Tribunal, we are grateful for the courtesy you always bestowed on us. To Justice Frederick Morris for finding Lennon and McMahon to be corrupt liars.

Finally, this book is a tribute to the Gardaí from the Donegal Division who had the bottle to present themselves and tell the truth.

1

The Early Days

I t was a bright afternoon sometime in 1971. Two men were standing at the back door of the family home telling Karen to pass a message to her father that 'the rebels had left the car'. They had parked it in a spot around the side of the house normally used by her mother. The sisters, Karen (9) and Adrienne (7), were glued to cartoons on television while their parents were away. Karen had seen the men arrive in the car and was surprised when they knocked on the back door. Visitors normally used the front. They left without coming in to wait.

Bernard and Liz McGlinchey were surprised to find the Northern Ireland registered car at the side of the house when they got home. They quizzed their daughters then summoned the Gardaí, who discovered that the car was packed with explosives. It seems the IRA intended to use the car in an attack across the border, but instead abandoned it in Letterkenny for some reason. The army was called in and removed the materials to Finner camp by helicopter for disposal.

Bernard McGlinchey was a Fianna Fáil member of Seanad Éireann, a member of the urban and county councils as well as

1

numerous statutory committees. He had more important things to do and therefore appointed his wife as the liaison between the family and the IRA should they decide to inquire after their car bomb. The younger members of the family, unaware of the serious situation, were dispatched to their grandmother's home. Bernard McGlinchey went to Dublin to engage in legislation for the nation.

Bernard and Elizabeth were married in 1957 and had five children, two sons and three daughters. In 1961 they built and opened a restaurant and snack bar on the Port Road in Letterkenny and called it The Golden Grill. Over the following years they added a dance hall and lounge bars and by 1968 decided to extend to larger premises across the road. Karen and Adrienne were third and fourth in line following their two brothers, growing up in Letterkenny, a medium-sized provincial town, while their younger sister Dolores, fulfilled her only ambition in life to marry at the earliest opportunity and have children. All the children worked in the business from an early age. Money was never handed over to them without having first being earned, a salutary lesson in financial management delivered at every opportunity. Sundays after Mass involved clearing tables and glasses to the kitchen, which was rewarded with the entrance money for the Sunday afternoon matinee to see *Batman*.

Donegal in the late Sixties and early Seventies was a county in turmoil. The city of Derry was a short seventeen miles away and the Troubles were on everyone's lips. The McGlinchey family enjoyed the comforts of a modern home built in 1968. It was a large American-styled house surrounded by three acres of well-manicured lawns tended carefully by a gardener. The family-run business was a success. There were holiday homes, island houses and boats. Later, the four eldest children attended the finest boarding schools, Clongowes Wood College and Mount Anville respectively.

Bernard McGlinchey had political ambitions. He was twenty two when he was first elected to Letterkenny Town Council as a member of the Fianna Fáil party, three years before he married Liz. He went on to become a county councillor in 1958, and Senator in 1961. He was part of the team of Donegal politicians and tally-men who were parachuted into key by-elections to secure Fianna Fáil victories. The late *Irish Times* journalist John Healy christened them the Donegal Mafia. The cadre of Donegal politicians, headed by Neil T Blaney, often met in Letterkenny, leading to a second nickname: the Golden Grill Parliament.

Bernard McGlinchey gave an example of the benefits of his political connections in an interview with a local newspaper to mark his retirement from public life. To get off the ground, the Golden Grill needed a licence. 'The law at the time stated that you had to prove the population of the civil parish had increased by thirty three-and-one-third percent. While the population of Letterkenny had doubled, the area stretched out to Glenswilly and Churchill, and as such my application for the licence would not have been granted.

'My solicitor said he had bad news for me — the law was against me. Well, I said back to him if the law is against me, we'll have to change the law. I was in the Senate at the time and Charlie Haughey was Minister for Justice and finalising the new Liquor Act. He inserted a sub-section which changed the law in the urban area.'

Bernard used to refer jokingly to the amendment, section 19 of the Intoxicating Liquor Act 1962, as 'the McGlinchey Act'.

Politics and Fianna Fáil came first in his life. Long into the night rumbling voices could be heard while strategies and schemes were plotted eagerly by some of the local honchos. He traversed the length and breadth of Ireland electioneering for by-elections, indulging in his passion for the party, and returning home to throw open the doors of the restaurant and bars for the aides who accompanied him.

The swimming pool served as the backdrop in the entertainment of national politicians who visited the McGlinchey home. It was landscaped with lights and trees and shrubs. Locals were invited to garden parties to mingle with the rich and powerful. For many people it was as close as they would come to meeting a government minister or a Taoiseach. Politics was part and parcel of the family life. It was the lifeblood of their father. Rising through the ranks of local politics, it wasn't long before he was propelled onto the national stage, but Bernard McGlinchey was always in the shadow of Neil T Blaney who by 1970 was a government minister and expected to remain so for a considerable time. The home had an open door for callers at all times of the day or night. Deals were done, backs were slapped and favours rendered. Someone's daughter may have needed an interview panel squared or a problematic planning application required the intervention of the Senator. Nothing was impossible. The first principle in politics was in knowing someone who knew someone. Politicians were on a pedestal with priests and doctors. No one enjoyed the respect and reverence afforded to him more than Bernard McGlinchey. He revelled in the simple homage paid to him by the plain folk. He was the mover and the shaker and he knew how to get things done. He knew the right people in the right places and moved in the right circles.

After the Arms Trial, Donegal homes split between the Blaneyite Independents and those who chose to remain loyal to Fianna Fáil. A bitter war was waged between opposing factions. Bernard McGlinchey sensed the prospect of standing as a candidate in a Dáil election.

McGlinchey had been a close friend and confidante of Blaney, a regular caller to the family home in Covehill. Now, with the former minister out of the party, his ambition was to take his Dáil seat. He courted friends within the party hierarchy.

Somehow, the Blaney political machine was getting word of Fianna Fáil plans. The McGlincheys suspected their telephone line was being monitored. A plan was hatched. Bernard McGlinchey and Liam Cunningham TD staged a telephone conversation discussing a fictitious plan to recruit an independent Donegal councillor into Fianna Fáil as an election candidate. When Blaney announced the news of the election days later, a Garda investigation traced the leak back to one of his supporters, James Patrick Hamilton, who worked in a local post office telephone exchange. Bernard McGlinchey called for a public inquiry into the affair in a Senate debate in 1973. 'I have an interest in it because the telephone that was tapped was mine,' he told the House. 'The Minister should investigate this matter because it had been proved in a court of law that my telephone was interfered with, and that while the political manipulator is not a member of this House, he certainly is a member of Dáil Éireann.'

Slowly and surely Bernard McGlinchey built up a power base in Letterkenny of people from all walks of life, all corners and creeds. He became Mr Fixit. He lavished treats on those closest to him. Christmas saw boxes of alcohol being delivered around town in appreciation for various acts of kindness shown to him throughout the year. The banks and clerks were given the selection of spirits and cigarettes, and the Garda station received their delivery in timely fashion, as did various council officials and numerous other organisations.

It wasn't unusual for Bernard to receive a phone call from one of the local Guards informing him of an imminent raid on the bars within minutes. Many of the local Gardaí were originally from the west of Ireland. Some tried to ingratiate themselves to him. Newly arrived from Templemore after completing the mandatory three or six month course, most Guards had never known or experienced the power that came with the uniform. The young recruits, fresh from their Mayo, Galway or Leitrim farms had suddenly, for the first time in their lives, discovered that people were obeying their commands. It was the day of the pint or a transfer and most Guards recognised if they wanted to climb the ladder of success within the force, crossing swords with Bernard McGlinchey was not going to augur well for their promotion prospects. Gardaí moved in concentric circles around him. Those on the outer edge were desperate to become members of the inner sanctum, and at any opportunity which might present itself, the ambitious Guard was ready, poised and waiting to pounce at a moment's notice.

Following the murder of Senator Billy Fox in 1974, the Gardaí provided personal security for public representatives from the border areas. This gave local Gardaí an insight into a lifestyle many of them could only dream about.

The system of Garda promotion involved a process of political recommendation. Behind closed doors, away from eavesdropping colleagues, there was a quiet word here and a whisper there. Cliques of Guards formed to curry favour with influential politicians. A word in the right place from a prominent politician could ensure a promotion — or wreck a career. Many Guards enjoyed the hospitality of Bernard McGlinchey. His generosity became infamous among the uniform section and while some were satisfied with the meals and drinks offered freely, others were enjoying the sumptuous lifestyle on the McGlinchey family island homes and boats.

In the 1970s, McGlinchey dominated the local political scene. It manifested itself in his business dealings, feeding an ego that enjoyed to a great extent the praise and respect heaped upon him by those who sought to reap the benefits of his contact and clout. When the rest of the country was being asked to tighten their belt, people in the corridors of power were shaping the future of Irish business and policing. During the local elections of the late Nineties, Bernard produced a record of the significant number of section four motions he had guided through Donegal County Council against the planners' advice. These motions benefited numerous people, civilians and Gardaí alike.

In the meantime, Bernard focused increasingly on his national career. Along with three other Fianna Fáil TDs — Ray McSharry, Brian Lenihan who later became Tánaiste, and Flor Crowley — he rented a house in Harold's Cross for their use while attending the Oireachtas. Charles J Haughey was and remains a close friend. The evidence of political influence in Garda affairs became most apparent during the phone tapping scandals of the Eighties.

The family worked in the business during school holidays and breaks. A healthy interest in politics was encouraged and the family eagerly engaged in current affairs subjects. Elections were the most exciting events. Canvassing throughout the county and pleading for votes created a better buzz than wondering what to wear to the local youth club dance. Leaflet drops and listening to those in the know about where votes would go and how they would transfer was intriguing. Getting to the count to take part in the tallies was the most gripping part of the election. The utmost concentration was required as lines were drawn and squares crossed using stubby pencils on sheets of tally paper. Watchful eyes stared as votes were being unfolded, gazes dropping immediately to the middle of the page looking for the single one after 'McGlinchey, Bernard'. As count results were announced the shouts and roars from partisan observers were deafening. Hostilities between Fianna Fáil and Independent Fianna Fáil were bitter and often spilled beyond the count centre. The disappointment was unbearable when for the third time he failed to take a Dáil seat. Haughey hauled him back to the Senate but by 1982, after three elections in eighteen months, the Coalition were not going to be so kind and he resigned himself to never attaining the Dáil seat he had for so long aspired to.

In 1983 Adrienne McGlinchey returned from London, where her father had funded her training as a Montessori teacher. She found a temporary position as a special needs teacher, dismissively referred to by Mr Justice Frederick Morris as teaching 'backward children'. To supplement the infrequent shifts she took a second job in the Golden Grill where she had worked prior to going to London.

Rosie O'Donnell, a childhood friend, also worked in the Grill. She lived on the outskirts of town. The road stretches for a couple of miles, with thirty to forty houses dotted along it. Rosie lived with her father and brothers in a charming cottage. The girls regularly visited each others homes. By the side of the cottage was a driveway and small car park serving a large house containing several flats.

Rosie and Adrienne were close friends. They had been on a camping holiday to the South of France together in 1981. Rosie had helped canvass for Adrienne's brother Ray in an election to the Ógra Fianna Fáil national executive. Meanwhile, Karen had trained and qualified as a nurse in the City Hospital in Belfast. By the early Eighties, Bernard McGlinchey had built a large home on the outskirts of Letterkenny in the townland of Bluebanks. The Garda cliques continued to gather huddled in whispered conversation with him in his sitting room.

Political life frequently claims a scalp and as with many political marriages this one fell, after almost twenty years, to the demands of public life. Bernard and Liz had separated in the 1970s. In response to the marital breakdown and as a matter of urgency, the local priests in Letterkenny sent separate church dues envelopes to each of them. In the 1980s, Liz contacted her solicitor, Alan Shatter, to regularise her situation. Mary Robinson had made a name for herself as a barrister and champion of human rights, the voice of women muted through decades of conventionality. She was the barrister who guided the various motions and applications through the High Court in Dublin, until the agreements were reached and signed.

The small town gossip that followed was part of the price of being a politically prominent family. Settlement figures were discussed, disputed and debated behind the shadowy squinting windows of the tittle-tattle classes. The family maintained a dignified silence.

In 1987 Adrienne and Karen decided to go into business together. The nightclubs attracted thousands of young people at weekends, but there were few eating places. They opened a restaurant opposite their father's nightclub, operating eighteen hours a day. During the day in Steers Restaurant they served hearty breakfasts, four-course lunches and steak dinners. To the nightclub crowd they supplied fast food.

Steers did well. Gardaí walking past frequently popped in for a coffee to pass the time. Casual banter was passed between the sisters and the Guards across the counter. Late night conversations were common in the quiet hours.

The sisters' social life dwindled as they worked to repay the large mortgage taken out to start up Steers. To break the monotony, Adrienne got involved in a charity cycle in aid of St Luke's Hospital, an annual trip from Galway to Letterkenny. The event attracted a large contingent from Letterkenny. Adrienne also took part in a Concern cycle around Donegal with members of the staff at Steers. The following year she joined the Foyle Paddlers Canoe Club in Derry with Anne Gallagher, a staff member, and they travelled in Adrienne's car to the various river meetings in the Derry environs.

The sisters built up a regular customer base, although the night shift was often a chaotic scramble as the crowds swelled outside the doors. Occasionally tempers frayed as arguments ignited between customers fuelled by numerous beers. There were Gardaí on duty as patrons exited the nightclub. They were quickly on hand to quell nasty situations.

Sometimes, prisoners in the station required food and the patrol car stopped by with a takeaway order. More often than not, the same Gardaí called in again after the rush hour for a more leisurely coffee. They took it in turns to work night shift and both girls worked Saturday, the busiest night. Steers became a popular rest area for Gardaí on foot patrol as they could easily observe street activity while sipping hot coffee. Sergeant John Costello rarely missed his lunchtime coffee break but it was generally the graveyard shift that attracted Gardaí as they passed by waiting for the end of their tour of duty. People such as Bobby Mullally, Declan Martin, John Rouse, Hugh Smith, Pauric Scanlon and Matt Tolan regularly called as the kitchens were being cleaned. Usually whichever Gardaí were on duty in the area popped in for coffee while the tills were being cashed up.

Members of staff who worked the late shift were always left home after their shift ended at 4 a.m. or later. Rosie O'Donnell's brother Mark was one of those who worked in Steers. Another of the O'Donnell brothers, a plumber, also did occasional work for the restaurant. Adrienne, Karen or Liz McGlinchey could often be seen driving back after leaving staff home in the early hours of the morning.

Most of the suppliers who delivered food to the restaurant were local, but there were a few from out of town. There was the bread man, the milk man, the fish man, the butcher, the vegetable man. One of the suppliers came from across the border. He always had a great sunny disposition and could pass hours chatting and drinking tea. His little business was soon adjusted to leave the restaurant to his last delivery of the day in Letterkenny because he spent so long telling jokes and entertaining Adrienne, and occasionally her mother as well. Adrienne and the supplier had a great relationship and they could often be heard laughing their hearty fill from outside.

In April 1990 the Labour Party and Democratic Left nominated Mary Robinson to stand in the Presidential election. Karen had admired Mrs Robinson since meeting her during her mother's separation settlement, and immediately wrote to her offering assistance and support in Donegal. Karen was invited to become her election agent in Donegal.

The election pitched McGlinchey against McGlinchey — Bernard was the Fianna Fáil election agent for Brian Lenihan. Both McGlincheys avoided the media interest in their own roles and concentrated on getting their candidates elected.

Karen mobilised her troops for the canvass. Posters were collected from Dublin and window space in the restaurant was used to promote the Robinson name. The car was postered and roof speakers rented from a local firm. The increased workload of juggling an election campaign and running a business became an enjoyable challenge. Adrienne managed to take part in a charity cycle with Anne Gallagher during the summer. Bobby Mullally was one of a number of Guards on the cycle. They had been talking about the cycle for weeks, swapping training stories, comparing cures for leg cramp or discussing the up-to-date cycle shorts available on the market.

During the Eighties and early Nineties Donegal became a sanctuary for many families from Northern Ireland trying to escape the Troubles, and for some it was a safe haven from the RUC wanted list. Most of the men became involved in the construction industry and within a short time had settled into the local community. Tradesmen were often difficult to contract and it wasn't unusual for local businesses and individuals to engage contractors originally from Northern Ireland.

After work at Steers, Adrienne often joined Mark or Rosie O'Donnell for tea. A couple of the men who lived nearby knew Mark worked late shifts in the restaurant and occasionally called in and asked for a lift home.

Unknown to Adrienne and Karen, a house near Rosie O'Donnell's cottage was under constant surveillance. Several Letterkenny detectives gave evidence at the Morris Tribunal that the security forces in Northern Ireland wanted some of the occupants, some of whom were builders by trade. 'They were subversives and they were wanted by the security forces in Northern Ireland for subversive activity,' Sgt Jim Leheny recalled.

It came as a shock to Adrienne to discover that Bobby Mullally, whom she knew as a casual acquaintance for years, claimed she had approached him in late 1987 offering information on subversive activity and informed him that the Provisional IRA were using her because she was a member of the McGlinchey family, a daughter of a senator, and as such the Provisional IRA were of the view that her car would not be stopped by the Gardaí.

The suggestion that she said her father, who was very well known in Letterkenny, was a senator in 1987 was somewhat curious, as he had lost his Senate seat in 1982. While Detective Garda Mullally said he was unsure whether he should take this seriously, he claimed she had associations with suspected members of the Provisional IRA. This information was reported to the collator at Letterkenny Garda station who in turn informed Chief Superintendent Ginty, the newly-appointed head of the division, fresh from Tralee. He in turn arranged for the Detective Superintendent, who at that time was John O'Halloran, now retired, to liaise with Detective Garda Mullally on any information coming from Adrienne McGlinchey.

Collator reports came thick and fast. Adrienne was reported no matter where she was. Movements of her car and the family car were noted, but collator reports drew no distinction. In 1990, a collator report noted that the car was sighted in the border town of Lifford, outside the Presidential election count. No mention was made that it had speakers on the roof and election posters for Mary Robinson on the windows. Karen McGlinchey, the Donegal election campaign manager for Mary Robinson, was attending the count in the community centre.

Collator reports are items of questionable intelligence. Any member of the public can make it into a collator report. In some cases, standing on a street corner could warrant an individual being recorded in a little Garda notebook and the collator informed. John Fitzgerald was the Detective Inspector at the time, and said that there was nothing exceptional about being in the collating system. He was not aware that Adrienne was in the system. Chief

Superintendent Sean Ginty said that the Gardaí would be doing well if one-tenth of collator reports led to anything useful.

Mullally was fascinated by the McGlinchey name and family. In his reports he always mentioned the ex-Senator. In 1989 he wrote 'It appears that she hates her father Bernard McGlinchey and goes out of her way to bring discredit to the name.' He also wrote 'I believe that it is very likely that the PIRA are and will use A McGlinchey and especially her vehicle in their activities in the county. I recommend that her car be put on the suspect list on the computer.' Bobby Mullally was promoted to sergeant in June 1990 and still works in Letterkenny Garda station.

Adrienne remained as open and friendly with Mullally as she was with anyone, oblivious to what was being written by Mullally and being reported by him to his superiors. Humouring his pride in his new promotion, she indulged his constant pestering to visit his new posting in the border village of Castlefinn.

Years later, at the Morris Tribunal, Bobby Mullally took the stand and gave evidence. In closed session, he told the Tribunal that Adrienne had approached him in late 1987 offering inform-ation on subversive activity. He said that Adrienne met with him and passed on information. Adrienne was never asked about Bobby Mullally when she gave evidence. He came forward to offer his evidence after she had completed her testimony, and she was not recalled to the stand. He never made a statement to the Carty inquiry or made himself available to be interviewed by Carty. It was mistakenly claimed that he had retired from An Garda Síochána, when in reality he was working on the same floor as the Carty team in Letterkenny Garda station during the time of the inquiry, according to evidence heard at the Morris Tribunal. All of Sergeant Mullally's evidence was heard in closed session. Through her barrister, Adrienne strenuously denied that she had been the source of information. In his report, Judge Morris found that Mullally 'gave his evidence in an honest and accurate manner' and accepted Mullally's evidence that Adrienne supplied him with information.

Detective Garda Michael Jennings is stationed in Letterkenny and has been attached to the detective branch since his appointment in 1978. He didn't believe Adrienne was in the IRA and he didn't see her associating with the IRA people that were in Letterkenny at that time.

The McGlinchey's marital breakdown was common knowledge. After the separation, the girls lived with Liz. Despite this, it was to Bernard that detectives went many years later, telling him that Adrienne was living with members of the Provisional IRA. They assured him that any embarrassing revelations of a family member's association with hardened republican terrorists wanted by the security forces in Northern Ireland would be kept within the closed and hallowed doors of the Garda Síochána, and would never be allowed to leak into the public arena. There would be no blemish on the family name.

A typical example is Detective Garda Joe Foley. 'I knew her father and brother quite well. Around the time [early 1991], I observed her car parked adjacent to the subversives' house outside Letterkenny. I did go to her father and I did say to him that I believed she may have been staying in that house.' Foley admitted that this was despite the fact he knew Rosie and Mark O'Donnell worked in Steers, and he was 'aware that she may on occasions have left some [of] those people home to that household'.

In 1999, Foley told the Carty team that Adrienne was living in the subversives' house. But in 2004 he admitted this was untrue, and that he could not remember seeing Adrienne in the company of any subversives, or going into their house, or leaving their house. He said she was not someone the IRA would use to do runs or errands and would find it 'extremely difficult to believe'.

Despite this, he had gone to Bernard McGlinchey and told him that he 'believed she may have been staying in that house'. Foley said the ex-senator 'was completely non-committal. It didn't surprise him I think in any way'.

Bernard McGlinchey's lack of surprise is hard to understand. Most likely he was already hearing stories from Guards about what his daughter was supposedly up to with the IRA.

Foley was not the only one to talk about the subversives' house. Other detectives like Martin Anderson, Matt Tolan and Hugh Smith also painted a picture of Adrienne somehow connected with the suspect house, although unlike Joe Foley, none of them went to the ex-senator to tell him of their 'concerns'. None of these detectives could remember seeing Adrienne ever actually enter the subversives' house. They saw her driving up there, driving back, they saw her car parked there.

The rolling stone was gathering moss. Mullally's reports had spread throughout the station. Garda Declan Martyn submitted a report stating that he saw her go into the Sinn Féin offices after midnight using a key to the building and exited carrying something. Adrienne flatly denies this. Indeed, she was never a member of Sinn Féin at any time. Sergeant Martyn, as he had then become, was not called to give evidence at the Morris Tribunal, thus denying Adrienne the opportunity to refute this charge in public.

Mullally was not the only one fascinated with the name of Bernard McGlinchey. Two other detectives also gave evidence that they received information from Adrienne. Hugh Smith and Matt Tolan told the Tribunal that Adrienne gave them information. They testified that Adrienne met with them in car parks in Letterkenny, and gave them information.

Detectives Smith and Tolan claimed they stopped Adrienne one night for a traffic offence, although they were in an unmarked vehicle and not in the traffic corps. 'We asked her who she was,' Smith said later. 'She said she was Adrienne McGlinchey, and I think she might have even referred that she was Bernard McGlinchey's daughter. I thought she was trying to use it as an excuse as to why we should even think of stopping her. She was abrupt in that.'

The road was narrow and must be driven with consideration and care, as it was barely the width of a car. On 12 October 1990 Smith and Tolan stopped Adrienne in her car. She knew them from their visits to Steers restaurant and was unconcerned about allowing them to look in her car, assuming she was in breach of some traffic law. One of the detectives removed two regular road maps from the pocket of the car, one of which was a map of Derry city used by her when she was involved in the canoe club. She was driving the family car, which was being used for electioneering. The boot and the rear seats were packed with posters and leaflets.

Smith and Tolan reported that the maps were marked. One was a map of Derry with markings and the other a map of Donegal with a mark on it. After some pressure applied by them, they said she told them that she was given a message on the streets of Strabane outside the Classic bar to deliver to the IRA in the subversives' house, and she also mentioned the name of a man living in the house. They said she gave them the maps to photocopy, and she waited by the car while they drove into Letterkenny, and copied the maps at the station. Smith said she gave three documents. Tolan said she gave two. Smith said Tolan searched the car and found the documentation. Tolan said, 'She appeared to conceal (the documentation) between the seats.' When Smith was asked to explain why this relevant, pertinent and significant detail was not in his statement, he stated, 'there is no particular reason why it's not there, like it's not a detailed statement.'

Tolan claimed that Adrienne used to hang around the Sinn Féin offices, a claim which was refuted by members of Sinn Féin, and that she was a lady who 'hung about a lot, she seemed to have very little else to do' although his partner Smith claimed she worked full-time in the family restaurant. This information was not referred to in any of his statements because 'there is no particular reason, it's not a full detailed statement'.

Once again, blissfully unaware of the reports being submitted by the Gardaí, Adrienne continued about her business to collect Mark O'Donnell, who was going to help her put up election posters around town. Less than a week later, Mary Robinson was conducting a tour of Donegal. An itinerary was put in place by Karen, which involved a parade through town accompanied by the town band, some visits around town, a press conference and an open invitation to a 'meet the candidate' party in the McGlinchey home. It was a resounding success.

At no stage was there ever a question of a security breach where Gardaí felt a member of the household involved in IRA activities compromised the safety of the Presidential candidate. This was three days before one of the most horrific murders perpetrated by the IRA.

Hugh Smith has made what is probably the most astonishing allegation of all. Patsy Gillespie, a Catholic canteen worker from Derry, was strapped to the steering wheel of a van while his family were held hostage. He was forced to drive to the border checkpoint at Coshquin where the bomb detonated, murdering Mr Gillespie and six soldiers, and injuring seventeen civilians in what Bishop

Edward Daly called 'a new threshold of evil' for the IRA.

Smith said that he was waiting outside a shop on Lower Main Street on the evening of the Coshquin attack, when Adrienne approached him. He said she gasped in horror that she didn't know the maps he had taken from her two weeks previously had anything to do with the Coshquin bomb. He said she told him: 'I didn't know there was a connection between the map and the bomb, I swear to God, I didn't know it.' Smith said he told her to keep walking and not to worry about it.

The detective said no one else witnessed this exchange. He was in the company of a member of the Technical Bureau from Dublin, but this Garda was inside a shop buying cigarettes when he met Adrienne. He said he had known this Dublin Garda for eight years, but he could not remember his name.

Smith's partner in Detective Unit B, Detective Garda Matt Tolan, was in Burt, and Smith said he told him what Adrienne said the next day. He also said he told Detective Sergeant Sylvie Henry and the Dublin Garda from the Technical Bureau about the conversation. What he did not do was report the conversation in writing. He did not mention it to the Carty team. He did not mention it to the Tribunal investigators when they interviewed him. The first mention on the record seems to be his evidence at the Morris Tribunal. Having made the allegation, he then backed away from it, telling the chairman that he 'felt when she said that she was putting two and two together but she didn't know from any other source that the map and the bomb was connected, she was assuming that'.

Smith went on to say that he met with Adrienne two weeks later, and she gave him photographs of the housing estate in Derry where Patsy Gillespie had lived.

Tolan said that Smith told him that during the conversation about Coshquin with Adrienne on the street, she said she would give him photographs. Smith was recalled to the stand about this, but was adamant that 'there was no mention of photographs, it was just a quick conversation, that was it'.

'It was at a subsequent meeting that the documents came up, but weren't produced,' he continued. This meeting was a couple of weeks later. Smith said that when he got the photographs, which contained directions to Mr Gillespie's home, he kept copies and handed the originals in to his superior, Detective Superintendent John McLoughlin. Despite a search by the Garda authorities, the original photographs could not be located.

Smith and Tolan said they handed in the photographs within two or three weeks of the Coshquin atrocity. Detective Sergeant Sylvie Henry said this was his recollection too. Yet McLoughlin said he didn't receive the photographs until January of the following year. In his journal, he described the photographs as 'maps'.

Seven people were arrested in connection with the Coshquin bombing, but not Adrienne McGlinchey, the one person who, according to Smith, had any knowledge of the attack. 'The Tribunal finds it hard to find any excuse for Detective Garda Smith, Detective Sergeant Henry, and especially Chief Superintendent John McLoughlin's failure to react to the knowledge that they had supposedly received,' Justice Morris said in his report. 'One of the worst terrorist outrages of these troubled years had occurred hours earlier. Someone who might reasonably have been believed to have been a courier for the perpetrators was known to them. She, it would appear, on their case, had delivered papers to a third party which possibly related to the event. Yet, no steps were taken to engage with Ms McGlinchey in relation to the matter. The Tribunal listened carefully for any justification in their answers to counsel's questions as to their lack of response. None was forthcoming. As the senior officer, Chief Superintendent McLoughlin's attitude to this matter was inexplicable and is regarded by the Tribunal as negligent.'

Adrienne was not recalled to the stand to answer questions about the evidence of Mullally, Smith and Tolan. Through her barrister Paul Murray, she told the Tribunal that she spoke to the detectives openly in Steers restaurant when they called in for a late night coffee, passing on the tall stories she had heard. The only maps she knew anything about were canoe maps from her involvement with the Foyle Paddlers, taken from her one night by Smith and Tolan.

Justice Morris decided that the maps only seemed significant with the benefit of hindsight. Despite the contradictions in their evidence, the judge decided that on the balance of probabilities he preferred the evidence of Detective Sergeant Sylvie Henry, Hugh Smith and Matt Tolan about the maps and photographs.

Following this incident, Smith and Tolan claimed she offered herself as an informant and they would regularly meet in a discreet area of the Court House car park. Tolan said the Court House car park could hold a couple of hundred cars, but the reality is that there are only fifty car spaces there. Tolan said if there was anybody present, she walked away and returned, or if a car came into the car park she waited until those people left and then approached them. They said she would first meet them in the car park of the Golden Grill, her father's nightclub opposite Steers restaurant. Tolan said she would not sit in the car. Smith said she would get into the car. They said they had upwards of thirty meetings with her but neither detective had a single scrap of paper with a note or memo to offer of any meeting. Tolan claimed she would loiter around the restaurant outside and when she saw their car approach she would gesture at them and they took this as a sign she wished to meet with them. In his closing submission for Adrienne, Paul Murray noted the remarkable coincidence that statements made by Tolan and Smith 'were for all intents and purposes identical'.

Hugh Smith was promoted to sergeant in 1991. Members of the Carty team stayed at his sizeable B & B while investigating Garda corruption in Donegal.

Adrienne never denied speaking to Smith and Tolan. Most of her days were taken up working hard during busy lunch hours and restocking and ordering new supplies. One of the suppliers had stirred up a bit of interest from local Gardaí, particularly Tolan who was keen to know what he was saying. Casual questions were asked about him. What was he saying? Where was he going?

It is possible that there was a degree of jealousy among some of the Gardaí at the easygoing relationship Adrienne enjoyed with the supplier. She had spurned the advances of one married detective. The supplier had very few contacts in Donegal and Adrienne offered to help him expand his business in the county. Occasionally after her shift ended she accompanied him to various hoteliers whom she knew to encourage new orders for his fledgling business. One day in January 1991, during a delivery, the supplier asked Adrienne if the flat at the upper rear portion of the building was available to rent as he had some friends who were looking for accommodation. He had been making a delivery in town when he met some friends who asked him if he knew where they could rent a flat. Not familiar with the property market he remembered that Adrienne was working and she would be the most likely person to know of availability.

The investigators from the Morris Tribunal interviewed the

supplier. He was not called to give his evidence, which would have greatly assisted the Tribunal.

Adrienne was unable to let the flat without first discussing it with Karen or her mother. They were on holiday in Hawaii and Karen was not due back for another couple of weeks. After the supplier left, Tolan came in and asked about the conversation. Tolan has since denied he convinced her to permit them to stay. She then called Hawaii and asked about the letting of the back flat to the friends of the supplier.

It soon became apparent there were strange activities occurring in the house opposite the restaurant. The large three-storey building dominated the landscape across the road. It was the movements behind one of the upper windows which had attracted the interest and attention of their neighbours opposite. Occasionally a flash would be reflected on the cross bar of the vertical blinds on the restaurant windows, which in turn was reflected in the floor to ceiling mirrors in the restaurant. Unknown to Adrienne, and following reports from Tolan, Gardaí arranged surveillance of the premises, and particularly of the back flat. After this, Tolan was given the cold shoulder by Adrienne.

The students who lived in a house next to the restaurant had noticed the presence of the National Surveillance Unit. Kevin Carty, who as assistant commissioner headed up the inquiry into Garda corruption in Donegal, was a member of the surveillance unit. The tenant in the first floor over the restaurant was approached by local Gardaí and asked if he would allow a listening device through to the flat at the rear. He refused and his friend brought the Garda request to the attention of Adrienne. He too noted the surveillance being carried out from across the road.

It seemed everyone in the area was aware of the presence of the surveillance unit and all the nearest neighbours were noting their movements with bemused intrigue. The residents of the Port Road were watching the watchers. Meanwhile the tenants in the back flat went about their quest for employment in Letterkenny, innocent of the interest they had generated. When Karen returned from her holiday she suggested that they find alternative accommodation.

2

Wrong Place, Wrong Time

The President was coming to lunch! That had been the mantra for weeks. Mrs Robinson was going to spend an hour with friends, have a bite to eat, and get a break from the business she was conducting in town. It was July 1991 and Karen had issued the invitation to the President when she learned of Mrs Robinson's planned visit to Letterkenny.

The success of the election campaign at the end of 1990 had been an inspiration to Mná Tír Chonaill. Mrs Robinson had been to their home as a candidate and indeed Karen and her mother had been to the Robinson home. The pride they felt that their President was going to honour them with a visit was overwhelming. Preparations for the visit began in earnest. Nothing was going to be left to chance. The house was painted and repairs carried out. The lawns were tended to perfection. No one expected Mrs Robinson to scrutinise every nook and cranny of their home or even notice paint or cracks, but they wanted to present their home in pristine condition.

A lot of people from Northern Ireland worked in the building trade in Donegal in the early 1990s, including the contractors doing up the McGlinchey home for the Presidential visit. With just over a week to go, the builders had abandoned scaffolding at the front of the house. Karen, Adrienne and Mrs McGlinchey had been invited to a garden party in Áras an Uachtaráin on Saturday 6 July 1991. Before leaving Letterkenny, a message was sent to have the scaffolding removed while they were away. They left Letterkenny on Friday afternoon, and arrived home on Sunday evening. The scaffolding was still there.

In the early hours of Monday morning, as the McGlincheys slept after their hectic weekend, several miles away a lorry primed with explosives was being prepared to cross the border.

The 'Wauchopes bomb' was intended to be a replica of the Coshquin bomb in terms of the carnage it would cause. The Wauchopes were a business family in Ballindrait, and the bomb got its name because it was found near their premises. Their young neighbours had been to a disco earlier in the night and became suspicious on their return home when they saw lights on in their neighbour's sheds. Concerned, they decided to investigate and foiled the preparation of a massive lorry bomb destined for Northern Ireland. They had caught the culprits in the act. It was the early hours of 8 July 1991. By the time Gardaí arrived, those involved had made good their escape. Gardaí mounted surveillance on known republican houses and suspects in an effort to apprehend the perpetrators.

At the Morris Tribunal, Detective Matt Tolan said he received a phone call from Adrienne McGlinchey to his ex-directory phone line at home that weekend, on the evening of Saturday 6 July 1991, telling him 'something big' was going to happen the following Monday. Detective Tolan filed no report of this information in 1991. He did not tell the Carty team when they came to Donegal in 1999. He did not mention it when investigators interviewed him for the Morris Tribunal. It was not until he took the stand at the Morris Tribunal that he first mentioned this conversation.

At the time, Adrienne was attending the garden party at the home of President Robinson in the Phoenix Park in Dublin. Mr Justice Morris decided that Adrienne had no knowledge of the 'Wauchopes bomb', but that she had called Detective Tolan, and it was 'pure coincidence' that there was a find the following Monday. This is the only time the detective said she ever called him at his unlisted home number.

Adrienne had worked the late shift after returning from Dublin. Her mother Liz was leaving for Dublin again and asked her to see about getting the scaffolding removed.

After breakfast, Adrienne and one of the part-time workers in Steers, Yvonne Devine, had planned to go training for a charity cycle, and were dressed in their cycling gear. Adrienne collected Yvonne Devine from her home and they drove to the builders to remind them again to remove the scaffolding. They missed the builder, and turned round to go back to town.

What Adrienne did not know was that another man living in the area was believed by local detectives to be a senior IRA figure.

It was 7.45 a.m. As she drove back into Letterkenny town centre, Adrienne saw a Garda car behind her, its headlights flashing. She pulled over outside the community centre. As the Guards got out, she recognised them as Martin Leonard and PJ Thornton.

'We were notified by communications centre in Letterkenny to check suspect houses in the area,' Garda PJ Thornton told the Tribunal years later. 'On our way up we met Adrienne McGlinchey. We met her car coming down, we turned the patrol car and followed them, and we arrested both of them on Pearse Road, Letterkenny.'

The Guards asked Adrienne where she had been, and she explained that she had been to the home of a builder to have some scaffolding removed. She was shocked when they said they were arresting the two of them under Section 30 of the Offences Against the State Act.

Records and interview notes relating to Adrienne's first arrest are missing. 'She was arrested in Letterkenny that morning under Section 30 of the Offences Against the State Act of 1939, having been found commuting between the flats at Crievesmith and the home of the then officer in command of the Red Tyrone Brigade PIRA,' according to Detective Matt Tolan. This was the first and only mention of her commuting to the Red Tyrone Brigade of the IRA.

Yet the arresting Garda, Martin Leonard, said the arrest was under the Firearms Act, as did a schedule of arrests provided to the Court of Criminal Appeal years later by the Director of Public Prosecutions. Judge Morris says the arrest was under Section 30. The discrepancy was not explored in his report.

When Garda Martin Leonard arrested Adrienne, he told her she would be interviewed after giving her details on arrival at Letterkenny Garda station. Two detectives introduced themselves as Noel McMahon and Danny Kelly and said they were from Buncrana. It was a day of firsts. It was the first time she was arrested, the first time she was ever inside a Garda station cell, and the first time she ever met Detective Garda Noel McMahon.

For a long time she thought something had happened to President Robinson. Most of the questions were about her visit to Áras an Uachtaráin. The questions seemed idiotic, as when she was asked had she drawn blueprints of the president's home and given them to anyone. Most of the time though, the two Guards engaged in general conversation. Adrienne had no links to any organisation and there was nothing she could contribute. Tired from lack of sleep and a hectic weekend, she sat waiting to be allowed home.

'She would talk about everything and everything except the reason she was arrested for,' Danny Kelly said. 'She knew nothing about that.'

As 3 p.m. approached she told the officers her shift would soon start and she needed to go home to change for work and started to leave the room. The detectives looked amused as they informed her she would not be leaving the station for some time. McMahon's version of this event was farcical. He claimed she climbed out the window of the interview room while in the presence of two detectives — who one would assume were well trained in the art of physical restraint — and attempted to scale a nine-foot-high fence. He went on to say that they had to rush out of the room and just got her before she escaped. Kelly made no reference to the incident.

IRA man Pearse McCauley is currently serving a sentence for the manslaughter of Garda Jerry McCabe. Days before, he had escaped from Brixton prison in London. McCauley is a half brother of Yvonne Devine's mother. Yvonne was questioned about his escape. The Guards were saying a shoe containing a gun had been posted from Letterkenny to Brixton prison for him.

Garda Martin Leonard later claimed, despite all the evidence to the contrary, that Adrienne was released within three hours of her arrest, which he felt proved she was protected by the Gardaí. He said he was on patrol around 10 a.m. when he received a message notifying him of the release. He could not recall how or from whom he received the message.

Leonard said his recollection was that Mary Robinson ('who went on to become President') had intervened. He said Mary

Robinson and Karen McGlinchey were in the Labour Party at the time. Leonard said he wasn't surprised because 'when someone is in political rings you're not surprised if something happens, when a phone call is made'.

Earlier, Leonard had said that 'representation was made by Karen McGlinchey to the Labour Party and in turn they communicated a concern to somebody in the Guards, and the reason given was that this communication justified the early release.'

Mary Robinson was not a member of the Labour Party in 1991. She was already President of Ireland and a person of the highest integrity and much respected by the McGlinchey family. Karen McGlinchey was not a member of the Labour Party in 1991 and made no attempt to contact the President or indeed the Labour Party to secure the early release of her sister. Despite having inaccuracies pointed out, Leonard remained adamant that the early release was something to do with the Labour Party, Mary Robinson and Karen McGlinchey.

Adrienne and Yvonne Devine were brought to the cells. Adrienne heard someone being brought into the cell between them. As the girls called out to each other the man in the middle cell asked them to identify themselves and the reason for their detention. Adrienne could hear the guffaws from his cell when she told him. She would spend almost fourteen hours in custody. No notes from her interviews with the two detectives survive.

Karen McGlinchey wondered what had happened to her sister when she didn't arrive for her shift at 3 p.m. They had never been strict with each other's times but if one was going to be delayed she usually called to say she would be late. As the hours ticked by, Karen's concern began to grow. She rang the hospital and the Garda station fearing Adrienne had been involved in an accident. Eventually she found out that Adrienne was in the station.

Breathless after running to the station, she was met in the front office by Detective Inspector John Fitzgerald. He brought her through to go to his office but she was so distraught at the notion of Adrienne being arrested that she broke down in tears. Asked if she had access to a solicitor, Fitzgerald said there was no need for one as she was going to be released without charge. Karen told him she would return with her mother, who was due back from Dublin.

His desk was large and uncluttered, the room cool and bright. Fitzgerald brought the two women through directly from the public office. He was pleasant and offered them coffee as they took the proffered seats. He was in his fifties, his once blond hair turning grey. He clasped his hands together.

'Adrienne was arrested this morning,' Detective Inspector John Fitzgerald told the two women. 'She was leaving an area which has been under surveillance by the Gardaí as there are known terrorist subversives living there.

'Members of the Provisional IRA were disturbed during the night putting together a lorry bomb and all known houses of suspects are being watched.'

'She was there because of me,' Mrs McGlinchey interrupted. 'She was to get the builders to take down the scaffolding in front of our house.'

'Adrienne was arrested leaving a house under Garda surveillance,' the detective inspector continued. 'She was arrested along with another female and a man. These people have been using her for quite a while to transport them to different places.'

Unknown to Karen or her mother, a report was furnished in December 1990 to the Crime & Security branch at Garda headquarters in Dublin and signed by Detective Inspector John Fitzgerald which said that Adrienne was 'a close associate of the PIRA members living in flats at Crievesmith at Letterkenny. She is the type that would do "runs" for the PIRA and as a result of information received from other sources regarding her activities, I am satisfied that she is doing "runs" for the PIRA.'

Fitzgerald smiled kindly at Liz and Karen. 'Everyone is tired,' he said. 'When you all get home, put on the kettle and have a nice cup of tea and say nothing. Stop at the shop and buy a packet of biscuits. Don't even bother mentioning this whole thing to Adrienne at all,' he advised them. 'It's over and done with. She's had a long day too. She will just need to forget about it.'

They waited calmly while she was fingerprinted before her release. There was an unreal sense of calm during the journey home with Adrienne. Everyone acted as if nothing had happened, just as they had been programmed. They drove home on auto-matic pilot, even stopping to buy a packet of Goldgrain biscuits as Fitzgerald had suggested.

Adrienne was tired. She had worked late, and spent most of the day in Garda cells and interview rooms. Karen and Liz still had Fitzgerald's words in their ears: 'These people have been using her for quite a while to transport them to different places.' In their heart of hearts they knew that the detente would never last. Tempers were boiling before the kettle and soon accusations and denials were being shouted, and it was inevitable that the house would soon shudder to the slamming of the front door.

Adrienne had strenuously denied that anyone had been in the car with her, other than Yvonne. 'I never transported anyone or delivered messages for anyone,' she told them. 'How could you be told such nonsense?' She was furious, but there was no point in trying to reason with her mother or her sister until they had calmed down. She walked out of the house.

Adrienne went to the Devine home. Yvonne's mother apolo-gised, believing the arrests were because of Pearse McCauley's escape. Adrienne spent the night in the flat over the restaurant.

Various officers commented on Adrienne's alleged involvement at that time with subversives. Detective Sergeant Jim Leheny, an officer of considerable experience of dealing with subversives, when asked many years later about allegations being made against Adrienne in relation to her being a member of the Provisional IRA, or an informer on the Provisional IRA, stated that it would be completely contrary to her family background. He said it would be totally out of character for her to get involved in an illegal or terrorist organisation.

Superintendent Kevin Lennon recalled that in 1991 he was a sergeant attached to the divisional traffic corps in Letterkenny. He said, 'I knew very little about her actually, other than when you would be out on patrol every time she'd move around the border there would be a "red alert" out on the radio system. An alert to say keep an eye out for a blond girl, at such a place, see what she's at.'

3

Blackmail

Adrienne had a sleepless night, tossing and turning. Her humour had not improved by morning and the stinging words still rang in her ears.

She decided to take a few days away with Yvonne Devine until the dust settled and Yvonne's mother suggested that they go to Bundoran. They settled on Buncrana.

Adrienne and Karen were joint signatories on a company account for the restaurant. The sisters occasionally used the account if they needed funds at short notice. Adrienne used the cash to pay for a B & B.

Adrienne had never had such a row with her family before. She felt guilty walking away on the busiest weekend of the year while everyone in the restaurant was working furiously, but she felt justified because of the row. She had always been the pacifist in the family, giving in to arguments when she could have held out and been more stubborn. But her nature was agreeable and considerate. Her easy tolerance in the face of adversity very often steered the business on an even keel during turbulent times. Spontaneity was not one of her attributes. She had to be persuaded to go on holiday or introduce new regimes in the restaurant, so when she decided to extend her stay in Buncrana and fund the holiday with a chequebook, dormant from her student days and containing less than a dozen cheques, it was an unusually impulsive decision seldom practised by her.

Passing a camping shop she eyed a tent in the window. By the end of the day, herself and Yvonne had found a field and pitched their new home, a four-man tent with pull-out canopy.

It was the release she had denied herself for years. All sense of responsibility vanished. No thought of work, staff or commitments bothered her. She felt deep hurt and a real sense of loneliness following the row with her mother and sister. She intended to make the most of the break.

Adrienne rarely drank alcohol. She had been hospitalised the previous April with a bleeding ulcer and as a result she had to be careful of the food and drink she consumed. But freed from the responsibilities of work, she cut loose on holidays. She brought herself to the notice of the local law within four days, and on 13 July 1991 she was arrested and brought to the station to sleep off the excesses of alcohol.

That night Adrienne heard screams coming from Yvonne's cell. The following morning Noel McMahon drove her back to the tent and told her Yvonne had gone home to Letterkenny. Yvonne returned to Buncrana within hours. She had visited her doctor in Letterkenny and told him she had been assaulted in Buncrana Garda station. Her doctor recorded the conversation in Yvonne's medical record.

Adrienne had exhausted her cheques, and sent Yvonne into the Bank of Ireland in Letterkenny. Yvonne requested a company chequebook for the restaurant. The teller asked if she required a standard business chequebook containing 50 cheques, or a larger 250-cheque book. She accepted the latter.

On 9 August 1991 Adrienne was found slumped asleep in a telephone box and brought to the Garda station. She was released the following morning. Her spending was out of control and her family were concerned. Detective Inspector John J Fitzgerald and Detective Matt Tolan visited Karen and Liz in Letterkenny. Fitzgerald told them Adrienne was living in a field in Buncrana. He said the Guards entered the tent without a search warrant and had suggested Adrienne was dealing drugs. He warned them not to disturb anything in the tent, but to locate and identify the tablets in question.

Locating the field was easy. There was one obvious landmark: a great big pink tent. New clothes littered the tent. The only drugs Karen saw were packets of Dramamine travel pills. Karen and Liz McGlinchey stuffed the tent into the boot of the car and returned to Letterkenny.

Undeterred by their homeless status, Adrienne and Yvonne searched the newspapers and found a flat for rent in the Crescent. A few cheques provided a deposit and soon they were living in the flat. It was a quiet, well-maintained, secluded area of residential private dwellings in an ideal location just off the main Letterkenny road, within minutes walking distance of the town centre of Buncrana.

John Mackey from Clonmany, a village north of Buncrana on the Inishowen peninsula, was their landlord. Within days, a two-bedroomed flat upstairs became available and the girls moved in. It was the middle flat of the three-storey building, with one entrance at the gable end, and the last in a row of red brick Victorian houses.

Adrienne was cashing cheques around the county, and Gardaí were telling her family that she was involved with paramilitaries. They claimed she was living with IRA members in Buncrana.

Karen and her mother were also told Adrienne was funding the local IRA with the cheques, and that it was her intention to have her share of the business liquidated.

Karen got the address from Letterkenny Gardaí and went to the IRA house, demanding to speak to her sister. Not surprisingly, the man who answered the door expressed bewilderment and told her he had never heard of Adrienne McGlinchey. He tried to shut the door but Karen wedged her foot in the door space, all the while threatening legal action for fraud. It was a less than satisfactory encounter.

The Guards in Buncrana required a statement of complaint from a company director, which would enable them to recover the chequebook. Karen and Liz were deeply distressed and worried. They sought the advice of their solicitor and he engaged a barrister. Sergeant Seamus Harron later confirmed to Tribunal investigators that a statement had been taken from Karen, as did Detective Michael Jennings, but the Garda statement is missing from Garda records in Letterkenny station.

One evening, a patrol car pulled in by Adrienne's flat. Two Letterkenny Gardaí emerged and knocked on the door of the unoccupied ground floor flat. The girls watched and waited, realising the Guards didn't know the correct address. Eventually they drove off. Adrienne had feared this day would come. She had persistently written cheques. A short while later they heard heavy knocking from below. This time it was Yvonne's mother and, reluctant to have a confrontation with the Guards in front of her mother, if and when they returned, they hid behind the curtain.

They watched as Mrs Devine left. The callers missed each other and a relay of knocking, waiting and leaving continued until one of the locals indicated to the Guards that the girls were in the upper flat. They watched, horrified, as all three heads were raised in their direction. The finger slowly lifted until it pointed directly at them. Both of them bolted out the door and raced across St Oran's Road to the grounds of the Mercy Convent, which provided a great vantage point to continue viewing proceedings without being detected.

The statue of the Blessed Virgin watched dispassionately. Yvonne had forgotten her cigarettes, and headed up the street to the shop. Hiding in the shrubbery, Adrienne kept watch. The Guards were at the flat, noses to the glass door, knocking loudly. She could see them muttering to themselves. Eventually, they moved to the front of the building.

It was chilly. A cyclist passed and she recognised him as a local Guard. The gods seemed to conspire against her. A car entered the convent grounds, and she froze as it drove towards her hideaway. Adrienne recognised the driver — Noel McMahon, the detective who had interviewed her the first time she was arrested. The next thirty seconds changed her life forever.

McMahon demanded to know why she was concealing herself in the shrubbery. She explained briefly that the Letterkenny Guards were at the flat. McMahon told her to sit tight for about twenty minutes before returning to the flat. He said he would get rid of the Guards, but asked her to come back to the same place the following evening. Relieved at the unexpected stay of execution, she readily agreed.

The next evening, she was in the same place when McMahon arrived. The greatest charade in the history of the Irish police force began with Adrienne waiting in the convent shrubbery, while the statue of Mary looked on. Adrienne's journey would see her passed off as the most important IRA informer An Garda Síochána had ever encountered.

McMahon was not alone. His partner Detective Garda Danny

Kelly went with him. The threesome headed north to a hotel in Ballyliffen. Kelly bought a round of drinks. He spotted someone he knew and went to have a chat, leaving Adrienne and Noel McMahon to their drinks.

Adrienne confided her troubles, the row after her arrest, the trouble surrounding the cheques. He told her about his life.

Born in Clones, Co. Monaghan, Noel McMahon joined An Garda Síochána in January 1978 and arrived in Buncrana after his six months training in Templemore Garda College. In 1980 he was transferred as a detective in the Special Detective Unit in Dublin Castle and within months married Sheenagh O'Doherty, a native of Buncrana. Sheenagh missed home, and in 1986 they transferred back to Donegal, first to Letterkenny, then Buncrana. They set up home there, but tragedy visited them in 1990 when their son Ross died in infancy.

The baby's grave was next to a Sinn Féin memorial. His disgust at the annual invasion and destruction of his son's burial place by the hordes of supporters celebrating militant republicanism was palpable. His pain was raw.

Noel McMahon loved being a detective. He didn't seek promotion or want a position of authority. His colleagues viewed him as an energetic, active police officer. But there was another side and it was a side that only a few people knew anything about. Among those was his wife, who over the years was subjected to enormous cruelty. Adrienne, too, was about to experience both sides of the McMahon coin.

This is a story of what ifs. What if she had not been arrested, what if there had not been a family row, what if she had not used the chequebook. What if, what if, what if.

McMahon hadn't much money with him and Danny Kelly had been buying the rounds. When Kelly returned to their table he remarked that Adrienne hadn't bought any drink at all. Reaching into her back pocket, she withdrew a bunch of cheques, asking if one would be accepted in the hotel. Dismayed, McMahon took them from her. Later, as they walked back to the car, he pulled her to one side and told her to meet him again the following evening —but not to mention the meeting to Danny Kelly.

The next evening, Adrienne didn't have to wait long. McMahon said they would take a spin. As the car approached a picturesque area frequented by golfers and sailboarders, he swung the car up a small side road and pulled to a stop. The drive was pleasant and McMahon was good company, laughing and joking. She felt she had found a friend she could talk to about her problems. Her life had nose-dived since her arrest in July.

A silence fell between them. McMahon turned to face her.

'I need information about your associates in the republican movement,' he told her bluntly.

Stunned, she assured him she knew nothing. But he became more insistent.

'I can't help you with the cheques unless you have something to give me in return,' he said. 'Danny Kelly was livid last night when you pulled that stunt with the cheques. He wants you handed over to the Letterkenny Guards.'

She could feel the tears welling up, frustration and panic closing in. McMahon was suddenly a different person. Angry. Irate. Cross. Demanding co-operation. She felt close to tears. He became calm and thoughtful again. Eventually, he spoke.

'Look, I know you've sacrificed your home, your family. You're in a bad spot because of the cheques. You need to understand, Karen has made a statement. There will be a prosecution, maybe a jail sentence. Do you want to end up in Limerick?' Limerick Prison was where female prisoners were usually incarcerated.

'I'm trying to help you, but Kelly will be a problem unless I can convince him you're giving us information on the local Provos.'

He explained the plan. He would give her information from Garda files. She would give it to Kelly. The most valuable asset a border detective could find was information on the IRA. If she could convince Kelly she had information, he wouldn't worry about a few cheques. The alternative was Limerick Prison.

She agreed to meet McMahon and Danny Kelly the following evening. He gave her a name, and told her to tell Kelly this person had stayed in a local Provo safe house the previous night. This would impress Kelly. Adrienne's anguish was acute. There was no risk for McMahon in the plan. No one would believe her even if she marched straight to the superintendent's office.

The next night, Adrienne waited as agreed. She was nervous. She worried that Danny Kelly would see through the pretence. But Noel McMahon was a good actor. He took the information as though completely surprised, glanced at his partner and nodded. As she walked back to the flat she gulped a great lungful of air. She had passed it off.

McMahon arranged to meet her again. He was at ease. 'Kelly was impressed,' he told her. 'He won't report you. You just have to pass on anything you hear about the Provos.'

'Don't worry, I'll give you a few bits to pass on,' he continued. 'It's the only way to keep Kelly on board.'

In the weeks that followed, passing information from Noel McMahon to Danny Kelly became routine. McMahon always acted as though hearing it for the first time. Afterwards, he would meet her alone and give an assessment of how she performed.

Spending her days in the back of a Garda car, passing snippets between the two detectives was not how Adrienne wanted to spend her life, but McMahon had other plans. He told her Danny was getting suspicious. 'He's been watching you, but he has never seen you near any Provos. Not even on the fringe with sympathisers. We need more.'

McMahon gave her the times of the local Garda patrols. She was to make sure she was seen walking from the safe house at Swilly Terrace. To add credibility, she was to have Yvonne accompany her. Telling Yvonne that this was the only way she could avoid prosecution, the two girls started a nightly jaunt to the safe house. When they spotted the Garda car, they raced away. Their odd behaviour raised eyebrows in Buncrana station. Back in Letterkenny, the Guards kept in contact with Adrienne's family. Reports of her working for the IRA were greeted with disbelief, but the Gardaí were persuasive.

Adrienne and Yvonne got jobs in Jay Bees textile factory in Carndonagh. McMahon did not share Adrienne's enthusiasm for her new career despite her eagerness to set about clearing her debt. Jay Bees specialised in the manufacture of ladies blouses. Delighted at securing employment and with no previous experience as a machinist, she set about her new job with great vigour. Carndonagh, a small village approximately ten miles from Buncrana, had no direct transport between the towns early in the morning, so Adrienne and Yvonne resorted to the daily trudge of hiking to work.

A prosecution was still hanging over her head but the guillotine would not come down unless Danny Kelly executed his threat to contact the Letterkenny Guards.

Noel McMahon gave her a new name to feed to Kelly. In meetings by the convent shrubbery, McMahon invented 'Shorty

Doherty'. 'Shorty' would be her source in the IRA. A biography was sketched out. 'Shorty' was from Derry, so the Guards would have no files on him. She would have had a fictitious affair with Shorty. Armed with the cover story, Adrienne filled Danny Kelly's head with fantastic stories and information, all of which came from 'Shorty'.

Of course, 'Shorty' never existed, except in McMahon's head. He is a ghost in Garda intelligence files. No detective or uniformed Garda ever saw 'Shorty'. Every mention of 'Shorty' in Garda files can be traced back to Adrienne or Noel McMahon. The Morris Tribunal even asked the PSNI if such a person existed. Incredibly, they found McMahon's phantom Provo had crossed the border.

'Extraordinarily enough, his name does appear on RUC files,' Tribunal lawyer Peter Charleton SC explained. 'These, however, were opened as a result of enquiries in 1993 from the Gardaí in Donegal.'

Kelly said Adrienne blamed 'Shorty' when she appeared bruised and beaten at their meetings. There was nothing he could do because he could not identify the man and she would not make an official complaint.

McMahon gave Adrienne money, telling her to get some cheap walkie-talkies and balaclavas in Derry. There was no point racing through the streets unless there was something to show if she was stopped and searched. It would give credence to her role in McMahon's imaginary band of revolutionaries.

Pressure continued to mount over the chequebook. She was increasingly worried about the outcome and one day decided to call in to a solicitor's office to see if the situation could be resolved. The solicitor told her he had a conflict of interest, because he did work for the DPP, and recommended she see a different solicitor. However, he too got back to her later to tell her he could not act on her behalf. At the Morris Tribunal, Peter Charleton SC theorised that 'the solicitor probably contacted the Gardaí and asked them about the issue of the cheques, hence the detective branch knowing.'

McMahon was incensed. She couldn't think what she had done to annoy him, but she knew she was in grave trouble. The verbal insults flowed like venom, spitting anger in her face. Cowering in the seat, she tried to think quickly but could only stammer out that she didn't know what he was talking about. With nostrils flaring, his eyes were furious, large and black, and lifting his hand, he bounced a stinging blow off her ear and the side of her face. Pleading with him, she sobbed that she was not trying to embarrass him. She was grateful to him for everything he had done for her. She was only trying to resolve the situation at home. She knew there was nowhere else for her to turn. Silence descended between them. She knew to say nothing. After a short time, he turned to her and explained that Danny Kelly was causing him problems. Running with bags left, right and centre, and feeding him information was no longer as convincing as the early days.

At the Morris Tribunal Karen confirmed for Tribunal barrister Peter Charleton that she wrote a letter to her own solicitor in November 1991 telling him of Adrienne's visits to Donegal solicitors to resolve her problems with the cheques. The first solicitor Adrienne contacted was Ciarán MacLochlainn, the state solicitor for Donegal, who prosecutes cases for the DPP in the county. Because he acted for the DPP in criminal cases, he had a conflict of interest — if her case ever went to court, he would be the solicitor working for the prosecution. Therefore he could not take her case. Adrienne cannot remember who the second solicitor was.

Tribunal investigators contacted Ciarán MacLochlainn while Adrienne was giving evidence at the Morris Tribunal. He faxed a letter to the Tribunal offices, confirming that she had visited him on Friday 13 September 1991. Ciarán MacLochlainn's fax went on to say that he lived near an IRA 'safe house' at the time, and 'observed Ms McGlinchey going to and coming from these premises, invariably accompanied by Ms Devine and invariably carrying plastic bags'.

Tribunal barrister Peter Charleton told Adrienne that Mr MacLochlainn would be called as a witness, and asked her what she would say if he gave this evidence. Adrienne agreed he could have seen her going up and down the street, but added, 'I guarantee he will not stand up here and say he ever seen me going into the house or coming out of it.' Detectives like Des Walsh said Adrienne was seen *near* the safe house in Buncrana, just as Letterkenny Guards said they saw her *near* the house outside Letterkenny. Every Guard questioned by the Tribunal agreed Adrienne had never actually gone *into* the safe house near Letterkenny, and Noel McMahon was the only Guard to say he ever saw her going into the safe house in Buncrana. However, Ciarán MacLochlainn was never called to give evidence before the Tribunal, and Adrienne's barrister never got the opportunity to clarify what he saw. .

McMahon told her it was time to expand the operation and bring Danny Kelly on board once and for all. The plan was simple enough. They would drive into the convent grounds. She was to wait until the lights of their car shone on her face. As soon as that happened, she was to drop the bag she was holding and run. The bag contained about two hundred bullets, provided by Noel McMahon. 'Tell Danny Kelly you're delivering them for Shorty. Insist he gives them back to you,' he told her. 'Whatever happens, get the bullets back from Kelly.'

It would be the first of many nights spent waiting at the convent to meet McMahon. Nights spent shivering in cold and rain, a bag ready to drop and run when a Garda car approached. In media reports and commentary, it was presented as slapstick, the adventures of a silly girl running around playing Provo. To Adrienne, it was all too serious. 'I cannot sit here and tell you that there were not funny moments looking back,' she said later. 'But I can tell you, at the beginning of all this here, there was nothing funny about standing and carrying bags in the rain and the gale, and being stopped by Guards, and being arrested, and being taken into a Garda station, and being told by Noel McMahon to get arrested at certain times, and spending the night in a cell. I do not think it was funny.'

The subtle manipulation of Adrienne by McMahon would evolve over time. Clutching the bag, she waited for the car. Nervously checking the contents, she felt the cold metal of the bullets against her fingers. If she could pull this off, it would be the last stunt. When the car pulled up the lights blinded her, and she dropped the bag and ran, just as she had been told. Danny Kelly jumped out of the car calling her name.

She returned looking suitably guilty. Kelly had the bag in his hand. She fell into the part McMahon had practised with her. She told him she needed the bullets back, but he was having none of it. Panic set in. McMahon had warned her to get the bullets back, but he remained silent. She told Kelly she would be in severe trouble if she didn't get the bullets back for Shorty.

Returning empty-handed to the flat, Adrienne was terrified McMahon was going to punish her for not getting the bullets back. Noel McMahon's mood at their next rendezvous was going to be critical to her future.

4

Trapped

'Your fingerprints are on the bullets.'

Adrienne was trapped. Kelly held the bullets, and they were enough to get her sent away on terrorist charges. Noel McMahon had her just where he wanted her. McMahon and Kelly applied pressure any time they wished. She felt constantly threatened and pressurised.

No report was written about the bullets. Nobody arrested her. Nothing was logged in the station property book. McMahon persuaded Kelly that Adrienne showed potential as an informer.

Kelly held on to the bullets in his locker in Buncrana Garda station until 1999. Early that year, the Carty inquiry team was sent to Donegal to investigate allegations against the Gardaí.

Kelly wrote a report to Supt Jackie O'Connor, a member of the Carty team, on 20 May 1999. This report makes no mention of receiving bullets from Adrienne. He described her as 'a Walter Mitty-type character' that liked to draw attention to herself.

In August 1999 Adrienne told the Carty team about the incident involving the bag of bullets and the years of blackmail and threats she endured.

Kelly then made a statement at Burnfoot Garda station on 29 August 1999. He signed the statement a few weeks later, on 15 September. In this statement he finally admitted that he had retained the bullets, and in September 1999, eight years after he received them, Sergeant Danny Kelly handed over the bullets to the custody of Inspector Ken Barker of the Carty team.

Barrister Paul Murray represented Adrienne at the Morris Tribunal. It's worth repeating here his questioning of Detective Kelly:

Murray: 'And can I suggest to you this: That it was only when Ms McGlinchey confirmed to the Carty team that she had bullets in her possession one time which you had taken from her, that you confirmed this to be the case?'

Kelly: 'That's correct, yes.'

Murray: 'What you said was, at question 138, page 46, Day 45: "The bullets I kept in my possession until such time as the Carty team asked me about them and I handed them over to them." If the Carty team hadn't asked the right question, would you have handed over the bullets?'

Kelly: 'I definitely would have if I had have been asked, yes, but if they hadn't been mentioned maybe I would not have handed them over.'

Murray 'Because you had been keeping absolutely silent about the bullets up to then?'

Kelly: 'Yes.'

In his report, Justice Morris complained about what he called the Trigger Syndrome. 'Provided counsel for the Tribunal is inspired to ask precisely the question that will ignite the item of information, then that piece of information will be revealed and disclosed. If counsel is not so inspired, that information will remain undisclosed. Asking such people for assistance in terms of a general narrative on a particular issue evokes no useful response.'

Danny Kelly's admission that if he had not been asked for them, he might not have handed over the bullets to the Carty team seems a perfect example of the Trigger Syndrome Mr Justice Morris criticised. Yet the judge concluded that Kelly's 'actions were wrong but his response to the Carty team inquiry was immediate. He did not make any attempt to disguise his misjudgement when giving evidence before the Tribunal.' Kelly has retired from the force since giving evidence to the Morris Tribunal.

That year, Adrienne didn't send a card to mark her mother's birthday, an event she never missed. In late October, Karen and Liz decided to go in search of her in Buncrana. They knew she had a job and a flat, but did not know the address. As they passed Buncrana Garda station, Karen decided to ask the Guards if they knew where she lived. She was astonished when the duty Guard was able to give her specific directions to the flat, pointing out the rear entrance, which was not visible from the front drive. Letterkenny Gardaí did not have such a keen community awareness.

Karen, Adrienne and Liz sat in the car talking for over an hour. Karen had refunded anyone who lost money on the cheques, and Adrienne had already agreed to pay back the money. Liz was shocked at Adrienne's appearance. She looked drained, her eyes ringed with darkness from lack of sleep. They pleaded with her to return to Letterkenny, where she could work with them in Steers instead of the drudgery of Jay Bees shirt factory.

But it was too late for Adrienne. McMahon had a new live threat, which he would use to persecute her with for many years. He had her fingerprints on bullets.

One thing led to another. When Kelly started to question her role as an activist McMahon sent her on bag dropping duties, and fed her information to pass to Kelly. When uniformed Guards started to discount her, he told her to be seen near the suspect Northerners living in the safe house. There seemed to be no end in sight.

In December 1991, Detective Michael Jennings from Letterkenny Garda station arrested Adrienne outside her flat early one morning as she left for work. It was totally unexpected. She was brought to Letterkenny and questioned about the cheques but was released without charge. Once again all records of the arrest, custody records and interview notes are missing.

Adrienne's barrister Paul Murray questioned Superintendent John Fitzgerald about the arrest at the Morris Tribunal. '[T]he person who compiled the report says that he has been unable to locate the custody record in relation to Ms McGlinchey's arrest in relation to those cheques,' he said. 'Do you find that surprising that any custody record in relation to anything should go missing?'

'Well, it shouldn't go missing. It shouldn't go missing,' Fitzgerald acknowledged.

Noel McMahon told Adrienne that he was the one who secured her release and the least she could do was to appreciate the work he was doing on her behalf and the difficult situation she had placed him in. At the Tribunal he said he told her there would be very little chance of a prosecution against the cheques.

She was told to carry holdall bags. Maps. Balaclavas. Bell wire. Telephone wire. Anything that would raise suspicion in the mind of a Garda already conditioned to think of her as an IRA sympathiser was dropped in front of their eyes at pre-arranged times and places. She knew exactly when the patrol would be around; it was just a matter of waiting. McMahon impressed on her the importance of getting the detectives and uniforms 'on board'.

Another opportunity soon presented itself to McMahon. A man who lived outside Letterkenny was already under surveillance on suspicion of being a leading IRA member. Coincidentally, Adrienne had first been arrested in this vicinity. McMahon dreamed up a relationship between this man and Adrienne. Snogging and pillow talk were among his favourite expressions to the Morris Tribunal and the Court of Criminal Appeal to describe how she was able to extract sensitive and quality inside information from him. Unfortunately for McMahon's romantic plot, the man married another woman in 1992, but luckily 'Shorty' was still in the background.

C77 forms are top secret documents used by Gardaí to send reports to Crime & Security, the Garda intelligence branch at headquarters in the Phoenix Park. Crime & Security (formerly known as C3) is, in effect, the Irish secret service. Three copies of a C77 form were sent to the Crime & Security branch, and one to the divisional officer in the area. Access to C77s was highly restricted in order to protect the identity of the alleged informer. As a further precaution, the alleged informer's name did not appear on the form. The forms are submitted without the knowledge of the alleged informer and the later identity of the individual is dependent solely upon the word of the submitting Garda.

Bobby Mullally identified five C77 forms as containing information he said came from Adrienne. Detectives Smith and Tolan also submitted C77s, which they later identified in 2004 as information they received from Adrienne in Letterkenny in the early 1990s. However, the judge noted that none of the evidence in the C77 forms the three detectives submitted to Garda HQ led to anything substantive. There were no arms finds, no arrests. He concluded that the vast bulk was 'based on small snippets of gossip'. To this was added pure invention.

Tolan and Smith were part of Unit B in Letterkenny detective branch. Detective Garda Noel McMahon also·worked in Unit B from September 1986 until October 1987. Between 1990 and 1991, Smith and Tolan submitted eight C77 forms. In 1991, Hugh Smith was promoted to sergeant. McMahon again teamed up with Matt Tolan and Hugh Smith on Unit B in 1997 and remained there until his suspension from An Garda Síochána in September 1999.

In Buncrana, the confidentiality of the C77 system was breached. A copy of every C77 was made available to the detective branch, to keep them on top of local crime and subversive activity. Kelly and McMahon decided to stop pooling their information. Kelly maintained that Adrienne was their informant and they wanted to keep her information secret and for themselves only. The C77s can relate to any information gleaned by a Garda on or off duty from any member of the public. Any number of forms relating to the same information from any number of Gardaí may be submitted.

In 1991 Kelly and McMahon submitted thirteen C77 reports. In 1992 they submitted only two. In 1993 they sent in a single C77. Garda headquarters was no longer privy to their information. Neither were Buncrana detectives.

For the first eight months after Adrienne moved to Buncrana, Kevin Lennon was a sergeant in the Letterkenny traffic corps. In March 1992 he was promoted to inspector and transferred to Buncrana. The friendship between Kevin Lennon and Noel McMahon was long-standing. They shared a flat together early in their career and McMahon is godfather of one of the Lennon children.

The Buncrana detectives felt that they were pushed to one side when Lennon arrived. It seemed to them that McMahon bypassed

the chain of command in favour of Lennon. Danny Kelly was side-
lined around this time — his unit sergeant told him 'Letterkenny
was taking over.' He was ordered to have no further contact with
Adrienne by Detective Sergeant Des Walsh some seven or eight
months after his initial contact. This coincides with Lennon's
arrival in Buncrana as a newly-appointed uniform Inspector in
March 1992, one year before his formal appointment to supervise
Noel McMahon. Tom Sreenan, a detective sergeant in Buncrana,
confirmed that Kevin Lennon took Noel McMahon 'on tow'
when he was sent as an inspector to Buncrana in March 1992.
Other detectives were edged out.

At the same time, the 'Hands Off' policy was born. Noel
McMahon was the golden boy in the Buncrana detective unit.
Sheenagh's description of her husband as a 'Starsky and Hutch
character' is illustrative. He already had a reputation in Donegal
as a top detective who had served with the elite ERU. Chief
Superintendent Sean Ginty, the most senior Garda in Donegal,
instructed his officers to pass along the ranks that Adrienne
McGlinchey was McMahon property. No one was to try and
muscle in on McMahon. There should be only one handler for
Adrienne, the Chief ordered. Guards in Buncrana and elsewhere
now knew Noel McMahon was dealing with Adrienne. 'Hands
Off' would become the whip to dispense control over the doubters
in the detective branch.

Garda David Murphy was on duty on 30 April 1992, on foot
patrol with Garda Frank Togher. Adrienne had been given more
bullets and was sent to drop them. The two Guards spotted
Adrienne and Yvonne hanging around the town and decided to
keep them under surveillance. They followed the girls to the old
disused church on St Mary's road and waited until they left the
area. Searching around, Murphy and Togher found a blue parka

coat and seven bullets lying on the ground. Kevin Lennon would deny that he had any involvement with Adrienne until May 1993, shortly before he was appointed to supervise Noel McMahon, but he wrote a report saying that the case for possession for these bullets was too weak to sustain a prosecution.

Experienced detectives had doubts about Adrienne.

Tom Sreenan said that 'the behaviour of the two girls was completely contrary to, or the opposite of terrorist activity, or anyone who would have knowledge of terrorist activity.' James Breslin said, 'it wouldn't be the behaviour that you would normally associate with someone as being a PIRA member, who would be a lot more discreet and wouldn't be bringing attention on themselves.'

McMahon told later investigations that he also expressed doubts, but not a single detective corroborated his claim.

McMahon insisted that Adrienne call him every day at home. The duty times of the various Guards, their units and any other relevant information was discussed. She was told who was on patrol and who was in the station. She maintained a convincing role, even though she would not relinquish her job in Carndonagh, which limited her availability to evenings and weekends only.

He held meetings with her near his home. There was an old dirt track at the back of his house where they could talk. Sheenagh McMahon often saw them from her kitchen window and was satisfied that her husband was a conscientious cop working to save lives.

McMahon had a bright idea. They were going to identify IRA bunkers, and the result was many nights searching the north Inishowen area for hidden arms dumps. Clonmany was a particular favourite. Invariably the bunker was a three or four-hour session in the pub.

Once, as they returned from a pub in Malin, McMahon was so drunk that he missed a corner and drove the car into a ditch. Unhurt, he dispatched her to a nearby farmhouse to get help. By coincidence, the woman of the house was the dental receptionist in Carndonagh, and recognised Adrienne as a customer from a few weeks earlier. The farmer attached a towrope to the car and used a tractor to pull out the car, but the rope broke and a branch swung back and smashed the window. Realising McMahon was too drunk to drive, he told Adrienne to take the car. She drove back to Buncrana while McMahon snored in the passenger seat. Once again McMahon had to report to his authorities that his search for the terrorist bunkers had yielded nothing of any intelligence value.

McMahon showed Adrienne a Garda booklet on IRA weaponry. The Provisional IRA used rocket launchers in their terrorist war against British army helicopters. They were successful because of the mobility of the weaponry, which helped them to evade capture. Mark numbers, such as mark twelve or mark fourteen, were used to identify the artillery weapons.

He told her to have copies of the objects made. Steel makers in north Donegal were unwittingly duped into making 'rockets' and tripods. Unable to take the book or detailed specifications she made rough drawings from memory. McMahon would not risk her being found with a Garda booklet in her possession. Numerous variations of tripods were constructed but most were of poor quality and crude workmanship.

On 7 July 1992 Detective Sergeant Des Walsh wrote a memo on Adrienne and Yvonne. He concluded that they were not members of the Provisional IRA. Two weeks later, Inspector Kevin Lennon submitted a report to Chief Ginty describing the girls as IRA members.

The day after Lennon sent in his report, Adrienne and Yvonne were hitchhiking outside Letterkenny when a detective branch car approached. They ran into a field. When they emerged they were arrested under Section 30 of the Offences Against the State Act. Adrienne had thrown away a sketch of a mortar and swivel mount taken from McMahon's book, which was found the following day and sent to the Garda Technical Bureau for identification. The pair were later released without charge.

One week later, Adrienne and Yvonne went to Lifford to pick up one of the tripods from a local engineering company. Jay Bees was closed for the summer holidays, and they brought the tent, camping out. They went to a pub for a quick drink, with the tripod in a black plastic bag.

The quick drink in the pub became several glasses. Some time after closing there was a knock on the pub door, and Adrienne answered. Garda Liam Tighe stood there. He asked her to open the bag. He didn't buy her explanation that the tripod was for her tent. The girls were hysterical with laughter. The Guard was unable to get any coherent response from them and every time he questioned them they collapsed in a heap of giddiness and laughter. Adrienne told him to contact Noel McMahon.

Garda Tighe told McMahon that he was investigating the suspicious nature of the tripod in the border town. He then contacted Superintendent John Fitzgerald at his home in Letterkenny. It was about 12.30 a.m. He moved the two girls to Letterkenny Garda station because Lifford had only one cell, and arranged for a detective to conduct interviews in the morning.

When Garda Tighe arrived for duty in the morning he was

amazed to learn that the pair had been released without being interviewed or charged. They went to bed in the cells, slept the night, got up in the morning and were allowed to walk out of the station, minus the tripod.

Superintendent Fitzgerald told Garda headquarters that Adrienne had been arrested in possession of part of a stand for a 'Mark 12 rocket'. The tripod remained in Garda custody until 2003, when it was handed over to the Morris Tribunal. Tribunal barrister Peter Charleton noted that it was quite unsteady and would hardly sustain the weight of an ice cream cone, let alone a rocket launcher.

1992 was a particularly busy year for Adrienne. While Noel McMahon was doing undercover work she was given her tasks to continue with. There were steel items and 'rockets' to be made. This involved travelling between Clonmany, Buncrana and Letterkenny. She also had to keep up the business of occasionally running about the town, otherwise suspicions would have been aroused as to why she had ceased her 'distraction activities'.

Sometime in late 1992, Garda John Murphy saw Adrienne turn down an alleyway carrying a black plastic bag, but when she was emerged she no longer carried the bag. Along with Garda Tom McDonagh and Garda Mick Galvin he searched the area and soon located the bag containing a tripod, which they returned to Buncrana station.

Garda Seamus Gordon was in the station orderly's chair. Around 2 a.m. Inspector Kevin Lennon and Detective Garda Noel McMahon arrived in to the day room, and there was a discussion between the Gardaí about taking the tripod to the Ballistics Section at Garda headquarters in Dublin. McMahon said they would deal with it. Gordon objected to McMahon muscling in to take the credit from the uniformed Guards who made the find. He demanded to know the reason for McMahon's interference.

Noel McMahon pulled out his gun, and cocked the hammer. 'This is the reason,' he snarled. Gordon froze, staring down the barrel of the detective's Smith & Wesson service revolver. Unable to move, he watched as McMahon cocked and released the hammer several times. Finally, Gordon heard a voice behind him telling McMahon to put the gun away. Lennon was standing behind him.

Lennon and McMahon left the day room. Lennon never reported the incident to his authorities. He claimed he verbally admonished McMahon for pointing his gun at another Guard. McMahon brushed it off as a joke. Gordon did not find it so amusing.

As far as McMahon was concerned, a balance had to be reached. Adrienne's actions had to look suspicious, but not quite serious enough to attract further action. Much of what she carried for 'stop and search' was useless and certainly not illegal. Adrienne was stopped with Army fatigue jackets, binoculars, balaclavas, electric wire and components. With the Guards conditioned to think of her as an IRA runner, every 'stop and search' added to her image, even if each one was innocent in itself. To build the picture, McMahon would also stage larger shows. Two weeks after she lost the tripod in Lifford, he decided it was time for a kidnap.

On 7 August 1992, McMahon told Adrienne to disappear for a few hours, and have Yvonne report a kidnapping. Superintendent John P O'Connor sent a report summarising what followed to Letterkenny at the time. Yvonne called to Buncrana station and said that three men with Dublin accents had taken Adrienne from the flat. Gardaí throughout the division were alerted to look for a small red car, as were the RUC.

Gardaí were put on full alert in the manhunt for the kidnappers of the valuable Garda intelligence source, as fears mounted that Adrienne would suffer the fate of many informers.

All the while Adrienne was sitting on the beach. After several hours spent shivering on the sand, she was so cold and hungry she made her way home.

McMahon was waiting for her. He was delighted with the operation, but angry that she hadn't stayed missing for long enough. Her credentials as an IRA informer were enhanced, particularly in the eyes of Supt O'Connor, who had arrived days earlier in Buncrana. He had until that time worked Letterkenny as an Inspector, and had never heard of Adrienne.

At the Morris Tribunal, Noel McMahon at first denied he was working the night Adrienne was kidnapped. When it was pointed out that O'Connor's report at the time said he interviewed the supposed kidnap victim, he then claimed the kidnap was a mis-understanding, the result of an argument between Adrienne and her boyfriend from Derry, the phantom Provo 'Shorty Doherty'.

Adrienne tried to explain in the following exchange at the Morris Tribunal how her fingerprints on the bullets were the precursor to her later activities, and were used by McMahon to persuade her to engage in such actions as he and Kevin Lennon directed.

Adrienne: 'Well, when you consider, say for instance, how did it progress from the bags to the … from walking in Swilly Terrace to carrying bags, I cannot really say, but it did. How did it progress from throwing a bag with a balaclava in it and a torch, to being shown the Garda manual of what to get made, how did it progress to that I can't say either. But it progressed from that, from steel objects, if that is what you want to say, from ammunition to steel objects, to a bag of fertiliser being put on my carpet, to bags of fertiliser in my flat, to bags of fertiliser in Noel McMahon's house. I can't say how it all progressed but I believe what he was telling me, that every Guard was out to get me and if I could convince them that I was this IRA woman or whatever then I would be grand.'

Peter Charleton SC: 'Yes?'

Adrienne: 'And it all went back to that bag of bullets.'

Peter Charleton SC: 'Okay.'

Adrienne: 'The real bag of bullets. The walking in Swilly Terrace would not have been as bad but it was the bag of bullets with my fingerprints.'

Adrienne gave Karen and Liz McGlinchey a key to her flat so that they could call when the girls were at work. One day Karen noticed that the panel of the bath was loose. As she bent to push it in, the panel loosened further. As she examined it, she saw steel pipes and bars. 'Just like a lazy plumber to leave his scrap lying around,' she thought. But beside the pipes she saw a car registration book.

Adrienne had bought a banger to travel to work in Carndonagh. It was untaxed, uninsured, and the problems with brakes, lights, and wipers were only the more noticeable mechanical defects. Tax and insurance weren't a worry for her though: the early morning jaunt over the mountain road to work took place in the shadow of the Garda patrol car providing security to the Post Office mail run. There was no possibility of a checkpoint on the route.

Karen and Liz found the car in a Letterkenny car park during Adrienne's next visit home. Karen decided to wait for Adrienne. As she walked around one side of the car, she met Letterkenny detectives walking around the other side. Fearing Adrienne would be caught stupidly driving the car uninsured or taxed, she sat in her car across from the car park with Liz, waiting for Adrienne and Yvonne. They wondered if the Guards were expecting a robbery at the nearby bank; there were quite a few of them sitting in unmarked cars.

Adrienne rumbled her sister and mother and agreed to get rid of the car. She left it in a garage in Newtowncunningham. Later she discovered that it was collected by Gardaí in Buncrana and taken to their yard where it rested — and rusted — for many months.

One evening, as McMahon and Adrienne sat in the car, he produced a small bag and a domestic coffee grinder. He told her to grind the contents of the bag. The grinder could only manage a cupful at a time and before long the motor burned out, but the first crushing of fertiliser was a success. By the time the faked explosives finds began in earnest in 1993, Justice Morris stated Lennon and McMahon had long since used Adrienne for their own ends.

In late 1992 Adrienne learned that there were very good quality walkie-talkies for sale. She told McMahon that the asking price was £100, including a battery charger. He gave her the money to buy them.

John 'Bobs' Kelly was a petty thief in Letterkenny and he had been arrested and questioned in connection with the theft of walkie-talkies and a battery charger from Letterkenny Fire Station. A hoax call left the station unattended and the thief or thieves had seized on the opportunity. John 'Bobs' Kelly was released without charge after denying any knowledge of the incident. He later told the Morris Tribunal that he had stored the walkie-talkies and charger at the request of the Devine brothers, Pearse and John Devine, brothers of Adrienne's flatmate Yvonne Devine. While there was no finding made by Justice Morris in relation to the incident involving the walkie-talkies, Pearse Devine emphatically denied any knowledge of them. However, in awarding costs to Mr Devine, Justice Morris stated that 'While the Tribunal has doubts as to whether Mr Devine told the whole truth in respect of the matters on which he gave evidence, it cannot go so far as to make a definite finding that he did not do so.'

On 23 December 1992 Adrienne and Yvonne were leaving a shop in Letterkenny when Garda Cyril Meehan stopped them. He searched the bag Adrienne was carrying and found two Motorola MX 1000 hand radio sets, and arrested the pair. Detective Sergeant Jim Leheny brought Adrienne in for interview and cautioned her, explaining that the radios were stolen property.

Adrienne insisted that he contact Noel McMahon, who would confirm that she had not stolen the radios. McMahon told Leheny he knew all about the radios, and asked him to release the girls from custody. Leheny refused to do so and insisted that he would investigate. McMahon then asked Leheny to contact Chief Ginty. The Chief ordered the pair released.

At the end of 1992, Ciara McLaughlin, Barney Logue and their baby son moved into the top floor flat above Adrienne and Yvonne. It wasn't long before the girls struck up a friendship. Ciara sat at her window and watched the comings and goings in the Crescent. She spent most of her time alone in the flat with her young baby, who slept for long periods of the day.

One night, within weeks of their arrival, the door burst open and two plain-clothes Guards rushed in. Realising they were in the wrong flat they immediately left without explanation. Ciara's father was so annoyed when he heard that he made a complaint to Buncrana Garda station the next day.

Detective Garda Noel Jones was sent to apologise on behalf of the Garda Síochána. Jones was sceptical about Adrienne, and he used the meeting to ask Ciara to keep an eye on the tenants in the flat below.

Ciara was a warm and open-hearted person. She enjoyed the company of the girls when they returned from work as she spent much of her day alone in the flat with her baby. Adrienne soon noticed Noel Jones' phone number lying on the mantelpiece in the top flat. McMahon was aware from the station that Jones had snippets of information. Ciara confided in Adrienne that Jones was giving her between five and ten pounds to pay for phone calls relating to any information about Adrienne. McMahon decided this could be to their advantage and used Adrienne as a conduit to pass information to Ciara to pass to Jones. Adrienne paid Ciara a further five or ten pounds supplied by Noel McMahon. The two of them would go to a local call box and call Jones. Standing beside her, Adrienne would dictate the information to be passed. Ciara, who had a particular penchant for the amusement arcade, was happy to take the cash from both sides.

Effectively, Detective Garda Noel McMahon was paying for selected information to be passed to Detective Garda Noel Jones.

5

The Daily Grind

Neither Barney Logue nor Ciara McLaughlin had a job, but Barney was a handyman and could turn his hand to anything. From a farming background, he enjoyed shooting rabbits.

Adrienne came to Ciara one night and asked if Barney could have a look at her coffee grinder, which wasn't working. Upon examining it, Barney realised that the motor was burned out. Some crushed powder lay at the bottom of the small container, and he realised that it was too much for the domestic grinder. He passed his suspicions to Ciara, who told Detective Garda Noel Jones. Ciara reported the movements of the girls and Jones asked her to follow them to see who they were meeting and talking to.

Yvonne and Adrienne would sit in Ciara's flat, watching the Guards watching their own flat. It was not the first time that the watchers were watched. The Buncrana detectives hiding in the convent shrubbery could be seen from the window.

Ciara looked forward to Adrienne and Yvonne's return from work. From time to time she joined the girls for a walk. Sometimes if Adrienne was carrying a bag and they were approached by a patrol car, the girls would split up and run. Ciara's excitement was tangible as the three girls bolted in different directions. Ciara didn't know why she was running but got such a buzz from the break in her daily humdrum routine.

'There were a couple of times they had bags and the Gardaí would chase them when I was there like. Twice that happened and to me it was fun getting chased. They were getting attention, so why shouldn't I?' Ciara told the Morris Tribunal.

'They were getting all the attention of the Gardaí and I wanted attention too,' she explained. 'They were the only ones I had. I wanted out of the flat away from my husband who was battering me, battering my children.'

Barney's father had a licensed shotgun, which Barney used. He was able to buy cartridges on his father's behalf. Adrienne asked him to get her some cartridges for clay pigeon and rabbit shooting. Barney made five or six journeys to the gun dealership in Carndonagh to get a mix of cartridges and .22 bullets. Ciara decided not to mention this to Detective Noel Jones in case Barney got into trouble.

Whenever the sceptics in detective branch expressed reservations, McMahon moved to extinguish doubts. Knowing the detectives were watching the flat, McMahon told her to hire an angle grinder and put on a show of assembling something in the flat. Detectives Jones and Breslin stopped her one night having observed her carrying a heavy bag along the Shore Road in Buncrana. Breslin asked her to open it and saw an angle grinder. McMahon had provided Adrienne's pre-rehearsed explanation that it was to fix her broken washing machine. The detectives were exasperated at such a ridiculous answer, but without any reason to arrest her, they had to let her go about her business. The angle grinder would have been more use to break up a washing machine than to repair it.

Black plastic bags were used as black out curtains, with enough space left for sparks to be seen in the darkness of night. Adrienne had no idea how to operate the angle grinder, but Barney gave her a lesson and soon sparks were flying through the sitting room. The machine was noisy and vibrated heavily. Barney disliked Garda Tom Rattigan, who visited his girlfriend in the ground floor flat, and was pleased to think the noise was going to drive him mad.

The routine was straightforward. When a Garda car entered the grounds of the Crescent, Ciara on look out duty upstairs would spot it and alert Adrienne by banging on the floor. The angle grinder would start. Soon she discovered it was not necessary to use the irons for sparking. Watching Coronation Street and waiting for the bang from upstairs, she could touch up one of the rockets, which provided even better special effects. Once, she got carried away and actually managed to burn a rocket. Years later at the Morris Tribunal, the distinctive scorch marks could still be seen along the side of the exhibit. Between the chinks, blue flashes could be clearly seen by the watchers, Detective Sergeant Tom Sreenan, Detective Garda James Breslin and Detective Garda Denis Doherty. This served to further establish her connection to the Provisional IRA.

'Generally, this would have to be seen to be believed, it was so strange,' said Francis Crawford, a resident of the Crescent. 'At times I used to say, this place is getting worse than Hawaii 5-O.' Before retiring at night he would take note of the parked cars in the driveway, and those which he was unsure of would be noted in his book. One night, when he was conducting his patrol of the Crescent, he was approached by a man who told him it was time for his bed. Crawford 'sort of knew by the gimp' that it was a Guard approaching, and decided it was indeed time for his bed.

Meanwhile, Adrienne had problems getting rockets made to

McMahon's specifications. She took notes from the Garda booklet but each time she got a new batch, he denounced them as rubbish. It was difficult to explain to engineering companies the precise detail of what she wanted. Christmas was coming and she decided to enlist Barney's help. She told him she was trying to get Christmas tree stands made for the shop in Letterkenny and drew out a diagram of what she was looking for. Barney Logue knew a fellow in Marion Park in Buncrana who might be able to construct what she needed. Everyone set off on the rocket mission but Barney was appointed to go to the man's house alone while the girls waited at a nearby phone box. He drew a diagram from his memory of the diagram that Adrienne had drawn for him and which she in turn had drawn from memory of McMahon's Garda booklet. It was a cylindrical shaped metal pipe with a fin-like stand welded on to the bottom. The pipe had holes perforated at regular intervals. He explained the requirements to the steel maker, and all that remained was for McMahon to fund the purchase of raw materials.

Adrienne had long suspected people were coming into her flat while they were at work. When she started grinding fertiliser for McMahon in the flat, he told her to sprinkle some of it on the carpet. He also told her to leave balaclavas, electric wiring, anything she carried in bags, lying around the flat. Adrienne now feels McMahon entered the flat while she was at work, and showed other Guards the exhibits in order to 'bring them on board'.

The Logues often observed Adrienne and Yvonne leaving for work early in the morning. Ciara had their movements timed to perfection. Adrienne would run out the back door, a mug of tea in her hand and would still drink from it as far as the gate where she left the cup until she returned in the evening. Her hair was usually wet as she washed it every morning but never had time to dry it.

Bags of fertiliser started appearing in her flat when she returned from work. The coffee grinders were burning out, and there were trips to Derry to buy more. McMahon always paid — he told her he was claiming the money from the Secret Service fund.

Once, Ciara and Barney heard a commotion from the girls' flat while they were at work. Barney went to investigate, and banged on the door. Suddenly a man jumped out the kitchen window, falling nine feet to the ground. Barney threw a rock after the fleeing intruder. He hit him on the leg but the man escaped. When Adrienne met McMahon that evening he was limping. He told her he was injured in the line of duty.

He told her to buy bags for the crushed fertiliser. All the local shop had in stock were plastic freezer bags. These raised suspicions in the minds of seasoned detectives when they were found later. It was a major departure from recognised IRA practice.

McMahon took health and safety at work into consideration and provided masks and gloves courtesy of An Garda Síochána. Adrienne's cough was becoming more troublesome and was noticed at home by her mother and sister who were blaming the textile factory where she worked. She developed an allergy to the fertiliser and the skin irritation was affecting her day job. McMahon had also taken precautions, and at times the pair could have been mistaken for scientists, minus the white coats. She used blue Garda scene-of-crime gloves for household cleaning because of their quality. There were boxes of gloves scattered throughout the flat, under the kitchen sink, in the bathroom and in the hot press.

McMahon told her to buy fertiliser in different stores. He bought some as well. She said it was for her mother's garden. McMahon used the same story about his garden, no doubt leading to speculation about the quality of lawns in Letterkenny and Buncrana. Many of the bags were bought in the Creamery in

Letterkenny. Adrienne had to replenish her stock of fertiliser and one day she explained to Barney that her mother's garden had been infested with some horticultural disease and she needed to collect a bag of fertiliser in the co-op in Carndonagh by taxi. It was another family day out for the McLaughlins who would otherwise have been restricted to the lonely flat all day. After loading up a taxi, Barney carried the bag up to the flat and left it inside the door.

The Buncrana Guards were split over her status. The senior officers were receiving reports describing her as an IRA suspect, but officers on the ground were sceptical. Detective Sergeant Tom Sreenan, Detectives Noel Jones, Jimmy Breslin and Denis Doherty took a keen interest in her activities. While not strictly placing her under observation they often watched the flat, especially at night.

Her days were filled. McMahon got more demanding but the grinding was a slow process. He was furious when she burned out a motor too quickly. For a long time she could not master the art, until McMahon figured out how to grind without burning out the motor. It required two machines. A cupful was ground and after fifteen minutes the machine was switched off to allow the motor to cool. While that was happening, a second machine was started and another cupful ground. Practice made perfect.

He brought her into his house one night. Sheenagh and the children were away visiting his sister. They sat on the floor in the family living room with the grinders, crushing fertiliser for the weekend. She slept overnight in the spare bedroom. Grinding at the McMahon household was done on many occasions.

His wife, who generally went to bed early, would never come into the room once she had retired for the night. She knew of Adrienne from her early visits to the house when they sat outside in the old dirt trail leading from the rear of the house.

One dusky evening Sheenagh was standing at her kitchen window. She saw two men make several trips around the back of the house. They carried black plastic bags, which appeared to be rather weighty. When they finished, Lennon came into the utility room, washed his hands, nodded a quick hello, and left.

When McMahon came in, he told Sheenagh there was a bomb out back, but not to worry. 'He brought me outside because when he said to me there was a bomb, of course, I suppose I was shocked and terribly, terribly worried and terribly, terribly concerned that it would blow the house up. Then he assured me it was not assembled, that is the word he used. He said, do not worry about it, it is not assembled.'

Lennon and McMahon variously claimed the bags contained cast-off clothes from Mrs Lennon, or 'pinkish velvet' curtains, or both. 'Pinkish velvet? I never had pinkish velvet up in the house,' was Sheenagh's indignant response when Lennon first described the curtains.

Noel McMahon claimed Sheenagh was too proud to accept charity from Mary Lennon, so the bomb story was invented to preserve domestic harmony. 'I might have passed some crazy comment to just put her off,' Noel McMahon told the Morris Tribunal. 'I did not want to insult the Lennons who were doing it out of kindness, or whatever, and that's simply what that was.'

Lennon was never slow to spin a wild story to discredit a witness. When the Carty team had first confronted him with Sheenagh's account of the bombs in the bags, he told them it was 'the hallucinated effects of binge drinking', and that she had also made allegations against a priest in Limerick. 'It is a fact that Mrs McMahon did send via the post to the same Father a condom suitable for an elephant,' he told the Carty team. It is clear that hallucinations were a problem for Lennon, not for Mrs McMahon.

The bags were gone the following day. McMahon's sister was visiting at the time and Sheenagh told her what her husband had said. Over the following months and years as the McMahons watched the evening news on television, McMahon would remark to his wife when a report of a bombing was aired that it was one of theirs. He would boast that Adrienne would have to be allowed to carry out some bombing missions so as not to arouse the suspicions of her IRA masters.

Inspector Kevin Lennon had transferred to Letterkenny in January 1993. On 18 May 1993 he was promoted to Detective Inspector and sent back to Buncrana. McMahon told Adrienne to get arrested that night.

Adrienne was getting impatient. Two uniformed Gardaí were on patrol duty, but they weren't taking the bait. The bag in her hand contained cartridges and a couple of pairs of gardening gloves. The patrol car passed her at least three times but failed to stop even though she had caught their eye. Usually there was a curiosity on the part of the Guards when she had a bag. Eventually they stopped and one Guard gave chase as fast as he could before recovering the bag near the station. She was almost on the grounds of the station when she was eventually arrested.

McMahon choreographed the evening. He arrived in the station day room with Lennon before the uniform Guards interviewed Adrienne. The two uniform Gardaí began to question Adrienne, but they were called away and told to search the area.

Sreenan's team took over. Detective Garda John O'Keefe asked the questions but during the course of the interview she told him she was being blackmailed. 'I did not take it seriously at the time,' he said later. 'Basically I felt it was an excuse she was making up in relation to her defence. I cannot totally disagree with her.' This is the first recorded complaint by Adrienne McGlinchey of her blackmail.

Detective Sergeant Sreenan and Detectives Jones and O'Keefe were all present when Adrienne passed on information McMahon had given her for them. But the following day when O'Keefe tried to follow up on the information he was warned of the 'Hands Off' policy by Superintendent J P O'Connor, who insisted that he did not want the other officers muscling in on McMahon territory.

O'Keefe felt that Lennon had taken McMahon under his wing. As a result of their friendship, McMahon had the ear of Lennon and he believed this caused a division in the unit.

On 9 June 1993 Detective Superintendent Denis Fitzpatrick wrote a memo to Chief Ginty about Adrienne and the apparent security risk she posed to herself. Denis Fitzpatrick was appointed Border Superintendent the year before, a detective rank in charge of coordinating anti-IRA operations across the border with the RUC. He had little experience of border policing. Fitzpatrick himself acknowledged his lack of training and experience. 'I didn't have any great insight into what the IRA did or did not do,' he told the Morris Tribunal.

'If Kevin Lennon said to me that the IRA are moving something, I accepted it … I thought he was the authority on IRA activity in Donegal.'

Unbeknownst to Adrienne, Lennon had spoken to Chief Ginty about the grinding of fertiliser in the flat using a coffee grinder. The minds of senior Garda officers were being carefully prepared for the finds to follow.

Fitzpatrick's memo to Chief Ginty suggested that the Guards 'lay off' her for six months. Her identity was too widely known among the Guards, he wrote, and she wasn't mindful of her own security.

Fitzpatrick and Ginty discussed the situation. Ginty told the Tribunal that he spoke to Kevin Lennon and that he expressed similar concerns. Lennon was adamant that she would be very difficult to get rid of, claiming that she was the one initiating contacts.

Following the Fitzpatrick memo, Lennon was officially appointed to supervise the handling of Adrienne McGlinchey by Noel McMahon.

McMahon told her he was taking her to a meeting with Lennon outside his house in Letterkenny. It was to be the start of many nights travelling from Buncrana.

Lennon was an authoritarian. He told her that the running around and getting arrested had to stop. McMahon gave her snippets to report to Lennon, just as he had for Danny Kelly. 'Lennon could have you jailed without a moment's hesitation, we have to get him on board,' he told her. 'I'm on your side. I can protect you from Sreenan and Lennon. Just don't let me down, I've put my head on the block for you.'

Like Fitzpatrick, Chief Ginty relied heavily on Lennon's experience and knowledge of the IRA. Lennon was always quick to promote himself as an authority on terrorist activity. When Lennon told him that Adrienne was using coffee grinders to crush fertiliser, Ginty thought the IRA were hard up in Donegal. The IRA had moved on since the early days of the Troubles when grinders were used in Belfast homes. The IRA rarely used fertiliser bombs in the Nineties, as Semtex was available in large quantities following shipments from Libya.

McMahon went to Letterkenny and checked the McGlinchey family home at Covehill when Adrienne's mother and sister went on holiday. The concrete garden sheds were hidden by trees and shrubs and rarely used. They were ideal for storage. The surveillance operation moved to Letterkenny for a time.

Back in 1970, Albert Luykx, a frequent visitor to Letterkenny, had installed a swimming pool in Bernard McGlinchey's front garden. Luykx, a Belgian arms dealer, became a household name in 1972 when he was acquitted of importing arms into Ireland with Neil T Blaney and Charles J Haughey, ministers in the government of the day.

The swimming pool had suffered over the years, and was seriously damaged by winter storms. Karen eventually had it filled with topsoil and used as a rose garden. Adrienne mentioned the converted pool to McMahon.

An anonymous male caller to the Garda station said that there was a bomb at the swimming pool and at the rear of the Oatfield factory. He claimed that the IRA had put a false roof on the pool and planted roses to disguise the explosives bunker underneath. The identity of the caller was never established. Perhaps it was a detective who wanted the chance to search the area, particularly the sheds where Adrienne was storing fertiliser.

Chief Supt Ginty issued a search warrant and set in motion a series of frantic calls. First, Lennon called McMahon to inform him of the impending search. Ginty then received a frantic telephone message from McMahon, telling him that a search of the McGlinchey home at Covehill would compromise Adrienne and get her into real trouble with the IRA. The Chief then had the search called off. Ginty later told Lennon to gather up the explosives at the earliest opportunity because he 'relied on Kevin and trusted him'. The thought that the IRA might investigate the loss of their bomb-making equipment and stores doesn't seem to have occurred to him He told the Morris Tribunal that perhaps he 'overshot the runway in leaving it entirely to Kevin Lennon to do so'.

McMahon warned Adrienne repeatedly that she should never keep ground and unground fertiliser stored in the same place. The unground fertiliser was kept in the concrete sheds by her mother's home in Covehill. McMahon said she should move some of the mixed stuff out and bring it to the attic of Karen's hostel business on the Port Road.

There was too much for one person to carry. Adrienne asked a local teenager to help her. They got a Dunnes Stores shopping trolley and loaded the trolley with the bags. They pushed the trolley along the laneway and heaved it up the steps, past the Letterkenny Urban District Council offices, along the side of the tennis court, down the steps at the boxing club and into the hostel by the rear entrance. When he climbed through to the attic, the young fellow realised that they would need a container on which to place the bags and she passed him a stainless steel tray from the kitchen below.

McMahon told Adrienne that this would impress Lennon greatly and would definitely get him 'on board'. Lennon would have to be convinced of her value if he was to keep Ginty off her back. Lennon never declared this as a find and there was never a report filed in the station or a telex to headquarters. It would have gone undetected except that they took photographs of the bags of fertiliser, which turned up as part of a fluke discovery of documents in 2002 in what became known as the 'Lennon locker'. Clearly visible was the stainless steel catering tray on which the bags sat, obviously in an attic.

Lennon claimed that Adrienne took the photos and gave them

to him, and that she refused to identify the location. He could not account for the fact that not a single report was filed in relation to them. McMahon denied any knowledge of the photos to Carty and Morris Tribunal investigators, and first told the Tribunal, 'No, I was never in the attic,' before changing his story to, 'Yes, sir, at some stage I was in the attic.'

McMahon could always be depended on to come up with a theory. According to McMahon, after the IRA had converted the swimming pool in the McGlinchey front garden into an arms bunker, he claimed they were contracted to work on the roof of the hostel building. He described it as a Chinese restaurant, but it was not until years later that the hostel was converted to a restaurant. McMahon could not see any problem in the IRA deciding to dump explosives in the attic of a building while doing renovations. How they planned to retrieve the explosives was never made clear.

Lennon was under pressure from Ginty and when he was suffering McMahon felt the pain. It was up to Adrienne to ensure Lennon was kept happy. McMahon brought her on jaunts around the county, looking for suitable dumps, an old house or shed. She was a terrible traveller, and swallowed Dramamine by the packet. Eventually he settled on an old house outside Donegal town on the Sligo road. It was ideal, an abandoned building on a corner in the townland of Ardchicken, just outside Donegal town.

6

Border Crossing

Anonymous calls about Adrienne were a common feature in the occurrence book in Buncrana Garda station. There was the man who informed Buncrana Gardaí about her clumsiness coming from the Crescent. The caller recounted how a blond woman had dropped three rifles from her bag as she exited on to the road. He said she quickly picked them up, wrapped them in her coat and went about her business.

Then there was the man who said that there were three men dressed in combat gear throwing stones at the window. Shouting followed when they were admitted to the flat.

There was also the man who informed the Gardaí that there were five or more men dressed in black seen coming through the hedge carrying bags and heading up into the flat.

Of course, there were no rifles, no men in combats, no men in black. Foundations were being laid, manipulating the minds of Gardaí into believing that there was strong circumstantial evidence to connect Adrienne to the IRA. The proof would soon follow.

First though, Ciara's enthusiasm for her role as a double agent was causing a problem for McMahon. Fertiliser had to be delivered, but all day Ciara sat at her window watching arrivals and departures. If she heard a rattle from Adrienne's flat, she would check it out and phone Jones. She was putting McMahon in jeopardy.

By coincidence, Sheenagh McMahon's grandmother lived in a bungalow in the Crescent and her garden shed could be seen from Ciara's window. McMahon had keys to the shed. From her window, Ciara saw men carrying heavy bags from the shed. She assumed the bags went to Adrienne's flat as there was nowhere else for them to go. She later identified the two men as Kevin Lennon and Noel McMahon.

The first time that Ciara saw fertiliser bags and white powder in Adrienne's flat she rang Noel Jones and told him. He submitted a report that 'On 23 August 1993 to the night of 3 September 1993, Ms McGlinchey had a number of bags containing a strong smelling granulated mixture, believed to be explosive. The bags were kept in McGlinchey's flat and removed on 3 September by a number of men.'

In the early hours of 7 September 1993 Adrienne was stopped and searched by Detective Noel Jones. Jones was perplexed. The finned steel cylinder she was carrying had no obvious purpose. After a cursory examination he returned it to her. However, he made a drawing from memory and submitted it to the Crime & Security Branch intelligence division at Garda headquarters.

Jones decided that he would speak to the Superintendent. He told O'Connor that he had doubts. Adrienne's behaviour just wasn't what the experienced detective expected from an IRA member. The Provos usually kept a low profile.

O'Connor was not amused and called a meeting with Sreenan, Doherty and Jones. 'I told the three that the policy and directions of "Hands Off" which all were informed of some months ago was still effective and must be observed,' he recorded in his diary. He reinforced the view from higher authority that they were not to interfere with Adrienne McGlinchey. His superiors were very impressed with the information emanating from her and he would not tolerate any further intrusion. He told them to stop interfering.

Later that day McMahon collected Adrienne and they drove to Letterkenny for an emergency meeting outside Lennon's house. Lennon was livid at the constant meddling by Jones. He came up with a plan to disengage Jones from Ciara. It would also make Lennon look good, and Jones look foolish. They told Adrienne to casually mention to Ciara that she was expecting a delivery later that evening. They returned to their own flat and within minutes Ciara came down the stairs. She excitedly felt about under the stone. She knew this was a place the girls used to leave their keys. Picking up the package, she could see wires protruding from it. There seemed to be bullets inside. She quickly went to the phone box opposite the station and called Jones. It was just a matter of waiting.

The envelope was left under a stone outside Adrienne's front door. It contained bullets, cartridges, two yards of electrical wiring and two notes filled with obscure gibberish.

The first note read: 'Adrian, enclosed within. Sorry, that's only thing I could take. Shortt did not give keys. Go over and find out from big Paddy. It would be if you collected the rest of belongings of this pack, even coming, walking in here with this I felt I stood out, called tonight 11.00! "West End" someone tell as usual or wait and try usual place. Stay of Church end, road running parallel would be best. Might be snag tonight but wait West End any way. Be careful with small pack. Don't put anywhere near heat at flat.'

The second shorter note read simply: 'We couldn't take it because it is daylight. It will be easier for you at weekend. Take everything individually.'

Adrienne sat in the dark as Jones skulked around, feeling under the stone for the package. He left after a few minutes clutching his prize and went straight to Superintendent O'Connor, telling him he had a source who had alerted him to the development at the flat. His boss was none too pleased. Jones had totally ignored his order of that morning. O'Connor told him to return the package with the bullets and reminded him again of the 'Hands Off' policy from the top. The detective photocopied the notes and left the envelope back where he got it. He figured there was a bigger picture, and he didn't 'need to know'.

Kevin Lennon wanted a package left over in Strabane so that he could demonstrate his intelligence-gathering skills to the RUC by alerting them to the 'hoax device'. Getting the RUC 'on board' would boost his standing on both sides of the border.

The plan was simple. There was a 'Hands Off' policy and he would make sure there was no Garda presence on the Donegal side of the border. McMahon went over the plan for the drop. If she could do this mission and convince Lennon, he told her, then she would be finished with everything. The thought that she might be arrested by the RUC never occurred to her. She believed him when he told her she had a clear run through. McMahon gave her a plastic lunch box filled with bullets. She added the bullets and cartridges from the envelope Jones had seen two days earlier. The box was so stuffed she struggled to close it.

Adrienne boarded the bus in Buncrana and went to Derry. From Derry she connected to the Strabane bus. Yvonne was brought along again, her family connections adding to the picture. As they walked past Wellworths she saw the steps down to the River Finn. She climbed down and as she left the box on the bottom step, she noticed her hands were shaking uncontrollably. She had completed her mission. Yvonne and Adrienne walked back through Strabane and into Lifford on the Donegal side of the border. Her heart was beating so loud she could feel it beating in her ears. She had been so calm going to Derry on the bus, but as she deposited the package, she was terrified someone would see her and raise the alarm. She rang McMahon from the coin box in Lifford to confirm the drop.

Sergeant Tom Sreenan was returning home from Dublin with his wife when he spotted the two girls sauntering over the bridge. He wondered to his wife what they were up to.

Lennon had already put the wheels in motion. He told Chief Ginty that the IRA had tasked Adrienne to make a drop in Strabane. She had to be allowed to do it, as it would boost her credibility within the IRA. On Ginty's order he informed RUC Detective Inspector Tim Donnelly and gave a description of the two girls. Donnelly put out a rummage patrol in the town. A major security alert followed in Strabane with most of the town centre being sealed off. By then, Adrienne was already in Lifford.

At the Morris Tribunal, Kevin Lennon and Noel McMahon told a complex story of ever-multiplying phone calls and consultations the day of the Strabane incident. Lennon claimed that after McMahon called him with the information that Adrienne was making a delivery for the IRA, he jumped into his car and drove the twenty-eight miles to Buncrana to look around the bus station and stop Adrienne if he found her. When he could not see her on the bus, he drove back to Letterkenny and contacted Ginty. When he was asked why he didn't simply pick up the phone and call Gardaí in Buncrana to check out the bus station, he said the wild goose chase was a decision he made 'in the agony of the moment'.

Lennon and McMahon couldn't agree on a story. It was a delivery, then it was a drop, then it was abandoned when Adrienne panicked. It was a device, then it was a package. Adrienne travelled by bus, but McMahon thought at one point she went by taxi. Lennon said there was no Garda checkpoint, but McMahon said that Lennon told him checkpoints were set up on both sides of border. At first McMahon didn't know what she was transporting, but then had 'a quick peek' inside the box.

This was the first major incident involving Adrienne since Lennon's official appointment as McMahon's supervisor. As intended, it cemented her IRA status in the minds of the senior management, particularly Border Superintendent Denis Fitzpatrick. Six months earlier, Fitzpatrick had wanted the Gardaí to 'lay off'. But in his view, she was now a valuable asset for the State in the war against terrorism.

When Noel McMahon was asked why he gave contradictory answers to the Carty team, he said his legal advice was to say nothing, but he 'did not want to sit there like a Provo and not answer questions' so he gave brief answers. He added that he was on 'fairly heavy medication at the time'.

Lennon also had to change his account of the incident when RUC Inspector Donnelly kindly made himself available to the Morris Tribunal.

One can only imagine the embarrassment suffered within senior management ranks of An Garda Síochána at the knowledge that the bullets contained in the lunch box dropped in Strabane had been in their hands only days beforehand.

The Morris Tribunal found that 'what really happened in relation to Strabane was that Kevin Lennon wanted a package left over in Strabane so that he could demonstrate his skill to the RUC by alerting them that it was there. His willing accomplice in this regard was Detective Garda McMahon.'

In his ruling on applications for costs, Justice Morris said 'the main allegations made by Ms McGlinchey concerning the corrupt activities on the part of Detective Garda McMahon and Superintendent Lennon concerning the "finds" and other matters, the subject matter of the Tribunal's terms of reference, were accepted by the Tribunal, for the simple reason that on each event her testimony was supported by cogent independent evidence. This enabled the Tribunal to independently accept the facts to which she had testified. In short the Tribunal found that in respect of the matters central to its inquiry Adrienne McGlinchey had told the truth.

'A situation was being engineered whereby Adrienne McGlinchey was being made to look like something she was not; a terrorist or someone with close and intimate relations within the "Provisional IRA" and thus trusted for criminal operations. The entire story told by Lennon and McMahon was a cover up,' Justice Morris said.

Noel Jones had indeed been made a fool. He had let the bullets slip out of his hands, and they had ended up in Northern Ireland, setting off a major security alert. When Ciara next called him with another snippet she had picked up, he didn't want to know and told her in less than polite terms to leave him alone.

RUC Inspector Tim Donnelly was used again to identify an IRA prototype weapon in the days after the Strabane crossing. Denis Fitzpatrick recalled Kevin Lennon coming and telling him that Adrienne McGlinchey gave him a steel tube, which she needed back within two hours. Lennon said it was part of some new IRA weapon. It was imperative that it was returned to her within the time frame allowed. Fitzpatrick said that he travelled to Derry with Lennon and the 'rocket'. He could vividly recall this, the first time he had met Inspector Donnelly in person.

Lennon later changed the story, claiming he got the item from Noel McMahon. McMahon gave evidence to the Court of Criminal Appeal that he gave three items to Fitzpatrick who took them to RUC headquarters in Belfast, because it was quicker to do this than to bring them to Dublin for examination, and time was a factor. He then changed this story, claiming he gave Lennon two items, and held on to one himself. McMahon then claimed that Fitzpatrick decided he was holding on to one of the 'rockets', and refused to give it back, so that it became a 'sort of an ornament in Superintendent Fitzpatrick's office'. The Carty team recovered one of the rocket exhibits in an office press in Letterkenny Garda station in 1999.

McMahon said that he made a decision 'off my own bat, just to err on the proper side' not to give the other rocket back to Adrienne, because he did not want it on his conscience if lives were lost through the weapon. Instead he 'fired it into the shed and it was lying there for I haven't a clue how long.' In 1999, Sheenagh McMahon handed two 'rockets' over to the Carty team.

Depending on which version of Lennon and McMahon's evidence one accepts, the IRA had been robbed of one, two, or three of their prototype weapons by one of their most trusted operatives. She had already lost a consignment of bullets and cartridges in Strabane only days beforehand. Yet, although Lennon was of the view that 'under no circumstances could you take a risk in having an informant executed', he decided they could keep the so-called rockets 'because then she could put the proposition that she lost one or that she was — whatever'.

Justice Morris concluded that, by refusing to return the rockets to her, Lennon and McMahon were 'virtually signing her death warrant'. Because they did so, they could not possibly have believed she was a genuine informer.

Noel McMahon gave Adrienne a shopping list. It was mainly circuit boards and other electrical components, which he specified. The electronics factory was located in an isolated area not easily accessible by public transport, outside the village of Crolly, once famous for the manufacturing of children's dolls. The young fellow at the front desk was very helpful and fulfilled the order as requested. Members of the public did not normally make a direct approach at the factory, but the girls had come so far and it was such a chilly afternoon that he felt obliged to assist them as best he could. While he went to make up the order, Adrienne doodled on a notepad headed with the company logo. When he returned, the assistant gave her the notepad to keep. As the girls stood in the cold afternoon hitch-hiking a lift back to Letterkenny, a local Garda patrol car came along and gave them a lift.

Garda John Murphy stopped Adrienne and Yvonne one night and found the circuit boards and small electrical parts and wires in a bag when he searched Adrienne. He made no arrest, but handed over the bag to the detective branch. No statements or follow up investigation or arrests resulted, but Chief Ginty sent Garda Murphy a written note of commendation. McMahon had once again choreographed an incident, allowing Murphy to receive the credit for a find of apparent bomb components in the possession of Adrienne McGlinchey.

Murphy stopped Adrienne another night and took one of her 'rockets' from her. Murphy had no idea what the item was but he knew she had a connection to the IRA and was dealing with McMahon. This was well known within the station. He called McMahon at home and the detective told him to bring the rocket to his house. He remembered leaving it in the utility room. When he delivered it, McMahon told him that Lennon would take care of it from there.

Ciara McLaughlin liked John Murphy. 'I used to fancy him,' she told the Tribunal. With Noel Jones disillusioned, she took to chatting to him, ad-libbing and inventing incidents. This wasn't part of McMahon's plan.

Noel Jones had been discouraged, but with Ciara on full alert to any activity in the Crescent, McMahon still couldn't get near Adrienne's flat. The plan he came up with was surreal. McMahon and Adrienne drove out a mountain road, and collected sheep manure from the fields. It was stuffed into a shoebox along with an old alarm clock. This would be a fertiliser bomb with a difference. The shoebox was left in a field outside the border town of Bridgend.

The shoebox in place, Adrienne called to Ciara in the upper flat. She felt sorry for the young girl as she told her about the package in the Bridgend field. 'I remember I went into the Garda station or I rang John Murphy ... to go and tell John Murphy that there was something left at Bridgend,' Ciara remembered.

John Murphy has denied that this conversation took place or that he ever went to Bridgend to collect the box and the sheep manure. Afterwards, Ciara tried desperately to contact him at the station, but every time she called she would be told he was busy or out on patrol.

Lennon recorded the hoax in his diary: 'Set up Ciara about gear moving to Bridgend. Traced her to station and followed her there with the story.'

7

Ardchicken

'Little piggy little piggy let us in,
We are the Gardaí and we want in.
We'll huff and we'll puff and...'

The flat was surrounded. Gardaí were banging and shouting at the door. Adrienne had been busy grinding fertiliser when she heard the loud knocking. She recognised Detective Sergeant Tom Sreenan and others through the glass panel. She turned on the outside light. Sreenan called in to her to open the door. Knowing that he had already been told to stay away, she refused to open the door. There was fertiliser everywhere, in the sitting room, in the bedroom, even in the hallway. Sreenan said he was getting a search warrant. He was taunting her at the door.

Terrified, Adrienne started grabbing the fertiliser and flushing it down the toilet as quickly as she could. It was going everywhere. She knew it was pointless. She was going to Limerick Prison for sure. In a blind panic, she ran the bath water and filled the bath with fertiliser. It billowed up everywhere, on her clothes, in her hair. Sreenan was teasing. Sreenan mocked her through the door. Looking out the window she could see no sign of Noel McMahon or Kevin Lennon. She was confused. McMahon had told her that the Buncrana Gardaí could not come near her.

It was 12 October 1993, one month after the Strabane crossing. Detective Sergeant Sreenan was still at the door. Her fear of Sreenan was immense. McMahon had told her that Sreenan was 'out to get her'. There was fertiliser in bags under the bed and in the wardrobe. She ran to the bathroom. Her hands were shaking. Sreenan was impatient, the banging insistent. She looked out. The 'Hands Off' policy was still in existence. She was supposed to be safe from the rest of them. Kevin Lennon had told her. Noel McMahon had told her.

The siege had begun with an anonymous call to Buncrana Garda station, reporting unusual noises coming from Flat 2 in the Crescent. Detective Garda Denis Doherty, Garda Catherine McGonigle and Detective Sergeant Tom Sreenan attended the scene along with some uniformed Guards. Someone said that a gun had been seen through a window. Sreenan decided to get a search warrant and went back to the station. He contacted Superintendent O'Connor, who in turn contacted Chief Superintendent Sean Ginty and Detective Inspector Kevin Lennon. O'Connor valued the advice of his detective inspector and rang him regularly, practically every day and night. Lennon told O'Connor that they would compromise an informer if they executed a search warrant. O'Connor made the decision not to grant the warrant. He called Lennon back with his decision, and recalled Lennon saying he would go to the scene.

Adrienne saw Garda John Murphy outside the flat. McMahon later told her that Murphy told him about the incident. Murphy denied this had happened. McMahon said he was almost one hundred per cent sure that Murphy contacted him and told him about the events unfolding at the flat. Murphy denied this too.

Sreenan returned to the flat. By this stage Adrienne guessed he had not yet got a warrant. She was in the bathroom, furiously flushing fertiliser down the toilet and the sink. The more she flushed, the more the powder sprayed. Outside, the Guards could hear the continuous sounds of running water.

Sreenan was taunting her with his little piggy routine. 'We will huff and we will puff,' he mocked. All sense and reason left her. Opening the window, she tossed a bag out on top of them and watched the powder float through the night air, settling on the steps and garden and uniforms below. She finished the sentence for him '…and we will blow it all over you!'

Eventually, unable to get a warrant, Sreenan had to call off the hounds. Noel McMahon made the most of it, phoning her at Jay Bee's the next day. 'You have no idea how much I had to do to keep them away from you,' he told her. 'You've no appreciation of what I'm going through, the strain you put on me. I'm the only one batting for you, I'm in your corner. After last night I hope you appreciate that.'

Later, he told her that the chief had reprimanded Tom Sreenan.

Superintendent O'Connor reminded Sreenan once again of the 'Hands Off' policy. Kevin Lennon had further boosted her status as an IRA informer, persuading O'Connor not to grant a warrant. The stash of crushed fertiliser and sugar lay undisturbed by the Gardaí, safe and ready for Ardchicken.

McMahon gave Adrienne money to buy a stockpile of fertiliser in the Creamery in Letterkenny. He had picked her up at the convent and drove to Letterkenny. He had a bottle of brandy and a bottle of vodka with him. He said that he needed to unwind, because Lennon had been ringing him all day confirming that the Chief had ordered everyone to back off and that this came 'from the top down in Dublin'.

He checked the concrete sheds to see what store of unground fertiliser was there, then told her she would have to purchase fertiliser in Buncrana and build up a store there as well.

Noel McMahon briefed Adrienne carefully to tell Lennon the IRA were using the sheds at her mother's home in Covehill, Letterkenny to store bomb-making equipment.

'If Lennon gets promoted, no one can touch you again,' he said. 'You need to build up the story like building blocks so he falls for it. If we make Lennon look good, his promotions will leave him in charge of the Division.'

'I hate doing this. It's taking over my life.'

'You're nearly there. This is the last one. This is the big mission. As soon as we got rid of this stuff, that's the end of it. No Guard will ever touch you after that.'

'I just want to get rid of it.'

'This is the last mission. Kevin Lennon will be satisfied and he can erase your record. You can forget the Guards then and get on with your life.'

It was an enticing dream.

The transfer of crushed fertiliser and icing sugar began. She could smell freedom. Kevin Lennon would be finally satisfied and she would have no further dealings with An Garda Síochána.

She fed the stories to Lennon as McMahon had told her. They travelled to Lennon's Letterkenny home on a regular basis, meeting outside his house at night. This story was gradually topped up as the days and weeks progressed and McMahon would tell her that Lennon was very impressed with her information. All she had to do was pull the whole operation off and she would have all her record wiped clean.

Ardchicken is a townland outside Donegal town. McMahon and Adrienne had already travelled there at night looking for a suitable location. The searching was usually done in McMahon's car.

Yvonne Devine agreed at the Morris Tribunal that in an interview with a member of the Carty team on 13 September 1999 she brought up the subject of Ardchicken and said 'Ardchicken, went twice by bus to Donegal town. Adrienne called them field trips, looking for suitable locations to leave fertiliser. Wasn't there when the fertiliser was actually brought to Donegal town.' However, in 2003 she testified that she was never in Ardchicken.

McMahon had identified an old house there after several night-time trips. On each trip he pointed out likely sites, and Adrienne would have to return in daylight to check them out. Eventually, he found a derelict building he was happy with. He said that as it was close to the Garda station, he couldn't be seen around the place.

The movement of crushed fertiliser to the family shed in Covehill was continuing in preparation for the drop at Ardchicken. The whirring sound of the grinder was constantly in her ears, both in Buncrana and Letterkenny. One weekend, alone in Covehill, she laid black refuse plastic sacks over the carpet and spent the entire time crushing and filling bags and stacking them in the shed. Karen and Liz discovered one of the bags of crushed fertiliser, left in a press in the sitting room. Karen thought it was cement, Liz thought it was putty. Adrienne reassured them by saying it was a whitewash mix, to be used to paint the outside of the flat at the Crescent.

McMahon called her every day at work, demanding that she come to the phone. He took over her life from the time she finished work at Jay Bees until she went back to work in the morning. He was putting the final touches to the plan and the movement from the shed began. The grinding took on a renewed urgency. There seemed to be fertiliser everywhere, in the shed and the flat, at McMahon's house and glasshouse. It was non-stop. Whirr! Fifteen minutes, then change grinders and another fifteen minutes. Whirr!

Finally, the consignment was ready. McMahon told her that she would have to drop the batches herself. 'I can't be seen there. It would be too suspicious if I'm seen near you, it would be very bad for you,' he told her. 'Don't worry, I have it from the Chief himself that no one will come near you. You're protected from the top down, no one can lay a hand on you.'

She made several trips to Donegal town. Lugging the heavy bags down by bus wasn't easy, but each bus journey was a day closer to being free of Noel McMahon. The bags were very heavy and as the bus left Donegal town she called the driver, pretending she had missed her stop in Donegal. The driver offered to remove the cases from the boot but she was concerned he would get suspicious about the weight and declined the help.

McMahon was impatient. His mood swings and drinking were becoming more extreme. Frustrated with the slow pace he made several trips himself, filling the car boot with bags stored in Letterkenny. He pulled in to the same spot across from the house as she had on the bus. She had to walk across to the house, making several journeys while he remained in the car in case he was seen, until she had carried across the entire consignment. The area was overgrown, full of briars, weeds and bushes. As on her previous visits she dumped the bags together.

Finally it was time to inform Lennon. Adrienne was nervous. This wasn't like showing Danny Kelly a bag of bullets. Lennon was clever and manipulative. Karen and Liz McGlinchey were away. The arrangement was to meet Kevin Lennon and Noel McMahon at the family home in Letterkenny. McMahon didn't want to be seen driving his car in Letterkenny, in case the local detective branch wondered what he was doing. McMahon and Lennon arrived together and they decided that Lennon would exchange his car for an unmarked red Garda car. Lennon sat at the bar counter in the sitting room and had a brandy. Adrienne had a drink to steady her fear of him, and they left for Donegal town. It was late and the vodka had made her tired. She wasn't feeling well, the mix of drink and travel sickness making her nauseous. She lay on the back seat determined to play out her role by pointing out the house to Lennon.

Adrienne awoke startled. Lennon's words rang in her ears. 'Pull in Mac, you've passed it.'

It took a moment to realise that Lennon knew the location. She was the person who was supposed to be pointing out the IRA store to him. Still half asleep, she tried to shake the fuzziness in her head. The only way Lennon could identify the house was if he had been there himself before or that Noel McMahon had given him a description on the way down. The latter seemed unlikely. McMahon would have told his boss that this was his first visit to the area as well. So if Lennon was here before, could he also be involved in the scam with McMahon?

At the Tribunal, McMahon had the cover story worked out. A local man whom the Gardaí suspected of IRA membership, together with two other IRA members, a man and woman, were involved. The Letterkenny IRA assembled the material in Inishowen and moved it south. Adrienne had been to the dump with the local suspect and another man, and while the second man unloaded the van, Adrienne and the suspect engaged in a quick cuddle in the laneway to deflect suspicion. They were the lookouts. This was McMahon's second version of how Adrienne found out about the dump. Earlier he said she had picked up the information from pillow talk with the local suspect.

At the Tribunal, Lennon and McMahon's version of events once again started to disintegrate. McMahon said that he went into the house first with his gun drawn in case there was someone there doing extra work on the bomb. He said that he came out and confirmed to Lennon that the bomb was there. Lennon said that the three of them went inside, Adrienne leading the way.

McMahon said there was a tap running out the back, which he turned off. He said this was a marker left by the IRA. It was 'a natural human instinct' to turn off a running tap, so the IRA would know if anyone came by the house. He turned it back on. Lennon said he turned off the tap and Adrienne told him to put it back on.

McMahon said that he did not see bags under the floorboards. Lennon said that he did.

Both detectives supplied the Tribunal with information they said Adrienne gave them about the find. None of this information was given to earlier inquiries.

After leaving the house they drove back to Letterkenny through Donegal town. Lennon did not go into the station there to notify them of the bomb destined for the RUC barracks in Beleek in Co Fermanagh. He said that he dropped McMahon and Adrienne off in Letterkenny and then he went home to bed. It wasn't until 9 a.m. the following morning that he contacted Superintendent Duffy in Ballyshannon Garda station to inform him of the bomb. He also spoke to Detective Superintendent Fitzpatrick in the morning.

The drama of 19 November 1993 was replayed on the RTÉ news the following day. Northwest correspondent Eileen Magnier appears to have the only photographic record of the bomb destined for Belleek. Adrienne watched the bulletin somewhat puzzled. The quantity shown on television was much greater than that which she had left and it appeared to be stored in a quite orderly fashion. She felt quite certain of one thing: household coffee grinders could not possibly have crushed the quantity of fertiliser that appeared on television. Other people must have been involved in crushing the fertiliser.

At the time, the Crime & Security Branch received no information at all about the source of the Garda tip-off on the find. None of the detailed information Kevin Lennon and Noel McMahon told the Tribunal they got from Adrienne about the find had been given to anyone on any previous occasion.

Within six weeks, Adrienne had apparently lost IRA prototype mortar weapons, IRA bullets for a training camp, and now a major IRA bomb destined for the RUC station in Belleek was uncovered. Yet no senior Garda seems to have worried that Adrienne might be discovered by an IRA investigation into the loss of the explosives store. Lennon said he told her to say the Guards stumbled across it.

When dealing with the Ardchicken incident in his report, Justice Morris stated: 'the Tribunal has carefully scrutinised the evidence given by Superintendent Lennon and rejects it completely.' Later, when awarding costs to the various parties, he said of Adrienne's evidence that 'the Tribunal found that in respect of the matters central to its inquiry Adrienne McGlinchey had told the truth.'

Analysis of samples at the National Forensic Science Laboratory revealed the fertiliser component of the homemade explosives was urea, an animal feed mixture which couldn't detonate a Christmas cracker. This did not set off any alarm bells about the find either.

Adrienne was able to relax at Christmas for the first time in a long time. On the night of the Jay Bees Christmas party the girls went to the Lake of Shadows hotel in Buncrana. They met Detective Inspector Tom Long. Adrienne hadn't seen him in a while and they struck up a conversation in the hotel lobby. Adrienne offered to buy him a drink and enquired after his family. Long declined the drink but instead bought the girls a drink. After some minutes chatting Long rejoined his company.

Detective Sergeant Tom Sreenan and his wife were also in the hotel that night. Sreenan met McMahon and told him about Long talking to the girls to see how McMahon would react to the news. McMahon went straight to the top. The following day Chief Superintendent Ginty contacted Long complaining that he had been trying to muscle in for information from the girls and that it was Detective McMahon who was dealing with Adrienne. He reinforced the 'Hands Off' policy message. Long was flabbergasted. Moreover, there was even a wild suggestion that Long had tried to entice Adrienne up to one of the hotel bedrooms with a bottle of vodka. Both Tom Long and Adrienne deny this suggestion.

Sreenan told how some time later he heard that a C77 in relation to the incident was sent to Crime & Security signed with his number. Sreenan knew that the only person who could have been responsible was the only person he told about the sighting: Noel McMahon.

Sheenagh McMahon was apparently also aware of the allegation and raised the issue with Tom Long when he came to take her statement in 1999. It seems that the allegation had been well circulated within Garda circles in Buncrana. Idle tongues do the devil's work.

Noel McMahon contacted Adrienne again in the New Year. He invited her to a party in his house on 6 January 1994.

She expected a house full of people at the party, but it was just a party for three. They were in the sitting room drinking, Kevin Lennon with his usual brandy. Within thirty minutes of arriving her head was swimming. The night became a vague blur. Everything was spinning. Adrienne vaguely remembers needing to use the bathroom. As she went into the hallway she could sense the room moving. She was swaying from side to side and in the distance she could make out a figure in pink moving towards her. Sheenagh McMahon directed her to the bathroom.

Sheenagh went into the sitting room. Lennon and McMahon were laughing. Lennon was pouring vodka and Coke into a tall glass for Adrienne. Sheenagh complained to them about what they were doing to her. Sometime later she watched from her bedroom window as they bundled her into the car. 'She will talk to you when she is drunk,' McMahon later told Sheenagh.

'I was to let on to her that she got sick in my hall,' Sheenagh recalled at the Tribunal. 'I believe on one or two occasions it probably was said to her and she was led to believe it. I thought it was a bit funny at the time, but it was not really funny.'

McMahon rang Adrienne a couple of days later. He was very angry. He said she told Lennon when she was drunk that she would do a movement of explosives to Derry. She was shocked, unable to remember anything about the night. She pleaded. Ardchicken was supposed to be the end.

'Lennon has your fingerprints on the find at Ardchicken,' McMahon told her. 'He'll have you in Limerick Prison if you cross him.

'You have to go through with it. Lennon has notified Fitzpatrick. If you don't follow through they'll ask awkward questions.'

She had no choice but to agree. Crossing Kevin Lennon was not an option.

8

The Brass at Bridgend

Bridgend is a border town a couple of miles from Derry. There is a massive combined British army border checkpoint and RUC base less than a mile away at Coshquinn. On a second road to Derry was another British army and RUC base, equally big, known as the Culmore checkpoint.

The holdall bags that McMahon had funded were being recycled so often that Gardaí were actually starting to recognise them. Lennon decided to put a stop to this and purchased new bags for Adrienne. He recorded the following in his diary: '£50 self, two bags, plus phone cards.' He put the odd case that he bought the bags for himself, although the phone cards on the same line are those he bought for Adrienne out of the Secret Service fund. Lennon and McMahon, of course, denied purchasing bags for Adrienne.

Noel McMahon told Adrienne to put fertiliser in the holdall bags and leave them behind a wall at Bridgend. The next night she was to repeat this performance leaving it in McCallion's builders' yard, also at Bridgend. She was to make sure that Yvonne accompanied her. Yvonne's family connection to IRA man Pearse McCauley always gave the operations a ring of authenticity.

McMahon told her that Detective Superintendent Denis Fitzpatrick would to be there to witness a live IRA operation. Fitzpatrick would disguise himself as a drunk, wearing a woolly cap. Denis Fitzpatrick denied this but the Morris report found that it was common for him to arrive in some form of disguise.

As far as Yvonne knew, they were going to Letterkenny to do some laundry at home, which was plausible to Yvonne since the Crescent flat had no washing machine. It was 11 January 1994, the anniversary of Noel McMahon joining the Guards.

They took a taxi from Buncrana and, as arranged with McMahon, arrived in Bridgend at around 9 p.m. It was normal for the girls to hitch-hike from the Bridgend roundabout to Letterkenny.

As Adrienne got the bags out of the boot, Yvonne paid the taxi. When she turned to call Adrienne, she saw her dumping the bags. Yvonne was furious. Adrienne had promised that there would be no more messing around. She walked ahead as Adrienne dumped the bags in the builders' yard.

Yvonne stopped short. She had spotted the Garda checkpoint near the Derry border, and shouted back to Adrienne. Adrienne had not been expecting this and fought a sense of panic. As she walked towards Yvonne, a drunk wearing a wearing a woolly cap passed by. Adrienne, believing he was the Border Superintendent Denis Fitzpatrick, was relieved to see him. If the Superintendent was here, then the plan was working.

They crossed the road and walked to a café. They ordered and settled in to watch the show unfold. Adrienne hadn't expected the checkpoint, so despite having been told by Noel McMahon to leave the area after the drop, she decided to wait until the coast was clear. McMahon had told her about Fitzpatrick, and that Lennon would be hiding in the trees. He never mentioned a checkpoint. She had heard twigs breaking underfoot when she was depositing the bags and assumed it was Lennon.

Soon the commotion began. She could see the flicker of the torchlights in the yard. Within thirty minutes the Gardaí had packed up for the night. They had collected the bags of fertiliser and Lennon had gone home happy. They went back out onto the road and hitched home. She felt she had been officially retired. She was emotionally drained, but she was free.

Some of the Donegal division's most senior officers were in Bridgend that night. Detective Inspector Lennon, Border Superintendent Denis Fitzpatrick and Superintendent J P O'Connor witnessed the 'frustration operation' put in place by the Gardaí. Fitzpatrick and O'Connor were not field officers. Fitzpatrick held the rank of detective superintendent, but had never trained as a detective and relied heavily on Lennon, who had never trained as a detective either.

Fitzpatrick and O'Connor believed that the bags were being transferred to Derry by Adrienne McGlinchey, and the checkpoint was set up to frustrate this operation, forcing her to drop the bags in Bridgend.

Fitzpatrick walked the road to the roundabout. He could make out the tail lights of the car reflecting someone at the boot. He made an anonymous phone call to Burnfoot Garda station that two youths were acting suspiciously at Bridgend. A radio message was sent out and a uniformed car at the checkpoint was dispatched to the area. The uniformed officers were not told what the cause of the suspicion was or what they were looking for.

Terence McMahon (no relation to Noel McMahon) was a student Garda on probation. During the course of the search of McCallion's yard, the rookie Guard discovered the holdall bags with freezer bags inside, and called his colleagues. At first he thought it might be a drugs find. He kicked the pallets, which were on top of the bags, away with his boot. In Templemore he had been trained to be aware of mercury tilt switches, which were often used by the IRA as booby traps. These would cause the bag, if moved or tilted one way or another, to explode automatically.

Terence McMahon's student notebook is the only contemporaneous record of the find at Bridgend. As at Ardchicken, no one took photographs and no one preserved the scene. There was no scene-of-crime examination.

As in Strabane, the RUC was notified. Denis Fitzpatrick recalled that on the morning of 11 January 1994, he received a phone call from his Derry counterpart telling him of a find of homemade explosives in a wheelie bin in the city that morning. It is possible that this find consisted of the bags Adrienne had deposited in Bridgend the previous night for McMahon, subsequently transported by persons unknown to Derry and deposited in the wheelie bin. Kevin Lennon came to him around 4 p.m. that afternoon and informed him of the transfer by taxi from Buncrana to Derry of homemade explosives to replace the store lost by the Derry IRA. Adrienne McGlinchey was the courier and would be accompanied by Yvonne Devine. Lennon told him the plan. The pair would travel by taxi as far as the roundabout in Bridgend. When they saw the checkpoint they would turn back, stop at McCallion's builders, and drop the bags. It would be a controlled frustration operation and the informant was aware of the plan.

Fitzpatrick called the RUC border superintendent in Derry and informed him of the plan. The RUC man said he would immediately go to the Culmore checkpoint. Although Fitzpatrick knew that the taxi was going in via Bridgend, he did not enlighten the RUC officer. Lennon claimed that he did not organise the operation for Bridgend. A diary entry found in the 'Lennon locker' read 'Organised Bridgend operation which resulted in explosives find in Bridgend, 95 pounds HME.' He explained this by saying that he made suggestions to his superiors.

After all the advance planning and involvement of the top brass, Lennon and McMahon had made the most elementary of mistakes. The checkpoint was set up about a quarter-of-a-mile from the roundabout, towards the Derry border. It was impossible for the girls to have seen it when they pulled up in the taxi, as the supposed cover story required. The taxi never came to the round-about. No one seemed to notice this until years later, when the Morris Tribunal looked into the affair.

Buncrana detectives were also involved that night. Detective Sergeant Des Walsh was told to man a checkpoint — his inform-ation was that there could be something going into Derry in a taxi. He was later told by radio that the substance had been dumped; he made his way to the scene. On his way, he saw Adrienne and Yvonne enter the café.

Manorstown Cross is a remote border outpost a couple of miles from Bridgend. Detective Gardaí Danny Kelly and John O'Keefe were ordered there and told to await further instructions. They were not told why they were there or what they were looking for. They sat in their car twiddling their thumbs, until they too got a call on the radio indicating that a drop had been made in Bridgend and that their assistance was required in the follow up search.

Sergeant Michael Murray is the Buncrana-based scene-of-crime examiner. He told the Tribunal that he received a call the morning after the drop summoning him to Burnfoot Garda station, where the three holdall bags were sitting in an office. He did not go directly to the scene of the crime, as one would expect of a scene-of-crime examiner. He was told that reference was made to

Adrienne McGlinchey who had been seen dropping the stuff off. He said the steps taken at a scene where there was a suggestion of homemade explosives should have been 'checked out to verify whether it was safe and to ensure that [it] doesn't pose any threat, number one to ourselves and number two then to the public'.

Murray said an Explosives Ordinance Disposal (EOD) officer normally did this but the officer Commandant White was already at the station 'or came shortly afterwards'. He did not take fingerprints from the surfaces of the plastic bags even though he conceded that the bags contained 'surfaces from which one could get a fingerprint'. He would never take fingerprints 'when scenes are not properly preserved or interfered with like that'. He could not clarify whether this rule was 'written down anywhere' or was to be 'found in (his) manual'.

Murray went on to say that he had to ask permission to take samples from the relevant bags because the Army EOD officer was going to destroy all the materials. He was surprised at the presence of the officer because the materials were in the station and therefore were regarded as safe. He could only assume that the EOD officer had permission to remove the material before Murray had the chance to take his samples.

Later on he went to the scene. He couldn't recall any Garda preserving the scene and he thought that he 'actually took measurements in relation to how far it was in and the actual gateway and that type of thing', adding that he 'would have made notes'. When he was asked to explain what happened the notebook he stated, 'well, normally, you know, files and things like that subsequently you would have retained them for up to four or five years. Then subsequently after that eventually, because of the amount of paperwork that has accumulated, eventually some of them would have to be disposed of.' When asked to do so by the

Carty team, he searched all of the relevant materials but 'didn't find any notes relating to that matter'. Despite evidence to the contrary and by Lennon's own admission later on, Murray could not place his detective inspector in Bridgend.

Commandant White expressed his surprise in a statement to the Morris Tribunal that the bags had been removed from the scene. Chief Superintendent Denis Fitzpatrick was of the view that Kevin Lennon had used Bridgend 'in order to boost his standing amongst his fellow officers'.

Once again a major departure from normal IRA operations had occurred. The IRA had apparently taken the enormous risk of delivering explosives by taxi through one of the biggest combined RUC and British Army checkpoints using a rather accident-prone operative. Once again Adrienne had lost an IRA cache. This loss was added to the long list of steel items, balaclavas, wires, circuit boards, bullets to Strabane, prototype weapons, and the bomb at Ardchicken.

Lennon was delighted at the success of the operation. He had conned and fooled the most senior officers in the division into believing he had his finger on the subversive pulse in Donegal. He was receiving the plaudits he believed he richly deserved. Word was spreading, his reputation in the fight against the IRA terrorism was growing. To add to their pride at their success, Detective Inspector Derek Browne of the RUC in Derry was invited on a guided tour of the area around Bridgend. They pointed out where they intercepted the bomb being transported from the South to the North. Lennon had already come to the notice of the RUC after the successful operation in Strabane and his acquisition of the prototype IRA rockets.

A few days after the incident at Bridgend, Tom Sreenan stopped Adrienne and said that he knew she had been involved in the dropping of the bags in Bridgend, and that she had done it for Lennon and McMahon. McMahon had already told her Sreenan was well in with the taxi men in Buncrana, but there was nothing he could do. The 'Hands Off' policy was in operation. McMahon told Adrienne that the best way to frustrate and confuse Sreenan was to tell every taxi driver 'you didn't see me' as she finished the trip. But she couldn't understand how he could have found out anything about the Bridgend drop because it was one of the few occasions where she got out and just said goodbye.

The Morris Tribunal concluded that the movement of ground-up fertiliser from Adrienne's flat to the roundabout at Bridgend was 'set up by Detective Garda Noel McMahon and Superintendent Kevin Lennon for the purpose of self-aggrandisement'.

Bridgend had gone off with little prior planning, even though Adrienne got mixed up and couldn't remember what exactly McMahon had told her to do. At the next meeting, McMahon said Lennon was 'hanging them out to dry'. 'Lennon is pushing me out,' he told her. 'All the Guards in Buncrana have turned against me. I need to get control or you're finished.

'Lennon is being smart. He wanted the brass to catch you red-handed carrying the bags in Bridgend. I'm sorry, I let Lennon walk you into Bridgend.'

By now, Adrienne was meeting Lennon on a regular basis. He was buying holdall bags for the fertiliser. Noel McMahon needed to regain control. Kevin Lennon was using her to promote himself at headquarters.

'Once Lennon has what he wants, you'll end up in prison,' he warned her. 'He has everything. He has your fingerprints. He has Fitzpatrick witnessing you doing the drop.

'Lennon's now the boss. Everyone is telling him what a great job he's doing.'

Noel McMahon no longer trusted Lennon. He was jealous and they seemed to have had some kind of row. McMahon said he needed something to keep in control of the situation, so he could protect her. Kevin Lennon didn't care about her. McMahon said he needed to convince everyone that he was the one in charge, that he was running the operation, not Lennon.

Adrienne saw little or nothing of either Lennon or McMahon for a couple of weeks until McMahon rang her at work. He told her to meet him that evening, that he wanted to introduce her to some friends. He collected her from the convent and brought her to the house in Porthaw, complaining for the entire journey that Lennon had taken all the glory for Ardchicken and he was going to use something on him to get him back. He said that he wanted to introduce her to two officers who he said were from the Royal Ulster Constabulary. He gave her an alias, which she was to use in front of them because he told her he did not want them to know or use her identity. When they arrived at the house, she was brought to greet them and after a short time she was told to leave the room. McMahon finished his meeting with the supposed RUC men and they departed shortly after that. They were introduced to her as Cyril and Alistair.

9

Charade

Noel McMahon lapsed into binge drinking, complaining that Lennon had become the golden boy in policing circles, both North and South.

Adrienne was worried sick. The top brass had seen her in Bridgend and the only person that stood between her and jail was Kevin Lennon. At any time he could click his fingers, and the keys would be thrown away for a very long time. There was a push on for the 'big one'. The 'big one' would end her worries forever, McMahon told her. He would ensure that Lennon kept his word.

McMahon took Adrienne to his house. They went to the garage and he showed her fertiliser there. He knew Yvonne wasn't at the flat so they moved the bags to the flat. He had two coffee grinders. Lennon wanted more and McMahon said she had to keep Lennon happy, this was the only way he could protect her from him.

Adrienne went home one weekend and she saw a Dictaphone tape recorder, which Karen used for making notes during election canvasses. There were a couple of mini diskettes. She had previously tried to record Lennon and McMahon in her home on the night of the Ardchicken find using an older tape recorder concealed in a drawer in the bar counter, but it didn't pick up their voices. McMahon had been promising her since the bullets and Danny Kelly in the convent in 1991 that the charade would end. Instead it snowballed, and with Lennon involved she feared she could become the sacrificial lamb.

She knew Lennon and McMahon were going to call to the flat. It had been arranged earlier. Yvonne wasn't there and she had the Dictaphone concealed. She realised that she would need security for herself. McMahon repeatedly threatened jail. Senior Guards had witnessed her making the drop in Bridgend. It left her in a very precarious position.

She switched on the Dictaphone before she answered the door so that it would record when they came in. The conversation turned to the Point Inn. Lennon was talking about the arrogance of Frank Shortt, the owner of the nightclub. Shortt held music raves and McMahon had conducted undercover surveillance work on alleged drug dealing in the club. She knew by the gist of the conversation that Lennon was aware of the activities of McMahon in the Point Inn. Before Ardchicken she always thought that Lennon was innocent of any involvement in the fake finds. After that night, she knew for definite that they had been plotting together.

Whirr! Fertiliser was ground and put in the freezer bags, and more fertiliser was bought. She would return from work and find a bag in her bedroom. On one occasion Lennon and McMahon carried fertiliser concealed in black plastic bags into the flat. It was the only time she saw Lennon carry it in. She was nervous buying fertiliser — she had bought so much that they must surely be suspicious. McMahon was buying it in the Co-Op to store in his glasshouse. Icing sugar came from the cash and carry, which

McMahon left in his kitchen at Porthaw. Sheenagh McMahon later confirmed that 'there was one occasion that Noel brought me in six bags or seven bags of icing sugar one time.'

Plans had been put in place for a party to celebrate Yvonne's forthcoming nineteenth birthday. The girls invited their friends and planned a great celebration. Adrienne hadn't told Lennon or McMahon about the party until the week before it. Eventually, as they sat in McMahon's car one night outside Lennon's house she summoned up the courage. Lennon was furious and demanded the plans be cancelled. There was nothing Adrienne could do. It was Yvonne's flat, she paid half the rent and if she wanted a party then she was going to have a party. They decided the only way to prevent people walking into her room was to fit a padlock to the door.

Coming home from work a day or two prior to the party on 11 March 1994, Adrienne found that a padlock had been fitted to her bedroom door. McMahon gave her the key later that evening, warning her that under no circumstances was she to allow anyone into the room, as if displaying a room full of nitrate pellets would somehow be something she would be proud of. The bedroom had become a strong room. Bags of fertiliser, ground and mixed and a couple of hundredweight bags of unopened Maxisward had been stored in the room. Several bags of icing sugar completed the booty. The wardrobe was bursting at the seams with the fertiliser, nice and neat in little freezer bags, ready for depositing in the 'big one', and there was even room under the bed for one of the so-called rockets.

There was a daily battle fought in the bedroom. Stepping over and around bags, applying Max Factor and avoiding Maxisward. Tripping up on welding irons. Coffee grinders were stacked under the sink and the stench was terrible. It wasn't that fertiliser itself had an offensive odour, but there was little ventilation in the small bedroom, save one window. One of the rockets had been stored under the bath, as the panel had slid off easily just as it had on many previous occasions. Adrienne drew a diagram of the rocket from memory for the Carty team in 1999, uncannily like rockets in the Garda booklet issued at the time.

The party began as the friends clocked out from work. Accompanied by some of their friends they made their way back to Buncrana. By evening word had spread through the surrounding pubs and clubs in Buncrana that there was a party in the Crescent. People just kept arriving. The party was a success. Lennon and McMahon had told Adrienne that one of them would remain in the flat below, occupied by the girlfriend of one of McMahon's colleagues, to make sure nothing happened to the explosives stash in the bedroom. The following morning there were bodies strewn throughout the flat. By late afternoon they were recovering, just in time to restart the party where they had left off. That night more people joined the party after the pubs closed. Adrienne had arranged to meet McMahon early on Sunday morning across in the convent grounds but he didn't turn up.

Casting their eye around the flat the next morning, Adrienne and Yvonne were horrified at the housekeeping disaster. Someone had released the fire extinguisher, and there was foam spray dripping from the wall in the hall. Igniting the contents of her bedroom would not have come close to the mess after the party. Neither girl could face the clean up. It would take a week of hard work. They decided to go to Letterkenny for the day and relax and start the clean up that night. But returning later than expected, after two nights with little sleep, they decided the cleaning blitz could wait until they returned from work on Monday evening.

The phone call from Noel McMahon came just after lunch, at around 2.10 p.m. on Monday 14 March 1994. McMahon was insistent with the secretary, demanding that Adrienne be brought immediately to the phone. The Jay Bees manager had issued a strict directive of no personal phone calls to the company line or on company time. The secretary ushered her in to the office, warned her that the male caller would not take no for an answer and begged her to keep low in case the manager spotted her. Adrienne bent down under the desk and kept an eye on the shop floor to detect the early return of the manager as McMahon screamed into the phone.

He wanted her undivided attention. She wanted to retain her job. McMahon ordered her to get outside and he would collect her. He said there had been some type of leak in the flat. Pleading sick, she clocked out, telling Yvonne that she had to go to Buncrana because there was a problem with a leak in the flat, and that Yvonne should not return to the flat after work but should go to Letterkenny instead.

McMahon brought her to his home in Porthaw, and she passed the time sitting in the front room. She amused herself playing patience on McMahon's computer, whittling away the afternoon and evening. Detective Inspector Lennon had directed his foot soldiers to capture her on sight, all the while knowing that she was in Noel McMahon's house. When the McMahon children came home from school they were quickly ushered into the kitchen. McMahon told her to wait until Lennon arrived.

Lennon and McMahon were busy spinning their web of deceit. As they drove to the flat, McMahon briefed her in what she was to say when they arrived at the flat and at the station. They would take her to Burnfoot Garda station so they could control the interviews. Detectives from Buncrana would not have access to her.

She would say nothing to anyone in her cell or the interview room unless they were present. A night in a cell no longer mattered to her. She had been through the charade so often that it was almost second nature. They would have more control outside Buncrana in determining which Guards would gain access to her.

When she got back to the flat, Adrienne stood at the front door flat and gazed at a slice of birthday cake, which had stuck to the Artex ceiling. She wondered how on earth it managed to hold fast. The remnants of the party were everywhere, and she regretted not cleaning the mess immediately after the party. But there was little point in self-recrimination. It had been a great party. It would be talked about at work for a long time. One wonders how she could think of that, when she was about to spend the night in a Garda cell.

Her clothes had been removed from the wardrobe and scattered throughout the bedroom. The Guards had wormed their way through the flat, invading the personal privacy of her bedroom. She went to get a change of clothes to bring along for the following morning. Gardaí were still removing fertiliser in freezer bags from the wardrobe while she casually put together a few items for her overnight stay. Lennon and McMahon drove her to Buncrana station before bringing her to Burnfoot Garda station. They were pleased with themselves. Rank is there to be pulled and the underlings executed their duties without question. They had made it look the part, even if the formalities such as arrest and search warrant were non-existent. Official procedures were not something adopted much by Lennon and his sidekick McMahon.

What had happened?

Vivienne Eccles, a tenant in the ground floor flat, lived with her young son and was involved with one of McMahon's colleagues, Tom Rattigan. She had reported a leak to her landlord

John Mackey, after she had found a pool of water in her kitchen. The landlord arrived within an hour and went directly to the girls' flat. He made his way to the bathroom and drawing a blank, decided to slide back the bath panel to check if there were any leaking pipes. Instead, he found fertiliser scattered on the floorboards and one of McMahon's rockets. Concerned, he made his way through the flat, finding more fertiliser and another rocket-like item, cylindrical in shape with fins attached at the lower end, sticking out from under her bed.

Mackey spotted Tom Rattigan's car in the driveway and sent his wife to the lower flat to summon the Guard. Declaring a bomb factory in one of his tenant's flats, Rattigan said he would get someone to deal with it. Mackey was happy to leave it in the Guard's hands.

Garda Rattigan was off duty, and left the scene unattended when he went to make a phone call. He was in a quandary. Noel McMahon was also off duty but they had been friends for years and he was the first person who came to his mind when he found the items. The call to McMahon's home was made from the call box directly across the road from Buncrana Garda station, but Rattigan did not alert his colleagues on duty only yards away. He did not return to the flat, but collected his car and left without preserving the scene.

Kevin Lennon was at a conference of senior officers in Letterkenny. Also there were Chief Superintendent Sean Ginty, Border Superintendent Denis Fitzpatrick, Superintendent John P O'Connor, and Inspector Patrick McMorrow, the acting District Officer.

Lennon had their ear. This was a time of security threats against the State, and ideas and strategies were pooled at the seminar, but no mention was made of the bomb factory that had just been found in the flat only yards from the Garda station in Buncrana. All the senior officers present emphatically denied that Lennon had informed them of the find.

The think tank was in full swing when Lennon got the phone call. McMahon gave him a run down on Mackey's discovery. But though he briefed Lennon, he did not notify Buncrana Garda station of the find of homemade explosives uncovered in Flat 2 of the Crescent. They decided during that phone call to embark on the greatest charade of all time to hoodwink and bamboozle concerned civilians into believing that Garda action was being taken. The landlord had put a spanner in the works. At least one of the neighbours knew about what was in the flat. It would have to appear to the public that a genuine search and investigation of what was described as a bomb factory in a flat in Buncrana was being legitimately conducted.

According to McMahon, all this was done to protect Adrienne's identity as a top Garda agent working inside the IRA. McMahon told Kevin Lennon that he would collect Adrienne from her work at Jay Bees in Carndonagh and bring her to his home in Porthaw, Buncrana. Meddlesome neighbours were not their only dilemma. It was a catch-22 situation. Detective Sergeant Tom Sreenan was on duty that day and he would insist on an investigation.

That evening, Lennon arrived in Buncrana Garda station having put together the final details of how they would capture and detain their agent without arousing suspicion. Brimming with confidence, Lennon moved the chess pieces. Detective James Breslin was sent to watch an IRA safe house when he came on duty, told to keep an eye on things there, and instructed to arrest the girls if he happened to see them. The wild goose chase had started.

Detective Sergeant Des Walsh came on duty around seven that evening. He was Lennon's mentor as much as Kevin Lennon was his protégé. Walsh, due to retire the following September, had groomed Lennon from his arrival as a new young Garda recruit and he saw great potential in him. Years later at the Morris Tribunal, Walsh claimed that he received a search warrant for the flat from Superintendent J P O'Connor, but O'Connor was not in Buncrana on the night. He was due to give evidence in the Special Criminal Court the next morning, and went straight from the Letterkenny conference to Dublin.

At the Tribunal, Des Walsh admitted that he lied to an internal disciplinary inquiry at Lennon's request, taking responsibility for the investigation file for the search and arrest. In fact no real investigation file was ever prepared.

By the time the search began, some eight or nine hours after the discovery by Mackey and Garda Rattigan, the contents of the flat were rearranged, and some removed.

No one could remember which uniformed Gardaí were present for the search, but everyone remembered that Garda Sarsfield, a now deceased member of the force, was definitely there. Garda Christy Galligan told the Tribunal that Sarsfield was recorded as the Member in Charge at Buncrana Garda station later that night. Sergeant Michael Murray claimed that only Des Walsh was present inside the flat with him.

Noel McMahon had been hovering outside the premises. Murray said that he conducted a thorough search of the premises on his hands and knees. He said that there was absolutely no sign of fertiliser or rockets in the bedroom, nor a sign of a rocket under the bath, but there were two suitcases in the bathroom and a number of bags located under the bath as well as two fifty-kilogram bags of agricultural fertiliser which he personally carried from the flat to his car, and transported to a locked store room at Buncrana station. He said that he held on to the materials for up to two years.

Justice Morris found that Sergeant Michael Murray and retired Sergeant Des Walsh and Noel McMahon 'withheld vital information in relation to this search from the Tribunal'.

Garda John Forkin first told the Tribunal that he knew nothing about the search, other than vaguely hearing something about it later. Adrienne recognised him as the Guard she passed at the flat entrance that night carrying fertiliser to a car, and Tribunal investigators subsequently interviewed him. His memory was jogged when it was put to him that he was recognised by a witness and he was recalled to the Tribunal on 19 January 2004. He remembered carrying a bag of fertiliser, which he found inside the hall door to the open boot of a patrol car, which had been reversed into the garden. He recalled meeting Kevin Lennon and Noel McMahon there. Walsh remembered McMahon bringing Adrienne to the flat in his car and Sergeant Michael Murray bringing her through the flat. Murray denied seeing her there.

Ciara McLaughlin from upstairs was causing a commotion about a bomb in the building. McMahon was having none of it. He bundled her in to her own flat and yelled at her not to come out until the following day.

Noel McMahon claimed that he found fertiliser in the bedroom. When Detective Garda Breslin got back from the wild goose chase watching an IRA safe house, he was assigned to interview Yvonne Devine in Buncrana Garda station. He recorded in his notebook that his questioning of her almost entirely related to fertiliser in the bedroom.

Legally, possession can be difficult to prove. If contraband is found in the kitchen or living room of a flat, then it could belong to anyone living in the house with access to the common living area. Proving that it belongs to a particular suspect can be difficult. On the other hand, contraband in a private area like a bedroom can more easily be proved to be in the possession of a suspect. Moving fertiliser from the bedroom — a private area — to the bathroom and hallway made it less likely that there would be a prosecution.

That night, a telex was sent by the Divisional Communications Centre in Letterkenny to Garda headquarters in the Phoenix Park following a report from Inspector Patrick McMorrow in Buncrana, indicating that the homemade explosives were found in the bedroom. He recalled that either scene-of-crime examiner Sergeant Murray or Detective Sergeant Walsh gave him the information. The Morris Tribunal decided that it was most likely Sergeant Murray. Walsh was in Burnfoot Garda station until almost midnight, ruling him out as the person who gave McMorrow the information.

The telex indicates that homemade explosives were found in a bedroom wardrobe, but makes was no mention of the rockets Mackey saw, or the two suitcases Sergeant Murray claimed were in the bathroom. Along with some welding rods and an angle iron there were large and small bags of fertiliser and icing sugar.

Garda Christy Galligan, the member in charge in Burnfoot Garda station recalled Lennon, McMahon and Walsh arriving at the same time. Adrienne's instructions were not to speak to any of the Guards. Walsh and McMahon commenced the interview process shortly after arrival. Walsh said later that anything and everything was discussed with the exception of the find. The following day Lennon and McMahon arrived and Adrienne was given magazines, Coke and sweets. Des Walsh took part in some of the interviewing. Passing the time, they discussed her acquiring shirts at reduced prices from the Montes shirt factory in Buncrana through an employee who regularly gave her a lift to work in the morning. McMahon said that they had put on a performance for Walsh to protect their top secret agent. Walsh said that she was never questioned in his presence.

Lennon was resting his feet on the table while he read his paper and Adrienne was engrossed in a women's magazine when a female officer startled them.

Irritated at the intrusion, Lennon decided that the local constabulary would require a little show. Banging on the table he shouted at her to tell the truth. He told her that at the next break when she left the room, she should complain about her treatment to the first Guard she met, which she duly did. Some time later, the member in charge, Garda Christy Galligan, came in to the interview room and advised her of the procedure for making a complaint to the Garda Complaints Board. As directed she said to Galligan that she was not happy with the 'mannerisms' of Inspector Lennon.

'If you take a suspect member of the IRA group, normally they would sit watching a point on the wall, but she wasn't,' Garda Galligan recalled later. 'There was a gay frivolity about the whole thing, it was kind of surreal.' McMahon and Lennon 'just kind of laughed, kind of ha-ha' when Adrienne said she wanted to make a complaint, he said.

By Tuesday afternoon it was time to go home. Lennon decided that a sufficient smoke screen had been put up and she was released. Genuine officers had been fooled into thinking a proper interrogation had taken place. People like Christy Galligan and James Breslin wrote statements for an investigation file. Walsh took their statements.

McMahon took her to Letterkenny where they met Lennon and they drove towards the home of the local man suspected of being in the IRA. Lennon said to walk back down towards Letterkenny and then go home. A short time later the patrol car from Letterkenny passed her. The script was complete.

A second telex went to Dublin the following day. It stated that an army explosives ordinance disposal (EOD) officer, Commandant Dowling, following samples taken for analysis, had destroyed the remainder of the find. Garda Forkin recalled going to Buncrana beach and observing the spreading of the fertiliser. Inspector McMorrow recalled meeting the EOD officer prior to the destruction of the materials. Yet Sergeant Murray claimed to have the entire find in a locked storeroom for two years. McMahon remembered bags lying against the shed door of the Garda station for years, dwindling as people helped themselves to the fertiliser for their front lawns or as it blew away in the wind.

Dr Sheila Willis, a director of the forensic science laboratory at Garda headquarters, received the samples from Sergeant Murray two days after the find, but noted that the delivering member told her the case might not go ahead.

Justice Morris found 'that from an early stage it was not intended that a full and proper investigation would be carried out in relation to the find at the flat. Sergeant Murray ensured that no proper forensic test of the samples took place such as would assist any future prosecution... Sergeant Murray was anxious to present himself to the Tribunal as both a truthful witness and as a member of An Garda Síochána who carried out his duties in a conscientious manner. The Tribunal is satisfied he was neither.'

And what of the missing rockets that Mackey saw? The Tribunal found that 'Detective Garda McMahon and Detective Inspector Lennon, in collaboration with other members of the

Gardaí who cannot be discovered, had the items removed from the flat before the "official" search began.' The reason for removal of the rockets was quite simple. Rockets had already been brought to the RUC in 1993 and passed off as prototype IRA weapons, which Adrienne only had for a short time. Their discovery, lying around her flat some six months after they were supposed to be handed back urgently to the IRA, would have raised serious questions. Headquarters in Dublin could not be allowed to see the obviously hoax munitions.

It was a setback, but Lennon and McMahon had managed to cover their tracks. They succeeded in hoodwinking their colleagues and even added further credibility to their three-in-one IRA informer, bomb manufacturer and courier. But in truth, the fertiliser, icing sugar, welding rods and rockets were 'under the control of Detective Garda Noel McMahon and Detective Inspector Lennon for use as and when required by them for the purpose of planting them for later discovery in locations in Donegal'.

10

'Please destroy this minute'

etective Sergeant Des Walsh contacted the landlord John Mackey, and he went to Buncrana Garda station the day after the find of 'rockets' in the flat. He wrote a statement, which he gave to Des Walsh, and while he was there he spoke to Lennon and another detective.

A few days later, as Mackey was coming out of a shop in Buncrana, a man he knew to be a Buncrana detective pulled up alongside him and asked him for a key to the flat. The detective, whose name he did not know, asked Mackey to allow the girls to remain in the flat for another while, as 'there might be bigger fish to be caught'. Mackey had had enough. He told Adrienne and Yvonne he wanted them to leave.

Lennon was doubly frustrated. Not only were the girls evicted, but the IRA were talking about a ceasefire. He needed more time. He said Chief Superintendent Sean Ginty was putting pressure on. He had been told a story that the fertiliser in the flat was being stored for someone else, which was why she escaped prosecution. Lennon and McMahon were singing from the same hymn sheet. McMahon, who was very stressed, said the chief was getting impatient because he was told it was part of a store for a major bomb to be used in the summer. Lennon and McMahon wanted the operation up and running again, but finding suitable accommodation proved difficult. Word travelled fast, and landlords were reluctant to let their premises to bomb-makers. The story was put round that there had been a drugs find after the birthday party, but this did little to ease the concerns of local property owners — no one was prepared to risk letting their premises, whether it was bombs or drugs. Reluctantly they moved out of Buncrana to the village of Ballyliffen, about ten miles away.

For Lennon and McMahon, access to Adrienne in Ballyliffen was not as easy as in Buncrana. She was now out of reach. Power is control and maintaining direct control was tricky. Adrienne's fear of Lennon was greater than ever. Although the successful handling of the Crescent find had buoyed him, he quickly resorted to his previous intimidating tactics. Matters weren't helped when some of the sceptics in Buncrana detective branch began snooping around Ballyliffen.

McMahon was assigned to protect a State witness outside Letterkenny, leaving Adrienne exposed to being confronted by Detective Noel Jones or Detective Sergeant Tom Sreenan. Lennon had a mobile phone, in those days still a rarity, a privilege of rank. He gave it to McMahon, and gave Adrienne phone cards so that she could call him at any time.

Detective Sergeant Sreenan and Detective Garda Denis Doherty Jones stuck out like two sore thumbs. Passing the window, Adrienne had caught sight of the detective branch car out of the corner of her eye. She had been in just about every Garda car in north Donegal and could recite their numbers backwards. She grabbed a phone card and went to the phone box to call

McMahon. He told her not to worry.

McMahon and Lennon called it a curiosity mission. Although the 'Hands Off' policy was still in force, they wanted to see if they could rustle up a reaction. The wait was short. Within ten minutes the radio crackled. Sreenan and Doherty were sent to investigate trouble in Muff, a village some twenty minutes drive away. Their suspicions were aroused when they arrived there and found nothing untoward. When they called in, they were immediately redirected to Moville, a village a further thirty minutes away. They knew not to push the issue any further. Adrienne was left alone.

Not long after they moved to Ballyliffen, Yvonne found a boyfriend. His regular house calls made it difficult for Adrienne to grind fertiliser. Then Yvonne had a fall, and was admitted to Letterkenny Hospital, ending up with a plaster cast on her foot. McMahon was delighted — flatmate and boyfriend were both safely out of the way. He arrived at the house with bags of fertiliser and coffee grinders, and soon they were back in business. They ground fertiliser for two days, which McMahon took away and kept at his house.

Whirr! Ready. Steady. Grind. Whirr! The daily routine after work was driving Adrienne crazy. McMahon was demanding a huge drop, the 'big one', before the ceasefire. They were still driving around looking for locations; the final explosives find would have to be far enough from Buncrana so that it could not be traced back to her. McMahon took her in the car around the Ballyshannon area looking for suitable places to drop the fertiliser. Donegal town had already been tried and tested and was a complete success.

But McMahon still worried about Tom Sreenan. The estate agent who let the house to the girls was also friendly with

Sreenan. What if Sreenan somehow got a key? McMahon didn't want the fertiliser left there. He kept the unprocessed fertiliser in his own glasshouse, and told Adrienne to move the ground fertiliser to her home in Letterkenny. 'Never keep crushed and uncrushed fertiliser together in the same place,' he told her.

Packing the small five kilogram bags into two holdall bags, she caught a bus to Letterkenny. As the bus passed by the family home, she asked the driver to stop. She tossed the bags down the small embankment to the scrub and bushes at the back of the property, planning to return later and bring them to one of the disused sheds at the back.

It was June 1994. The local and European election campaign was in full swing. The McGlinchey house was busy. Karen McGlinchey was a candidate for the local town council. European candidate, Senator Ann Gallagher and her driver were staying in the McGlinchey home while canvassing in Donegal. Election workers were coming and going.

Adrienne couldn't pick up the holdall bags right away, but she knew they would be safe. The McGlinchey family home ran up against the wall of Oatfields sweet factory, which was closed for the weekend. The bags lay on the Covehill side of the boundary wall and the tall bushes sheltered them from public view. When she finally got away to retrieve the bags, they were gone. She assumed McMahon had removed them, as he was the only person who would know they were there, although she could not remember having confirmed with him that they were at the bottom of the garden. She thought no more about it.

Noel McMahon was working on protection duty. On 4 June 1994, at 6 a.m. he relieved Garda Martin Leonard, who was working the same duty. Having completed his shift, Leonard drove back to Letterkenny, but instead of going home, he headed to the Garda station.

Martin Leonard was not a detective. He was a uniformed Garda, assigned to the Letterkenny traffic corps. Three years before, he had been the Garda who arrested Adrienne McGlinchey for the first time, as she returned from a futile trip to the builder to have scaffolding removed.

Leonard had never in his career made a find of explosives. That morning, a man walking his dog noticed the two holdall bags lying down the embankment. He was in the Garda station telling Garda P J Thornton all about it, when Leonard arrived. Incredibly, the concerned citizen had identified the contents as being homemade explosives. He declined to make a statement or give his name, and went on his way. The time was 6.45 a.m.

As Leonard passed, he overheard the conversation. Although he was off duty, he offered to pop down in his car with Thornton and retrieve the explosives. They found the bags contained crushed fertiliser, not heroin or cocaine as they first suspected. Standard operating procedure with a find of explosives would be to cordon the area and notify the Explosives Ordnance Officer in case of booby traps. Instead, they bundled a bag each into the boot of the car.

Leonard never sought favour or credit — or even overtime expenses — for his over-riding sense of duty. The work done, he went home. He had been off duty since 6 a.m. Garda Thornton could take care of the paperwork.

Thornton was hungry. Finding the bags was a feather in his cap, and the exhilaration had generated an appetite. The canteen was usually closed at weekends, but he managed to commandeer a breakfast that Saturday morning.

After breakfast, Thornton said he went in search of detective branch members, to tell them about his discovery. He later recalled mentioning it to the station orderly when he first came back with the bags. For many years, he could not remember which detective he had given a verbal report of the find to, but in 2003 he remembered that in fact he had spoken to Detective Sergeant Jim Leheny.

Martin Leonard was by his own admission 'naturally curious'. Yet he too could not recall anything about the fate of the find in later inquiries, except that detective branch had taken over. Happily, he too had a sudden recollection in 2003 that Garda Thornton told him at the time that he had spoken to Detective Sergeant Jim Leheny.

In his interim report, Justice Morris was highly critical of the way Garda Martin Leonard and Garda P J Thornton handled this find. 'They ignored appropriate procedures which should apply to such a find,' the judge wrote. 'They did not preserve the scene. They did not inform the station and request assistance or the attendance of a scene-of-crime officer. They simply brought the bags to the station. The Tribunal is satisfied that this behaviour is totally inexcusable and contrary to proper police practice and procedure.

'When the Gardaí brought the two bags to the station they did not enter the find or cause it to be entered in the occurrence book which exists for that purpose. This would have given every member on duty at the station the relevant information in respect of the find.'

Neither Leonard nor Thornton made a written statement about the find. The bags ended up in the station gymnasium, where they gathered dust for years. Justice Morris concluded that Garda Leonard and Garda Thornton 'have not given the full story in relation to this find'.

Detective Sergeant Jim Leheny told the Tribunal that he did not learn about the find from Garda Thornton on the day it happened. He was in Dublin for most of the following week to give evidence in a court case and heard nothing until he got back to Donegal. He said he thought that Detective Garda Martin Moylan, who had been in Dublin with him giving evidence, told him about it after seeing a telex describing the find on his return.

The telex itself is a mystery. The find was made in the early morning according to Leonard and Thornton, yet the telex was not sent until after midnight. The time of the find was given as 11.25 p.m. The telex said that the Gardaí had recovered two holdall bags and three cardboard boxes. Leonard and Thornton said they recovered only bags.

Every telex sent from the divisional communications centre must be recorded. No one below the rank of Superintendent or Acting Superintendent is permitted into the telex room. No telex can be sent without a written authorisation from the Superintendent. After sending, the original note and a copy go to the Chief Superintendent for his attention and signature. It is then filed in the divisional communications centre. No copy of this telex could be found in Letterkenny. The copy used by the Morris Tribunal was that stored in Garda headquarters in Phoenix Park, where it was received.

Whether Jim Leheny learned about the find the day it happened, or after he returned from Dublin, he ordered two detectives, Pádraig Cafferkey and Martin Anderson to go to the area of the find and carry out a 'discreet search' — a Garda euphemism for a covert search carried out without the authority of a search warrant.

One week later, the local and European election count was in full swing in the Letterkenny community centre. It was a hot sunny day, Friday 10 June. Karen was running for a seat on the Town Council, and Adrienne visited her in the count centre. As she walked across the car park on her way out of the community centre where the count was taking place, a car pulled up beside her. The events that followed became the subject of the terms of reference of the Morris Tribunal.

Over the years, McMahon had told Adrienne many stories of corruption. These two finds in June 1994 were referred to at the Morris Tribunal as the Oatfield find and the Covehill find, despite the fact that both finds took place on the McGlinchey family property at Covehill.

P J Thornton told the Tribunal that the bags he and Garda Martin Leonard recovered were on the Covehill side of the boundary fence with the sweet factory. Adrienne had unwittingly set in motion a series of events, which despite inquiries by the Carty team and the Morris Tribunal, would never be fully resolved. It wasn't until the terms of reference for Morris were published that she even realised that there had been officially recorded finds in June 1994.

On Monday 13 June, three days after the local election count and one day after the European election count in Bundoran, a telex was sent to Garda headquarters at 3.24 p.m. The telex described a find 'during a routine search of vacant sheds at Covehill, Letterkenny', which the McGlinchey family property, stored in cardboard boxes. It said that the find took place at 8 a.m. that Monday morning. The information was not to be released to the press. The Gardaí are not usually so publicity shy, particularly when it came to trumpeting successes against the IRA. No one in the Letterkenny detective branch has admitted to making the find of 13 June 1994 despite extensive inquiries by the Carty team and the Morris Tribunal.

The only record of the second telex is in Garda headquarters in the Phoenix Park, Dublin. No record of the second telex could be found in the divisional office or anywhere else in Letterkenny Garda station, not even in the 'Lennon locker'.

No investigation was ever carried out into the finds. No one remembers sending the telexes. Superintendent John Fitzgerald recorded in his journal a find of explosives on 4 June. He had no record of the second find. No Garda has come forward to claim responsibility for making the find described in this telex. No one knows who authorised the sending of the telexes. No forensic evidence was taken from this find, or that on 4 June. No copies of the telexes were filed in Letterkenny. No investigation files were prepared. No statements were taken. Oddest of all, no one can understand how the cardboard boxes involved in the second find are mentioned in the first telex sent nine days earlier.

The fertiliser lay in the Garda gymnasium for years, until about a week before the arrival of the Carty team at Letterkenny Garda station in 1999, when someone decided the old gym really needed a good clean out. The holdall bags containing the crushed fertiliser, including any forensic evidence, were disposed of. Some people remember seeing the bags lying there for years, some people cannot recall them. No one knows who disposed of them and Superintendent Fitzgerald didn't even remember where in the Garda station the gym was located.

Kevin Lennon sent Jim Leheny a memo asking him 'not to go near McGlinchey or the property in Letterkenny this weekend or until we discuss the matter further. It appears that she is having some problems with the Provos at present over the last two finds. Please destroy this minute.' Leheny did not destroy the note, and instead held on to it for a rainy day, producing it when the forecast got gloomy for Lennon.

Justice Morris concluded that this note showed Lennon 'had some knowledge of these finds which was much deeper than that of Detective Sergeant Leheny'. The note discouraged Leheny from investigating further.

Jim Leheny gave a detailed analysis of the June 1994 finds at the Morris Tribunal. He told Justice Morris that he felt two or three men in Letterkenny Garda station knew the origins of the cardboard boxes. 'Based on the note, I have no doubt but Superintendent Lennon is fully aware of everything in relation to the both finds,' he continued. 'Garda P J Thornton, whom I have known for years and I always found him to be a reliable member and I have no dispute with the man ever, and I held him always in the highest esteem. I think the man is confused or else he is put into a position, which he now finds himself in, that he cannot talk his way out of it.

'I am concerned of the role of Martin Leonard in this find and I base that on the fact that on the previous night he was on a protection post. That protection post was in operation for approximately three to four months, following an arrest I made in the previous March. The post was manned by two armed men. To take up duty at the post, you didn't have to report to the station or you didn't have to report back to the Garda station, you went and you signed on at the post.

'Here we have Garda Leonard coming in at a quarter-past-six in the morning, into the Garda station after completing an eight-hour tour of duty, which was a tour of duty where a member had to be one hundred per cent alert, because there was a threat to this person's life and it was a dangerous post. He goes with Garda

Thornton to the scene, in response to a man calling to the Garda station with a dog reporting a find. There is no record in the station occurrence book, the name of the man isn't known, and it is at a peculiar hour of the morning for this man to be out walking with a dog at six o'clock in Letterkenny.

'Garda Thornton stated he was an observer in the car, he doesn't know who the driver was, he didn't know who the station orderly was. He failed to report it to the sergeant, his unit sergeant, who is Sergeant Bernie O'Reilly. He failed to report it to Detective Garda Jennings when he came on duty and he failed to report it to Sergeant Costello, the sergeant in charge of the station when he came on at ten o'clock.

'The district office is actually where he should have then have reported to, which was manned. He stated that he brought the explosives into the Day Room first and he was waiting on me. That member wouldn't have an idea of when I was coming on duty, if I had availed of a day's leave or what time I would appear at. The volume of people were coming into the station and to his solicitor he stated that 30 to 40 people at that hour of the morning would be passing through the Day Room, going to their various offices.

'This is a Saturday morning. There is no civilians in the office, they don't report to the Garda station on a Saturday morning. It would be only a skeleton staff with the divisional office and in the district office stairs. And that's the corridor they were going down.

'If you were going to the traffic corps or the Detective Branch you would go the opposite direction. He then stated that he was going for breakfast to the canteen, which is next door to the gymnasium and that he took the bags out there. I stand to be corrected on a lot of issues, this is me recalling from his evidence.

And that he put the two bags of explosives out in the foyer outside the back door, that was between the back door coming out of the station and the door leading into the canteen, and that would be the door that I would go up the stairs to the office and directly under the Chief Superintendent's office.

'There is two pillars there, so was midway out there, where people going into the canteen — the canteen was open and that he went to canteen for breakfast. The canteen in Letterkenny Garda station is contracted out to civilians and it only operates from Monday to Friday, so if he had to avail of breakfast in the canteen on a Saturday morning he had to bring in his own food to cook it there. I find that very strange.

'And in the canteen, if he was there, he wouldn't have [seen] the explosives unless he sat by the window. If he was sitting back at the table, he wouldn't have — and I think he is put into a position where he now finds he cannot talk him out of.

'I don't think it's of his making. I think, in my opinion, that Garda Leonard has an input into this. When Garda Leonard was relieved that morning at 6 a.m., I stand to be corrected; he was relieved by Detective Garda Noel McMahon, on the post.

'Another factor in relation to Garda Leonard, he continued on duty and he didn't terminate duty until after 7 p.m., which would have entitled him to claim overtime,' Leheny continued. 'And there he didn't put in any claim in respect of claiming for extra duty performed in seizing this explosives and that would have been granted to him and paid to him without authority, the fact that he went to a scene and explosives were recovered and that's only my theory on it. My theory is that the stuff was taken to the station and put into the gym and nobody was told. And that somebody then later that evening was told and this telex was drafted up and sent off.

'How the person that sent the draft, that communicated this information to the Communication Centre, hasn't been identified, is another mystery.'

Kevin Lennon denied to every inquiry — including to members of the Tribunal legal team during interviews — all knowledge of the second find in June 1994, but his note to Jim Leheny, produced to the Tribunal, proved that he was aware of the finds.

Detective Gardaí Martin Anderson and Patrick Cafferkey admit they conducted a 'discreet search' of the McGlinchey lands on the instructions of their Detective Sergeant Jim Leheny, and denied they received three cardboard boxes of ground fertiliser and icing sugar. Although a 'by the book' detective, Anderson did not seek a Section 29 warrant to lawfully enter the family lands and search it in June 1994.

Anderson and Leheny attended the Central Criminal Court in Dublin between 6 June and 9 June 1994. They returned to duty on 10 June. Anderson and Cafferkey were working from 2 p.m. until 10 p.m. that evening. Anderson said that the search took place 'on Thursday or Friday', and he started work around 2 p.m. or 2.30 p.m. that day and it was a follow-up search to the find on 4 June 1994. Anderson said that they parked their car in the car park of Oatfield car park, which is not open at weekends. Since he was in Dublin on Thursday, this means that the search must have taken place on Friday, the day of the election count, 10 June 1994.

Anderson had a problem with the layout of the land and the sheds. In 1999, he accompanied Inspector Hugh Coll and once again without permission entered the family lands. It had been developed since 1994. In 1997, a planning application clearly showed the two concrete sheds to the west of the family home, and the proposal to demolish them. In 1998 a new house was built between the family home and Oatfield. A 10' x 4' garden shed was

Former Detective Garda Noel McMahon who was found to have lied to the Morris Tribunal in an effort to mislead the Tribunal. Subject to some very minor exceptions, his evidence was rejected in respect of all the central matters considered by the Tribunal. He attempted to mislead the Tribunal in relation to his knowledge of, or involvement in, each of the findings of the Tribunal's Term of Reference. He gave a misleading and untruthful account of his dealings with Adrienne McGlinchey and Superintendent Kevin Lennon. The chairman was satisfied that this was done in a calculated way in an attempt to prevent the Tribunal ascertaining the truth. He retired from An Garda Síochána following the damning report of Chairman Frederick Morris. Photo: Empics

Sisters Adrienne and Karen McGlinchey as they left the Court of Criminal Appeal after giving evidence in the successful Frank Shortt application for a miscarriage of justice. Photo: Collins Photo Agency

Garda Martin Leonard of Letterkenny Garda station told the Morris Tribunal: 'It is the nature of the Gardaí, we don't name the names — we don't want to get anybody into trouble in the Garda Síochána internal matters.' Photo: Photocall Ireland

Yvonne Devine, a former flatmate of Adrienne's in Buncrana during the 1990s. Photo: Photocall Ireland

View of the front of the flats at the Crescent in Buncrana. The middle bay window is the sitting room of Adrienne's flat and the side 'garden' leads to her flat entrance.

View of the rear flats of the Crescent from the convent grounds.

A Garda carrying evidence into the Donegal Town courtroom at the start of the Morris Tribunal. Photo: Empics

The roundabout at Bridgend leading to the border between Donegal and Derry. A find of homemade explosives was made on 11 January 1994. The find was made behind the sheds next to the group of trees beside the buses at the rear right of the photo. The foreground shows the road leading to the border. Gardaí had set up a checkpoint a quarter of a mile from the roundabout towards Derry to 'intercept' the delivery of the bomb to Derry. The Tribunal discovered that it would have been impossible for Adrienne to see the checkpoint and therefore the delivery had to have been a 'drop' to impress the senior officers present.

Shed at Rathfrangan, Rossnowlagh, where the second find of homemade explosives was made on 18 July 1994. This is the shed to which Justice Morris found that Lennon and McMahon had transported the materials to be found later.

Photo of a shotgun found among documents belonging to Kevin Lennon in Letterkenny Garda station in 2002.

The landmark Camel's Hump checkpoint in Strabane being dismantled by British army personnel as security measures were scaled down in 1999. Photo: Empics

Former Detective Garda Noel McMahon sits at his legal team's table awaiting the start of the explosives module. Photo: Irish Times

Sheenagh McMahon, estranged wife of Detective McMahon, gave evidence concerning her husband and former Superintendent Kevin Lennon at the Morris Tribunal. Photo: Photocall Ireland

Members of the Garda Commissioner's legal team: Patrick Marrinan SC and Eamonn Leahy SC who sadly passed away during the hearings in Donegal in 2003. Photo: Empics

Superintendent Hugh Coll, a senior member of the Carty team who conducted interviews with Adrienne over a period in excess of forty days. Photo: Empics

Retired Garda Tom Sreenan, who used nursery rhymes to try and persuade Adrienne to open her flat to him. Photo: Photocall Ireland

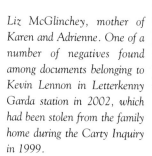

Liz McGlinchey, mother of Karen and Adrienne. One of a number of negatives found among documents belonging to Kevin Lennon in Letterkenny Garda station in 2002, which had been stolen from the family home during the Carty Inquiry in 1999.

Adrienne arriving to give her evidence to the Morris Tribunal. Photo: Photocall Ireland

Bill Shipsey SC and Adrienne exit the Morris Tribunal during a break in the hearing. Photo: Empics

'Superintendent Lennon lied to the Tribunal on almost every issue on which he gave evidence. He lied about the nature and extent of his involvement with Adrienne McGlinchey and Detective Garda Noel McMahon. He lied about his knowledge and involvement in the finds and other matters which were the subject matter of the Tribunal's Inquiry. He attempted to mislead the Tribunal on all of the central issues. On these, his evidence was rejected in total. In these circumstances, Superintendent Lennon is not entitled to his costs. I would add that the idea that the people of Ireland should be asked to pay him €40.00 per hour for the

many hours that he undoubtedly spent trying to deceive the Tribunal and prevent it getting to the truth, is unrealistic.' Chairman Frederick Morris, July 2004. The government, on foot of the damning report, later sacked Kevin Lennon. Photo: Photocall Ireland

Peter Charleton SC

'The past cannot be changed. The truth reflects reality without adding anything to it or taking anything from it. Reality, because it has happened, is beyond any power. The only honest answer is to reflect reality in truth.' Morris Tribunal introductory remarks by Peter Charleton. Photo: Irish Times

Ciara McLaughlin lived in the flat above Adrienne and Yvonne Devine in the Crescent in Buncrana. She was given money for phone calls by Detective Noel Jones to inform him of Adrienne's movements. Photo: Irish Times

Eleanor McDermott was given a threatening message to pass to Adrienne during the Carty Inquiry. Photo: Empics

Joint border patrol checkpoint by RUC and British Army. Photo: Pacemaker Press

The hearing rooms of the Morris Tribunal in Clonskeagh, Dublin. Photo: Irish Times

A large cache of homemade explosives stored in Adrienne's bedroom in Buncrana. This photo was found among documents belonging to Kevin Lennon in Letterkenny Garda station in 2002. He told the Tribunal that he was unable to identify the location, but agreed with Peter Charleton SC that the toiletries on the sink suggested it was probably a lady's bedroom.

Letterkenny Garda station. Photo: Irish Times

Photo of a shotgun, one from a number of photo albums found among documents that were the property of Kevin Lennon in 2002 in Letterkenny Garda station.

Chairman of the Morris Tribunal, Mr Justice Frederick Morris.

'The Tribunal is of the view that every member of An Garda Síochána should be immediately obliged to account for any action taken by him or her as a member of An Garda Síochána or while on a designated duty.

'Within the context of the powers vested in An Garda Síochána and the need for a disciplined force, any member who does not comply should be suspended. It should be a specific breach of discipline to fail to account in that regard and one, which, in the Tribunal's view, merits dismissal.' Photo: Photocall Ireland bought in 2002 and placed at the east side of the new house. At the Tribunal, Anderson identified the new sheds to the east of the new house as the ones he had (unsuccessfully) searched in June 1994.

Under direct examination he told Tribunal barrister Paul McDermott SC that the day of the election count was 13 June. The thirteenth was the day that the telex was sent, but the day of the count was the date which was being nominated as the actual day of the find. In the following exchange with Paul McDermott, Detective Garda Anderson denied involvement in the Covehill find of homemade explosives:

Paul McDermott: I wonder if I could take you then to 13 June 1994; was that the date of the count of local elections?

D/Gda Martin Anderson: So I'm told. I checked it, I checked it, it was, yeah.

Paul McDermott: Were you on the lands that day?

D/Gda Martin Anderson: Pardon?

Paul McDermott: Were you carrying out the search that day? Is that the day you were carrying out the search?

D/Gda Martin Anderson: No, I wasn't carrying out a search that day.

Paul McDermott: Did you attend again at the shed or in the vicinity of the shed on the McGlinchey lands on that day?

D/Gda Martin Anderson: No, I didn't.

Paul McDermott: With your colleague Detective Garda Cafferkey?

D/Gda Martin Anderson: No, I didn't.

Paul McDermott: Did you meet Adrienne McGlinchey that day?

D/Gda Martin Anderson: I may have seen her but I wasn't talking to her.

Paul McDermott: Were you in a patrol car that day with Detective Garda Cafferkey?

D/Gda Martin Anderson: I'd say I was.

Paul McDermott: Do you recall stopping in the car near some car park at Letterkenny at any stage and talking to Ms McGlinchey?

D/Gda Martin Anderson: I wasn't told, that didn't happen.

Paul McDermott: Was there any encounter between yourself and your colleague Detective Garda Cafferkey asking Ms McGlinchey had she any more fertiliser?

D/Gda Martin Anderson: That never happened.

Paul McDermott: Was there any occasion upon which fertiliser was handed over to you by Ms McGlinchey?

D/Gda Martin Anderson: No.

There was one particularly interesting fact about the find of 13 or 10 June, whichever day one decides it occurred on. The three cardboard boxes were already described in the earlier telex, which was sent on 5 June but had not yet been officially 'found'. The telex was put to Anderson for his opinion.

Paul McDermott: There is one document apparently relating to this find on 13th June. The Carty team originally thought there wasn't any documentation but they have in fact unearthed this. This is a message from Letterkenny for the information of Assistant Commissioner Crime & Security: 'Telex message 294. Subject; explosives find at Covehill, Letterkenny, County Donegal. At 8 a.m. on 13th

June 1994, during the course of a routine search of a vacant shed at Covehill, Letterkenny, D Branch members found the following: Approximately 112 pounds of finally ground fertiliser. It was contained in 14-pound plastic bags, which were stored in cardboard box. The fertiliser has been examined and samples will be forwarded to the Technical Bureau for examination. This information is not to be given to the press. Any further developments will be reported. Message ends. Sender, Divisional Communications Centre, Letterkenny.'

Now, that signifies that there was a vacant shed at Covehill, searched by Detective Branch members and in it was found ground fertiliser in the amounts set out in the telex. Now, what do you know about that find?

D/Gda Martin Anderson: I had no knowledge of that find until recently.

Paul McDermott: How can that be?

D/Gda Martin Anderson: I don't know. I only heard of that recently.

Paul McDermott: Well, if it was significant enough to inform Crime & Security in Dublin about this, was it not a matter of significance in Letterkenny Garda station?

D/Gda Martin Anderson: It should be but I didn't hear anything about it.

Paul McDermott: You had been searching the sheds within days of this?

D/Gda Martin Anderson: I searched the sheds, the grounds there, we found nothing. That was the first — that only came to light to me just a few weeks ago.

Paul McDermott: The Detective Branch is interested in investigating finds of explosive; isn't that right?

D/Gda Martin Anderson: That's correct.

Paul McDermott: If one assumes that, and one assumes that you went out to see if you could find more explosives in addition to the holdall bags, if there was a find on the 13th following your search, is that not something you were interested in?

D/Gda Martin Anderson: It would be but I know nothing about that find.

Paul McDermott: Well, do you think it never happened?

D/Gda Martin Anderson: I can't answer you that.

Paul McDermott: Well, if it had happened, wouldn't you have known about it?

D/Gda Martin Anderson: I should have known about it if it happened. I'm here on oath, I didn't know anything about that find.

Although it was admirable that Anderson wanted to remind the great Irish public that he was under oath, it seems that he was wasting his breath as far as the chairman was concerned. Tribunal counsel continued to try to unearth the truth about the find of homemade explosives at Covehill.

Paul McDermott: You see, a person might be surprised if there were a find on 13th June, which occurred perhaps a number of days after a search, that the persons who were investigating the find on 13th June, didn't even try to put a time frame as to when the material may have arrived in the shed at Covehill, by asking the people who searched the premises a few days earlier to confirm with them that nothing had been found and try and pinpoint the date upon which they searched the premises?

D/Gda Martin Anderson: I couldn't indicate what date I searched the place, first of all, I knew it was searched, that place, sometime, but I couldn't say exactly when I searched it.

Paul McDermott: It was a number of days after 4th?

D/Gda Martin Anderson: It was sometime after 4th, it could be a fortnight or three weeks, I don't know.

Paul McDermott: Well, sorry, you told us yesterday it was a follow-up search as you understood to the 4th, to the find on the 4th?

D/Gda Martin Anderson: Yeah, but I didn't know anything about this other find.

Paul McDermott: But the logic of that is, if it's a follow-up search to the 4th, it must have happened before the 13th, because otherwise it would be a follow-up search to a find on the 13th?

D/Gda Martin Anderson: Well, all I can say is, I went down and searched that place and I had no knowledge of this other find, whatsoever.

Paul McDermott: In any event, nobody came to you to ask you about the day of the week that you had attended or the time of the day that you had attended to search the shed at Covehill?

D/Gda Martin Anderson: Nobody asked me, all I done was report back to Jim Leheny and that was it.

Paul McDermott: The suggestion made by Adrienne McGlinchey is that she handed you material which is much the same description as that in the telex?

D/Gda Martin Anderson: That's completely untrue.

Paul McDermott: We can take it then, that you didn't bring such material to the Garda station and file it as a find at Covehill on the 13th?

D/Gda Martin Anderson: No, certainly not.

Paul McDermott: What then is your explanation in relation to this mystery find on 13th June 1994?

D/Gda Martin Anderson: I don't know. As I said already, I only became aware of that in the last few weeks.

Paul McDermott: Well, do you know from working in Letterkenny Garda station, whether it is a mystery to all of your other colleagues who were present at Letterkenny Garda station in June of 1994?

D/Gda Martin Anderson: I know some of them there that have no idea, no idea.

Paul McDermott: Who has no idea?

D/Gda Martin Anderson: Matt Tolan.

Paul McDermott: Yes?

D/Gda Martin Anderson: And Hugh Smith.

Paul McDermott : And yourself?

D/Gda Martin Anderson: And myself.

Paul McDermott: And Detective Garda Cafferkey?

D/Gda Martin Anderson : Cafferkey, yeah.

Paul McDermott: Who else?

D/Gda Martin Anderson: That's all I can remember talking about it to.

In summary, Mr Justice Morris concluded that 'no member of the Garda Síochána on duty on the 4th, the 10th, or the 13th of June 1994 called before the Tribunal has given a satisfactory explanation of their involvement in respect of these events. The Tribunal is satisfied that most of them have withheld information from the Tribunal and failed and neglected to give a full and true account of what happened.'

In 1999, the Carty team had conducted hundreds of hours of

interviews with Adrienne over several months, filling thousands of pages of statements and memos. Not a single note, line or scrap of paper exists to suggest that even one question was posed to her by the Carty team about the events surrounding the find of cardboard boxes on 13 June 1994. The only reference in any statement to the find of holdall bags on 4 June is in a statement from June 1999, in which she told them '(the stuff) was left behind Oatfield factory. Sometime afterwards I learned from the Guards that they had found the ground-down fertiliser behind Oatfield.' There were no follow up questions about what she had learned, who she had learned it from, or even when she learned this. She was never asked about a second find.

In reaching his conclusions, Justice Morris was wary of accepting uncorroborated testimony. In all of the finds in the terms of reference, evidence was available from other sources to buttress Adrienne's evidence. Evidence from scene-of-crime officers, from the Gardaí who made the finds, even limited forensic analysis in some cases. This was not the case in the June 1994 finds.

No one is able to say who sent the telexes. No one admits to making the second find. In the end, Justice Morris didn't know quite what to believe. He found that Gardaí P J Thornton and Martin Leonard, retired Detective Sergeant Jim Leheny and Detective Gardaí Pádraig Cafferkey and Martin Anderson and Kevin Lennon had not told the true and complete story of those events.

In his ruling on applications for costs, Justice Morris said 'the main allegations made by Ms McGlinchey concerning the corrupt activities on the part of Detective Garda McMahon and Superintendent Lennon concerning the "finds" and other matters, the subject matter of the Tribunal's terms of reference, were accepted by the Tribunal, for the simple reason that on each event her testimony was supported by cogent independent evidence. This enabled the Tribunal to independently accept the facts to which she had testified. In short the Tribunal found that in respect of the matters central to its inquiry Adrienne McGlinchey had told the truth.'

11

The 'Big One'

On Friday 10 June 1994 a considerable change of senior personnel in Letterkenny Garda station took place.

Superintendent John Fitzgerald was in Ballybofey. The senior inspector, Detective Inspector McLoin took time off from 7 June to use up his last few days of leave, and retired on 10 June. Chief Superintendent Sean Ginty left Letterkenny Garda station to work for the United Nations in Cyprus the same day. Inspector Jim Gallagher was attending a court case in Dublin, while Chief Superintendent Denis Fitzpatrick, who was to take over from Sean Ginty, was leaving to do an FBI course. Chief Superintendent Noel Anderson, who would be in temporary charge until Fitzpatrick got back from the USA, did not arrive until some days later.

So, on 10 June 1994, Detective Inspector Kevin Lennon was the Acting District Officer in Letterkenny. He wrote a letter to his Chief Superintendent. The letter survives only in one photocopy, and is illegible in some parts.

In the letter, Lennon outlined a detailed plan by the Provisional IRA to attack a military checkpoint at Belleek, a town on the south Donegal/Fermanagh border. The attack would involve 'remote control' and 'necessitate a house takeover in the Ballyshannon area, where the final phase of completion of the device will be carried out prior to transportation to the target area'.

Lennon said that he hoped to thwart the planned IRA attack by working with the superintendent in charge of the Ballyshannon district, and confidently predicted that he would 'be in a position over the coming week to identify the location of the device, now in the early stages of assembly'.

'I request that no written correspondence in relation to this matter be returned to me and I undertake to inform all concerned of any developments. The RUC should be notified when the superintendent at Ballyshannon has been briefed,' he concluded.

The IRA ceasefire was imminent. A meeting of Sinn Féin had taken place in a Donegal hotel in April 1994 and there was a groundswell of support for the peace initiative.

While the country prayed and hoped for an end to the misery, in Donegal there were those who viewed the new dawning of peace with less than overwhelming enthusiasm. Noel McMahon had a new urgency. There had to be one final drop, the 'big one'.

Every year, the Orange Order celebrated the victory of William of Orange at the Battle of The Boyne in Rossnowlagh in Co. Donegal. It was and remains a popular day out for families to enjoy the parades and the bands through the tiny seaside village. The parade is always held on the Saturday prior to the main Northern Ireland marches and always passes off peacefully. It made the perfect backdrop for Lennon and McMahon to bow out of their campaign of deluding the nation, many of whom actually believed the Garda mission statement of achieving 'the highest level of Personal Protection, Community Commitment and State Security'.

Three years previously, Kevin Lennon had been a sergeant in the traffic corps in Letterkenny. Now he was the shining star, heavily relied upon by senior Garda management for his opinion on counter-terrorist strategy. Noel McMahon was basking in Lennon's glow and living under the protection of his friend and senior officer. The authoritarian Lennon commanded respect. Detectives like Tom Sreenan feared demotion if they were seen to interfere in the activities of Adrienne, McMahon and Lennon, while others suspected the reward for asking awkward questions would be a transfer to a remote post until the end of their career.

Adrienne and Yvonne had moved again. The house in Ballyliffen was compromised by the friendship between Detective Sreenan and the estate agent. Clonmany was a little town some ten miles away and she found a house away from the main village. It had an outdoor shed, ideal for dry storage. The grinding operation was taking every spare moment. McMahon told her that Kevin Lennon had him under intense pressure to have everything in place for the Twelfth parades. This would be the last job. This time she knew it was really going to be the last. The ceasefire would secure her freedom. There was extensive media speculation during the summer of an imminent announcement from the IRA Army Council of a truce.

Lennon and McMahon had taken over her life. Days had turned to months, which turned to years at their beck and call. Occasionally they argued and she found herself in the middle. McMahon complained that Lennon had taken the glory for his work. At other times he speculated on Kevin Lennon's promotion to Superintendent, and then to Assistant Commissioner. He expected Lennon would one day be enthroned in the Phoenix Park as the Garda Commissioner. McMahon fancied himself as an Assistant Commissioner in human resources. Adrienne just wanted to be left alone.

Work in the factory was a relief from the constant humming and whirring, which continued into the early hours each night. McMahon joined her at the house and they gradually filled bags and stored them in the shed.

When it was time to select a location, they toured Ballyshannon and Bundoran, checking out derelict houses, barns and sheds. She lost track of the buildings he checked out. Every boreen and by-road along the south Donegal coast was inspected. It was long and tiring, but finally they settled on an old house at the side of the road in Rossnowlagh, in a townland called Ardeelin, part of the marching route for the Twelfth parade. McMahon had suggested a caravan in the holiday park but it was impossible to locate an unused caravan.

Kevin Lennon wanted the find to be the biggest and most convincing. The Orangemen would give greater credence to his scheme. The prospect of the Gardaí foiling a major terrorist plot against the Orange Order would be a coup from which Lennon would reap benefits for years. Analysts would comment on the brilliance of Garda intelligence, which saved countless lives, and on the predictability of the IRA committing one final atrocity to satisfy the militants who had not yet gravitated towards peace.

Lennon was busy preparing the officers in south Donegal and the RUC for the bomb. He had already submitted his letter of 10 June. On 8 July he went to Bundoran with Chief Superintendent Noel Anderson to meet Superintendent Duffy from Ballyshannon. Duffy recalled Lennon and the Chief arriving into his office. They travelled together with Detective Sergeant Aidan Murray to Bundoran. Out of earshot of the other officers Lennon told Duffy of the supposed IRA plan.

'There was going to be a bomb attack on the British Army checkpoint at Rosscor,' Duffy later recalled being told. 'The IRA were planning the attack by means of a bomb loaded into a caravan, towed to the checkpoint and that the caravan would be dropped at the checkpoint and detonated.'

Duffy, for his own reasons, chose to drive to Fermanagh that evening to inform RUC Superintendent McFarlane, rather than going through the normal channels of speaking with the border superintendent. He did not inform Crime & Security at Garda headquarters, assuming that Lennon had already done so.

The girls had been saving for a holiday during the summer break in August. After her eviction from the Crescent by John Mackey, Adrienne had to dip into their holiday fund to pay the deposit for the new house. She complained to McMahon about being evicted because they had used her flat to store their 'explosives' and the loss of her deposit in the Crescent. It was always a struggle making ends meet on the minimal income, and she had not taken a holiday since 1991.

There was a desperation about Noel McMahon. He could sit grinding on the floor with a bottle of brandy beside him, swigging between crushing cycles. They were at his house. Sheenagh was away. McMahon was filling the freezer bags with the ground fertiliser. He then took away each bag as it was filled. Then he would start all over again.

At one stage, he ran out of brandy and he told Adrienne to carry on while he drove to town to replenish his bar. He warned her not to answer the door to anyone. Adrienne took the opportunity to have a look around the house in his absence, wandering from room to room. Suddenly, she saw the lights of an approaching car and feared he had caught her snooping. She waited for him to enter the house, but after some minutes she looked out the window and saw two Gardaí. She recognised one of two men carrying black bags and going to the garage as being a local Garda. After they left she went into the garage and opened the bags. They contained carrier bags of ground fertiliser and at that point she realised that she was not the only person involved in the crushing and preparation of homemade explosives for the hoax finds.

At the rear end of McMahon's home at Porthaw, Buncrana, there was a glasshouse which had become a storehouse for bags of crushed and uncrushed fertiliser. It was stacked in piles on the floor. McMahon had also purchased fertiliser, which he later told the Carty team was for use on his garden.

McMahon repeatedly denied to the many inquiries that followed that he had ever stored fertiliser for use in hoax bombs in 1993 or 1994. Unfortunately for McMahon, his lie was uncovered in his own discovery of documents to the Morris Tribunal, because he produced the cheque receipt for the purchase of the glasshouse in 1993. Sergeant Michael Murray, the scene-of-crime examiner from Buncrana, testified that the glasshouse lay unassembled until he helped build it in 1995. He told the Tribunal that 'up to February of 1995, there was no glasshouse there. But I was aware at that stage that Noel McMahon had purchased the frame to erect the glasshouse, which was lying out at the back of the garage. There was no glasshouse in existence during my friendship with him up to that time.'

So harsh were the criticisms of Sgt Murray by Justice Morris in his interim report, that his legal team did not even bother to apply for costs.

Taxis were used to transport the bags of fertiliser from Co-Ops and shops where they were purchased. The demand to get as much as possible ground in time for the Orange parade was ever present but by the week of the parades, he had to postpone the official Garda discovery of an IRA cache of homemade explosives because there was not enough in place.

McMahon told her that they had kept an eye on the house at Ardeelin during the march. He laughed as he described an Orangeman who came into the overgrown garden and relieved himself. McMahon said in his own evidence that Adrienne had told him the story, replacing the Guards with IRA watchers. The Rossnowlagh parade took place on 9 July, the day after the meeting between Duffy, Lennon, Murray and Anderson in Bundoran. Kevin Lennon was present in Rossnowlagh during the Orange march.

Six days later, Lennon wrote a secret report addressed to Chief Superintendent Noel Anderson. Once again, he outlined how 'secret intelligence' from a 'reliable source' pointed to an IRA attack on the British Army checkpoint at Belleek. The attack would be launched from Ballyshannon. This time Lennon had more detail on the operation. The IRA had moved homemade explosives into the area and planned to load them into a caravan in the Rossnowlagh Caravan Park, Ballyshannon. 'They have inspected the caravan and entered it by means of picking the lock,' he added.

The IRA would take over a local house to load, arm and prime the caravan bomb, and tow it to Belleek using a car with false number plates matching those of 'a respected person in the locality, thereby arousing no suspicion'. Lennon described how the driver would use a foot pedal to release the caravan. This would give the IRA bomber fifteen seconds to accelerate out of range before detonation.

Lennon concluded that 'the plan I believe will be disrupted early next week when I believe I will have learned the location of the explosive mix.'

'I also believe I will be in a position to identify the area where the house take-over is planned,' he continued. 'Superintendent Duffy of Ballyshannon station will be briefed in full and is aware at this time that I have carried out some duties in his district in this regard.'

The letter has some curious features. The caravan bomb which Lennon describes had never been used in the history of the Troubles. The IRA are not noted for suicide missions, which is what a fifteen-second getaway amounts to. The release of the caravan bomb, even with the fifteen-second interval before detonation, would certainly have aroused the suspicions of the professional soldiers manning the border garrison, who, without doubt, would have opened fire in self-defence.

Throughout all the inquiries since 1999, at no stage did Kevin Lennon ever suggest that he was in receipt of any information about Rossnowlagh prior to 18 July 1994, the day of the find. At the Court of Criminal Appeal in 2002 he started the narrative on the night of the Rossnowlagh find. The reports he wrote at the time were never submitted to Crime & Security Branch, the Garda intelligence agency. Noel McMahon also began his story on the night of the find. Cross-examining Adrienne, his barrister said: 'Noel McMahon's position is this: He knew nothing and heard nothing from you about Rossnowlagh until 18th of July when you told him there was stuff down there. You went down that night with Kevin Lennon and saw this stuff. You then told him you knew about this because you had been there on a previous occasion with a number of men in a van who were unloading stuff into the house, and that the reason you were there was to pretend to be kissing one of the men in the front seat of the van if any car or passer-by along, so as to deflect any attention from the activities that you were engaging in.'

McMahon, in his initial evidence, never mentioned receiving earlier information. There was no talk about caravans, or pedal devices, or houses being taken over, or locks being picked. On the contrary, he claimed that the first he knew was from a sudden phone call from Adrienne on the night of the find.

Freelance journalist Gerard Cunningham covered the Morris Tribunal for several national and provincial media outlets. Vincent Browne interviewed him on RTÉ on the night that McMahon gave the evidence described above. Cunningham pointed out the discrepancies between Superintendent Duffy's evidence some months previously in relation to Lennon's prior information weeks before the find, and the position adopted by McMahon where the first word he received was on the night of the find.

The following day McMahon apologised to the chairman, Justice Morris for misleading the Tribunal. Explaining that he was tired and confused the previous day, McMahon said he now remembered receiving information around ten days before the find. He proceeded to describe in fine detail the plan by IRA members from Letterkenny to use a caravan to blow up the checkpoint at Roscor in Belleek, Co. Fermanagh. This memory recovery was remarkable, reversing what he had told the Carty inquiry, his evidence to the Court of Criminal Appeal, the instructions given to his legal counsel during the cross-examination of Adrienne, and his own evidence the previous day.

'This change of evidence was seismic as far as Detective Garda McMahon was concerned,' Justice Morris noted in his report.

To suggest that a journalist on a talk show could have influenced a change in testimony would be speculation. But whatever the reason, Justice Morris found that Noel McMahon 'amended his evidence so as to dovetail with the report which had been sent in by Detective Inspector Lennon. This was done, the Tribunal is satisfied, in an effort to iron out the contradiction between them.'

The evening of 17 July was balmy and warm. Noel McMahon had set the deadline for the final removal of ground fertiliser to Rossnowlagh. The find would be made the following day. Adrienne had her shopping list. He told her to fill a drum with diesel and leave it in Letterkenny. There was a beer keg, found lying abandoned in the council yard. McMahon wanted it included in the drop. The house had been chosen weeks beforehand. A dilapidated shed further up the road would also be used.

Despite the many trips to Rossnowlagh, Adrienne could not recall leaving explosives in the old house. She clearly recalls being in the house on at least one occasion, but has no memory of dropping fertiliser in the house.

The undercover van used by Gardaí in the Inishowen area was always kept behind McMahon's house. On the night of 17 July 1994, McMahon loaded it with the ground fertiliser. They drove to Letterkenny and collected Kevin Lennon. They collected the drum of diesel and a beer keg.

They drove to Rossnowlagh. Lennon stopped in Donegal and he went into an off-licence to buy some vodka for Adrienne, which he said would help to relax her. There was light banter between the three on the journey. Both men had their official weapons with them, which lent authenticity to the operation in the event that they were disturbed by an unexpected patrol. Comparisons were made between the guns and she was given possession of both guns as they drove through the night.

Lennon denied stopping in Donegal for vodka on the way to Rossnowlagh but recalled that there was a stop on the way back for chips. The issue of a stop for vodka in Donegal town became more credible when McMahon recalled that Adrienne was 'pole-axed drunk', a strangely unsolicited proposition to make when they were denying they stopped for vodka. The vodka also explains Adrienne's lack of a clear memory of the night.

In Rossnowlagh they pulled off the narrow country road onto a dirt track, barely the width of the van. Working quickly Lennon and McMahon unloaded the diesel, fertiliser and sugar. In total they left a three-and-a-half hundredweight bag of ground fertiliser, eighty-four pounds of icing sugar, twelve gallons of diesel oil and a beer keg. Lennon was nervous, terrified of being caught in the act. Adrienne's memory is that they left after unloading and drove back to Letterkenny without going to the house at Ardeelin.

As they left Donegal town going north to Letterkenny they passed through the mountain pass of Barnesmore Gap. McMahon spotted a Garda checkpoint. He stopped some yards from the marked patrol car. It was the early hours of the morning. Lennon told her to hide behind the curtain between the front seats and the back. Peeking around the curtain she saw McMahon flashing his warrant card at the Garda. As he got back into the van, he laughed that they did not recognise Lennon. The remainder of the journey was uneventful.

Later investigations into the personnel involved in the checkpoint could not establish the Gardaí involved. No Guard has ever come forward and admitted being present the night a large quantity of subversive material was discovered in Rossnowlagh. A checkpoint may not necessarily be recorded in the relevant station and investigations relied totally on the truthfulness and memory of the Gardaí. Lennon said they were stopped in the surveillance van on another occasion around that time, when he claimed Adrienne was in the Ballintra area with them.

Adrienne watched the RTÉ news bulletin with some amusement the following day. Superintendent Duffy discussed with emotion the diligent work carried out by Gardaí, which undoubtedly resulted in the saving of lives. Prior to the Ardchicken and Rossnowlagh finds the largest cache of homemade explosives uncovered by Superintendent Duffy's division in south Donegal amounted to a mere four-and-a-half pounds, whereas within the space of eight months they had unearthed two finds of around three-quarters of a ton.

Kevin Lennon and Noel McMahon both claimed that they travelled to Rossnowlagh in Kevin Lennon's car, not the surveillance van. Lennon told the Court of Criminal Appeal that he would have claimed mileage expenses for the use of his private car, but by the time he got to the witness box at the Morris Tribunal he did not think he had made a claim.

Lennon said he told Adrienne to have a cover story ready for the IRA to explain the loss of yet another cache of explosives. He said she was very concerned about her safety because an alleged informer had been murdered in Fermanagh the previous week. He claimed that at all times he considered her personal safety and adopted a unique method of detecting any IRA surveillance, circling a roundabout three times to spot anyone following, with Adrienne lying down in the back seat. As a further anti surveillance precaution, Adrienne was told to lie down on the back seat when they drove through the towns of Donegal and Ballybofey.

Once again, they couldn't agree a story. Lennon said that they went to the shed first, then the house. McMahon said that they went to the house first. Lennon said that he took up a covering position at the door of the shed, handgun drawn, while Adrienne went inside and counted the bags. McMahon said that Lennon never went inside the shed. McMahon said that he feared for his personal safety entering an IRA store, but also said that he knew the IRA didn't work at night. He said that Adrienne gave him the names of two Letterkenny IRA members — who had also been behind the Ardchicken find, he claimed — but said he asked that no arrests be made in case it landed Adrienne 'in real trouble'. On the face of it, an accident-prone IRA informer, two-timing lover of senior Republican personnel, manufacturer of explosives, and courier had lost another huge cache of explosives and ammunition. But despite the fearsome reputation of the IRA internal security checks, no one seems to have worried that the constant losses would land Adrienne 'in real trouble'.

Both McMahon and Lennon remembered that Adrienne was hungry. McMahon told the Court of Criminal Appeal that he went into the chip shop beside a Donegal town nightclub. Lennon said that he was the one who went into the chip shop. He placed the time at around 2 a.m., as he recalled the patrons milling around the street after the disco. He managed to find a quiet spot away from the hundreds of people on the well-lit main street.

Neither officer contacted Donegal Garda station to inform them of the supposed IRA dump in Rossnowlagh. Lennon said that informing Gardaí in Donegal town might have compromised the security of his informant.

As in the previous hoaxes masterminded by Lennon and McMahon, there were major departures from normal IRA procedure. Storing explosive at two locations for an attack on a single target was alien to the IRA. The shed was owned by a local farmer and in regular use. They were destined to store hay within a few days. The first the farmer heard about the use of his shed was on television the following day. No statement was taken from him until the Carty inquiry was set up in 1999. Lennon had 'conditioned' Duffy to expect a major find by submitting the reports weeks beforehand.

Lennon moved quickly. He grabbed a few hours sleep and by 10 a.m. he was back in south Donegal. He met with Superintendent Michael Duffy in his office in Ballyshannon and told him that he had been up most if not all the previous night at the scene of a major find of homemade explosives in Rossnowlagh. The two men left in Duffy's car and drove slowly past the house and shed, which Lennon had indicated were the sites. After Lennon left for Letterkenny, Duffy retraced the route with two of his sergeants, instructing them to take two search parties and recover the explosives at separate times. The first find made at the house was at 3.30 p.m. on 18 July and Duffy subsequently forwarded a report to Letterkenny indicating that a further find was expected the following day. However, the sergeant who was to make the second find went off duty and the search party, unaware of Duffy's instructions, made the second recovery at 8.50 p.m. Telexes were generated from Letterkenny Divisional Communications. The reports found their way to Garda headquarters and from there by some route up to the authorities in Northern Ireland. This in turn brought a response from the Northern Ireland Office.

The day after the finds, the Right Honourable Sir John Wheeler DL MP from the Northern Ireland Office wrote to Justice Minister Maire Geoghegan-Quinn congratulating her on the invaluable counter-terrorist work of the Gardaí. He added, 'I understand that the Gardaí are hopeful of making arrests following the operation.' Of course no arrests were planned, as the finds were the work of the Gardaí.

By 3 August 1994 a chain of correspondence flowed through the ranks. An official in the Department of Justice was directed by the Minister to forward a copy of Sir John Wheeler's letter to the Garda Commissioner. He in turn gave it to the Deputy Commissioner of Operations. It was passed to an assistant commissioner who sent it down the line to the chief superintendent at Letterkenny. On 18 August the detective superintendent on behalf of the assistant commissioner wrote: 'The attached correspondence above is forwarded for your attention and that of other members involved in this case. Please return when noted by all concerned.' Chief Superintendent Fitzpatrick and a Sergeant McFadden, and various members of the search party involved in uncovering the find, noted the congratulations. It was also reported on RTÉ News.

Against best police practice, Duffy instructed the removal of the explosive material to the store in Ballyshannon and some time later the ground fertiliser was spread over his garden, that of another officer and over waste ground in Bundoran. No investigation file exists for the find.

Lennon and McMahon were buoyed up by the success of their bogus operation. Adrienne was unaware of the attention it received from the ranks of the governments and was busy preparing to take her long planned holiday in Lanzarote with Yvonne Devine in August 1994.

On her return she learned hat the IRA had announced the long-awaited ceasefire. She had experienced normality while she was away. Prior to each find, she had always been told it would be the last. On each occasion Noel McMahon had told her it was necessary to bring someone on board. First it was Danny Kelly, then the local Guards in Buncrana, then Kevin Lennon. Lennon had bullied her constantly to maintain the charade. The threat of a long prison term was ever present. The RUC were used by

Lennon to impress Fitzpatrick and the Garda authorities. She knew she had no way out and would always be at the beck and call of McMahon and Lennon. Refusing them wasn't an option.

The Tribunal found that Lennon's intelligence reports of 10 June and 15 July 1994 were 'invented by Detective Inspector Lennon with a view to the creation of hoax finds in Rossnowlagh'. Justice Morris also found that for months in advance of the finds Adrienne McGlinchey, Kevin Lennon and Noel McMahon made preparations on the ground, which involved the grinding and transportation of fertiliser and other materials to Rossnowlagh, and included the grinding of fertiliser by Adrienne and McMahon. The judge found that 'she could not have done it on her own.' He was satisfied that along with Adrienne, Detective Inspector Kevin Lennon and Detective Garda Noel McMahon were involved in the movement of the material to the shed at Rossnowlagh on 17 July 1994.

12

Leprechauns in New York

Shortly after her return from Lanzarote, Noel McMahon brought Adrienne to his home at Porthaw.

She stared aghast at the contraption in his back yard. As he explained that it was a 'barrack buster' she felt the old fear return. She thought that with the ceasefire there would be no further drops. She had no ground fertiliser left, every last ounce had been used in Rossnowlagh. But McMahon was at a loose end. He was drinking heavily. She had no idea what schemes he and Lennon had plotted while she was away. Her reaction when she saw the huge lump of steel and metal was a hope that he did not intend her to carry it somewhere. She had to get away.

On a visit to her family, her mother told her a story she had heard on the radio of a businessman importing a field of Mayo turf to the United States. A personal crisis, which had befallen one of the girls some time previously, required re-evaluation of their income. The idea of doing something on a much smaller scale was born. Adrienne and Yvonne got excited at the prospect that they could succeed in the Irish pubs throughout New York. They developed the idea, settling on the Christmas season in New York.

The Irish in the Big Apple would have a few dollars more to spend and would be probably be a little homesick as their friends flew home during the holidays.

Once they made the decision to go to New York, they set to work. In the shirt factory, little bags were attached to finished blouses containing spare buttons. This gave them an idea. They used their machining skills to create small string bags to hold tiny pieces of turf. They bought a secondhand sewing machine in Letterkenny at a bargain price of £50. With some green, white and gold material they created the turf purses.

The bags were being sewn together at every opportunity, a tricolour of green, white and gold against a white background. It would never be a 'must have' fashion accessory, but within the Irish-American community there would be nostalgic smiles.

Their boss allowed them to use the machines during their lunch break and they enlisted the assistance of their friends. The machinists were working as intensely during their lunch hour creating the turf purses as they were during the morning sewing blouses for Next and Dunnes Stores. Occasionally a bag was inadvertently sewn onto the arm of a blouse destined for Next and discovered in the quality control section.

As autumn drew near the shorter evenings were taken up with planning their trip. The machine was brought back to Letterkenny at weekends so that valuable time would not be lost. The entire family got involved in the enterprise. Karen went to the printers in Letterkenny and had a couple of hundred cardboard tags printed with the slogan 'Keep The Home Fires Burning' against a background of a map of Ireland, and 'Bogged in Ireland'. These were attached to the purses. Karen rang the embassy in Dublin and was told that it was acceptable to bring small chips of peat briquette into the USA. Adrienne's mother recorded the totals as they were being completed. The purses were bagged into lots of one-hundred and seventy-five.

To complete the entrepreneurial image, it was decided to have a visual selling aid which would capture the attention and imagination of potential purchasers. They went to a local dress-maker and had two leprechaun costumes made. Bright green trousers of calf length tapered at the bottom with long white socks and a bright green pointed cover for over their shoes. A dazzling red jacket topped with large shiny buttons was held together with a huge belt and silver buckle. To complete the costume there were beards and pointed pixie hats colour coordinated with their outfit. Nods of approval were given to the girls as they strutted across the kitchen at home at the first showing of their outfits. By mid-November everything was in place. The plane tickets were bought as an early Christmas present from Adrienne's mother.

The editor of the *New York Voice*, Niall O'Dowd shared a friend with Karen and her mother who knew him from his days in the Irish media. He was contacted in November 1994 to do a story about the girls who would be seen in New York bars in early December selling their turf purses in their Leprechaun outfits. A reservation was made in 'The Big Apple Hostel' in New York and at the end of November 1994 they departed for two weeks.

McMahon had her tormented when she told him of her trip. He was like a spoiled child. She didn't tell him of the reason for going or that they would be selling purses in the Irish bars in Queens and the Bronx. She didn't tell him of the Leprechaun out-fits either. He thought she was going on a holiday paid for by her mother as a Christmas present. McMahon was envious of her trip and wanted to go as well. But he just wanted to go the States on his own. He told her that she did not have to worry about him tagging along with her. He had never been to America and he wanted to see New York, experience the life there, and sample the famous hospitality offered to the Irish, particularly to the Gardaí from their colleagues in the New York Police Department. Thinking aloud, he proposed that she would say she was getting counterfeit plates and he could say he had to go too. The secret service fund would probably finance the trip if it were of benefit to the national security of the State, he reasoned.

But she was free from her tormentors and she was not going to engage in any more of their deceptions. The ceasefire was holding and as long as it did she had breathing space. McMahon became dangerously obsessed with the trip. Adrienne spent less and less time in Buncrana and regularly came home during the week as the date of their departure loomed.

Jet lag notwithstanding, they donned the leprechaun outfits on their first night in the hostel and set off for the Irish bars. They found Donegal pubs and received a wonderful reception from the local Irish. The bags were a bargain at a dollar each. Fortunes were not going to be made, however, and the streets were not paved in gold. Whatever was made was reinvested in Payless shoe stores and bargain basements. Their original idea of saving money had in the short term slipped their minds as they enjoyed everything the stores in Manhattan had to offer.

Surprisingly for the time of year, their dormitory of six beds was full every night for the duration of their stay. By night they traveled by subway to the Bronx and Queens from Manhattan. The local Irish from Mizen to Malin were very welcoming and even the local cops bought the purses. It was quick lemonades here and there before moving on to more lucrative and greener pastures. Adrienne had learned from her early days in Buncrana that alcohol did not agree with her.

Their usual mode of transport around New York was the

subway, which was the fastest and most convenient way of getting around the city. One night as they were returning, there was a commotion in the carriage in which they were travelling. Two drunks had started a brawl and had created a scene. Although initially apprehensive they were startled when several men pulled out guns and badges. It appeared there were more cops than customers on the train providing security for the travelling public. In her next phone call home, Adrienne related to her mother the experience of the previous night, which eased her concerns of her daughter travelling on subways late at night.

On another occasion they had become disorientated as they made their way through the streets of New York and stopped sharply in their tracks, turning around to look for the correct street. Two gentlemen almost bumped into them and were very helpful in accompanying them to their destination. Americans are famous for their hospitality, but generosity with their time to strangers is not so common. The girls returned home prior to Christmas through Heathrow and Belfast airports. They were never on any occasion stopped, searched or questioned by anyone either in America, England or Belfast.

McMahon had not been sanctioned to go on the trip, much to his chagrin. But in the trip he and Lennon saw the opportunity to further their careers while enhancing her status as a senior IRA figure. Lennon contacted the Crime & Security Branch at Garda headquarters and informed them of her travel plans. They in turn notified their American counterparts. The FBI surveillance was in place from the moment the pair arrived in New York.

A briefing document to the chief superintendent in Letterkenny was submitted by Detective Inspector Lennon, dated 24 November 1994, from the detective superintendent's office.

It included a reference to a suggestion that anti-peace factions had held secret meetings in Letterkenny in the previous few weeks, which were attended by a number of individuals. It continued:

'It is understood that this faction had buried weapons and explosives in bunkers in the Letterkenny area. I am endeavouring to have the locations identified if possible. I'm also advised that these units of the IRA, despite being stood down, were extremely active in the past three weeks and are continuing to manufacture and store devices. Other activists, unknown to my source, have visited the Letterkenny area and remained overnight. They were having secret training camps during this time. Two weeks ago sixteen loaves of sandwiches and other food supplies were made available to them.'

The report also noted that 'a peace rally was held at Letterkenny on 12 November 1994. Many were directed not to attend this rally, while others did attend as a face-saving exercise.

'In the near future two persons from the IRA will travel to America on an all-expenses-paid trip. They will be given the sum of £1,000 spending money for the holiday in the USA. There it is believed they will obtain plans or drawings of some type of device and take them back to Belfast via Heathrow. At Heathrow the plans or drawings will be taken possession of by a third party. I am endeavouring to arrange that I might get photocopies of these items.'

Lennon said that he would monitor the situation, and said that his information came from 'a previously reliable and prudent source'.

McMahon later said that Adrienne was instructed to bring back counterfeiting plates, but it appeared she was unable to acquire this item because he claimed no one contacted her while in the States. It is not known if any of the British security services were contacted while she was travelling home through Heathrow Airport.

Chief Fitzpatrick wrote on 12 December 1994 to the Assistant Commissioner of Crime & Security Branch in Dublin and he referred to the Lennon report of 24 November 1994. He reported, 'Adrienne McGlinchey and Yvonne Devine were travelling to New York that evening, 1/12/94, via Belfast and Heathrow. They were given £1,000. The tickets were organised by a named person [the wife of an IRA activist] and that they would be meeting people in Manhattan, New York, where they would be collecting items undescribed, which would be handed over by them on their return at Heathrow. The identity of the receiver at Heathrow was unknown.'

Other reports followed, and on 29 December 1994 Lennon met with Chief Superintendent Diffley at Crime & Security Branch to discuss the matter.

Laden with Payless shoes, low cost Levi's jeans and duty-free perfumes, the girls returned after their two-week break, unaware and oblivious to the security operation that had been put in place by McMahon and Lennon. Within days of their arrival the FBI had established that there was nothing subversive about the activities of the girls.

It has since been reported that the Garda report to the FBI, which sparked an international security alert, caused serious problems for the peace process in Northern Ireland. Unsure as to the reason for the so-called IRA operatives operating in New York as leprechauns, but certain that there were no subversive intentions, the various security agencies could not rule out the possibility that the girls were a diversion for the real buyers of a missile system in New York. The British government through MI5 and the RUC were unable to verify the reports emanating from Ireland, though they sent shock waves through the British secret services. The IRA commitment to the peace had become highly doubtful.

The interim Morris Report found that 'the circumstances detailed of the trip to New York by Adrienne and Yvonne conform to the worst of their behaviour during the Buncrana period.' Evidence relating to the trip was given in both private and public session. There was nothing in the selling of souvenir purses in New York bars that required the Garda Commissioner to claim privilege. It was an innocent trip undertaken by two girls unaware of yet another deplorable abuse of their names and characters by members of the Gardaí.

'To have failed to have asked appropriate questions was negligence on the part of the Crime & Security Branch of An Garda Síochána,' the Morris report concluded.

13

Moving On

Adrienne and Yvonne returned from their American trip, back to work in the shirt factory.

McMahon put it to Adrienne one night that he had a friend in Monaghan who required a favour, which was to duplicate the Rossnowlagh find. He envisaged the return to operations of happily grinding fertiliser while swigging brandy. It was early in 1995. He had bought a bag of fertiliser and it was at his house. She refused point blank. Circumstances had changed. McMahon brought her to see Lennon and they threatened to have Yvonne Devine arrested, and for the first time in years Adrienne summoned up the strength and courage to say no. She expected serious consequences, but she had come to the end of the line and no longer cared.

Fed up with small town gossip at work they decided to leave Jay Bees and got a job in Fruit of the Loom in Milford, a small town some ten miles from Letterkenny. Adrienne was selfishly happy to have an excuse to make the final break from Buncrana. Yvonne got a flat alone and Adrienne moved back home. McMahon made no further contact throughout 1995.

Karen McGlinchey was active in local politics. In the late summer of 1995, she received letters making serious allegations about an interview process within Co. Donegal VEC. The issue was also hotly debated in the local press. In September 1995, Detective Inspector Kevin Lennon called into her shop in Letterkenny, asking for her file on the VEC issue. She remembered Adrienne had mentioned his name several times, and asked him if he was the same Kevin Lennon that was based in Buncrana. Lennon denied he knew Adrienne, which Karen found surprising as she had the impression her sister was well known in Buncrana, particularly in Garda circles. When Adrienne returned that evening from working in Milford, Karen mentioned Lennon's visit. Adrienne was amazed when she heard Lennon had denied knowledge of her. She told Karen she had proof that Lennon knew her and produced three mini-cassette tapes. She played a short extract of one of the tapes and Karen immediately recognised Lennon's voice. At Adrienne's request, Karen took possession of the three tapes and placed them in an envelope for safe keeping for her sister. They lay in the envelope until they were recovered in 1999.

Towards the end of 1995, Yvonne asked to move into a room in the youth hostel owned by Karen where she stayed for over a year. In early 1996, Adrienne left Fruit of the Loom to rejoin the family business while Yvonne remained working there. Some months later, Yvonne left the factory and began a FÁS course, but continued living in the hostel.

The family were delighted that Adrienne was home again. It became a matter of concern when incidents, which would occur from time to time as would be expected in late night business, were not being thoroughly investigated by members of the Gardaí if Adrienne was the person who made the report.

In 1997, Detective Garda McMahon called upon Adrienne while on temporary transfer to Letterkenny. The reason for his transfer to Letterkenny soon became clear. There had been incidents where he had misused his official weapon. Lennon had been promoted in 1996 to Superintendent in Buncrana. Detective Sergeant Leheny had transferred to Buncrana when Detective Sergeant Des Walsh retired. Leheny would not tolerate McMahon's behaviour and there was a clash of personalities.

During this time two extraordinary letters, known as the 'letters of satisfaction' were composed. Sheenagh McMahon handed one in to the Morris Tribunal. Sheenagh told the Tribunal that her husband said that the letter was 'the biggest mistake Kevin Lennon had made in his life'. She took it with her when they separated, and handed it in to the Carty team. The note is in Kevin Lennon's handwriting.

A suggestion had been made that McMahon could have Lennon suspended on a whim. McMahon set about proving to Lennon, his friend and superior, that he was not making any allegations about him to Leheny or anyone else and drafted a document, which later became known as 'The Letter of Satisfaction'. It was the most extraordinary letter for any member of whatever rank of the Garda Síochána to compose and sign. There were two versions of the letter, one being in the handwriting of Superintendent Kevin Lennon, which read as follows:

> I have worked with Superintendent Lennon as D/Inspector, we have worked on sensitive operations, we have carried out all operations to the best of our ability. I have never known Superintendent Lennon, while in any rank, to take part in or authorise either accompanied by me or otherwise (a) any unlawful activity or operation (b) to act illegally

during the course duty on or off duty (c) to act illegally while participating in any operation.

The second letter is a typewritten note giving Lennon a glowing reference and stating, 'I do not know anything that would endanger his career or that I could say about him to endanger his career.' McMahon's signature appears at the bottom of the letter. Sgt Jim Leheny said he found the letter, a photocopy of an original and date stamped 26 March 1996, lying beside a computer in Buncrana detective unit. He handed it in to the Carty team in 1999.

McMahon said that he wrote the typed letter because Leheny was spreading gossip about Lennon, and he wanted to reassure his old friend and boss. He said that Lennon then wrote out the handwritten letter as a draft for an improved letter, but he never got around to typing up the final draft.

The Tribunal decided that the letters were evidence of McMahon and Lennon 'sharing a guilty mind in relation to their past activities.'

It would be fair to say that there were those in the Garda Síochána in Buncrana who had waited in the long grass for McMahon for years. With Lennon back in Letterkenny McMahon was exposed to the harsh reality that the job required a certain discipline and application, which he lacked. The new regime under Leheny proved difficult for him. Without his friend Lennon to support and protect him in Buncrana, he had become a liability in Lennon's pursuit of the rank of Commissioner of An Garda Síochána. In 1997 he transferred to Letterkenny, following in the footsteps of Lennon. McMahon bought a house and his wife

Sheenagh and the boys moved after completing the sale of their home in Porthaw, Buncrana.

In 1997 McMahon was introduced to Karen McGlinchey. As well as operating the youth hostel, which she opened in the early Nineties, and a shop, Karen had also converted Steers into a teashop. McMahon stopped in for a chat. Karen was taken back by his personal derogatory comments to a female French member of staff within minutes of meeting her. Although he was laughing, they were the type of comments usually made between friends of long standing. At other times Karen noticed him involved in doublespeak with Adrienne. While he talked to Karen about the tourist season, he turned to Adrienne and said she was his 'Inishowen terrorist, I mean tourist.' Adrienne was clearly upset by his comments, but his threatening manner was camouflaged by the constant smiling and knowing glances he passed to her. Ironically, Sheenagh McMahon gave evidence of similar comments made to her. 'I am not sure whether there was drink involved that night or not but I remember Noel slagging her off that night and referring to her as the tourist rather than the terrorist to me and he thought this was very funny. I did not stay, I just went on down to bed.'

As Karen got to know McMahon over the next few years, she was puzzled by his behaviour, which was considerably different from the conduct of other Guards she knew. There was something she could not quite put her finger on. She knew he was consistently absent from work through alcohol abuse, and often wondered how someone could be allowed to take days and weeks from work without fear of reprimand.

In the years after Adrienne left Inishowen, McMahon slid into the dark horror of alcohol abuse. He had systematically abused her both physical and emotionally and she was still a hostage to his demands. He phoned her constantly demanding she call to his house. Occasionally, when she went to the house, both McMahon and Sheenagh were locked in alcohol-fuelled arguments. One or other of the McMahons always involved Adrienne in their rows, which became more frequent and violent. Torn between phone calls she tried to distance herself from becoming embroiled in their personal relationship, but offered support to the McMahon children, who were clearly suffering.

McMahon had become almost fanatical in his recording of conversations with Leheny. Adrienne was in his house in Letterkenny and there were notes spread around the floor. Through bouts of drink-filled duty, which he spent hovering around the business, he began to confide in Adrienne details of his relationship with Lennon and other members of the Gardaí. He recounted an occasion when he and Detective Sergeant Leheny had collected a prisoner in north Inishowen to bring to Buncrana. On the journey McMahon and Leheny started to argue, and it evolved into a physical fight by the time they returned to Buncrana Garda station. Leheny also gave evidence of this incident to the Tribunal.

In 1998, McMahon asked Adrienne to arrange a summer job for his son in the sweetshop. A Tribunal barrister pointed out that a detective would hardly allow his teenage son to work for someone he truly believed was a member of the IRA. Sheenagh McMahon gave evidence of a conversation she had in 1999 with a retired Buncrana detective, Des Walsh.

Paul Murray: If I can just conclude with a couple of questions. You said on the TV3 programme that you thought Adrienne McGlinchey was an informer?

Sheenagh McMahon: Yes.

Paul Murray: Past tense, you thought she was an informer?

Sheenagh McMahon: Yes that is because Des Walsh told me she wasn't.

Later, she recalled the summer job her son was given a year previously.

Paul Murray: She maintains that she was never a member of the IRA, nor an informer?

Sheenagh McMahon: Yes, I agree with her.

Paul Murray: By 1998, am I correct in thinking, the relationship between you and her was this: that she found a job for you in a cinema, is that so?

Sheenagh McMahon: She did, yes.

Paul Murray: She gave a job to your son?

Sheenagh McMahon: Yes.

The McMahons had very few friends in Letterkenny. Adrienne helped Sheenagh McMahon find a job, to help her integrate into the new town and make friends. Children are resilient and can adapt reasonably quickly to new schools, making friends quickly, and her husband had his colleagues at work, but Sheenagh was lonely and was excited at the prospect of starting the new job, which Adrienne found in the local cinema. Unfortunately for Sheenagh, the night she was to begin she was unable to take up the position because of bruising to her face.

At times Noel and Sheenagh tried to stop drinking but it usually only involved one and never the two at the same time, which always made it difficult for the other person. McMahon had checked into hospital for treatment of his alcohol abuse but the commitment was never strong enough and he invariably reverted to his old ways. His jealousy of Lennon was consuming him.

Lennon had been awarded the Garda Síochána divisional merit award in 1995, more commonly known as the Policeman of the Year Award, which McMahon had expected to receive. In her testimony to the Court of Criminal Appeal, Sheenagh McMahon said that Lennon's wife had called one day and told her that her husband Noel was going to receive the award. McMahon had been proposed for the award jointly with another Garda officer in recognition of their work in the Point Inn. The McMahons were very excited about the award coming to them and told their family and friends about the honour. They were devastated when they learned that Lennon was the recipient. The record as to who nominated Lennon for the award was mislaid in Garda headquarters. Lennon had taken the glory once again.

McMahon complained incessantly to Adrienne about being left on the bottom rung. Bottles of brandy were being consumed daily and his mind was degenerating into a craze-filled obsession with Kevin Lennon. This fixation with Lennon was mirrored in Sheenagh's conversations. She constantly claimed that Lennon had used her husband to get to the position he was in and had left Noel languishing at the bottom. She blamed him for the problems in their marriage and their alcohol dependency.

McMahon was telling his wife snippets of his activities involving Adrienne. One night she asked Adrienne about an incident involving Noel and their family car, which she said had the back window shot out. Horrified, Adrienne told McMahon to tell his wife the truth, that it came about as a result of an accident because he was drunk. Adrienne was caught between them. There were constant demands on her time by one or both of them. One minute Sheenagh would call her on her mobile telephone while Noel could be on the landline and vice versa. They were wearing her down and the pressure was starting to mount. When she tried to distance herself from them, they would reel her back in. McMahon would stop at the shop insisting that Adrienne sit in the car while he unburdened his seemingly never-ending list of problems. He told her all sorts of stories about people, Guards and his own crises in life.

There were times when Adrienne went to his house and McMahon had notes written and posted all over the floor. He talked about bribes and backhanders and there were allegations of extra-marital affairs. All the while he was recording the information in his notebook. McMahon later gave evidence to the Tribunal that these notes and allegations were what prompted the letter of satisfaction. She was becoming more disturbed at his behaviour. Although Adrienne was becoming concerned, she indulged his grumbles, hoping that they would resolve their marriage differences and life could return to normal.

Adrienne started receiving disturbing anonymous telephone calls on her mobile phone. It started with hang-ups, but gradually the caller got more daring and hung on breathing deeply into the phone without speaking. Her number was widely known by staff and friends alike.

One day, Karen received a call from a friend who told her that there was an obscene voicemail greeting on Adrienne's mobile telephone. Karen phoned to check, and heard a male voice say, 'If this is the Ulster Bank, you can fuck off. You're not getting any money out of me.' Shocked at the message, Karen told her sister immediately. They did not know how someone could access her phone unless she had left it somewhere. At first she thought it was a poor joke played on her by someone working in the bank, but friends in the bank assured her this would not be considered a prank and advised her to notify the Gardaí.

She played the answer machine for McMahon and he took the

phone, telling her that they had special equipment in the Garda station that might identify the culprit. The following day he told her that the Eircell network lost power in Donegal and that the message was wiped from the machine before they could make a recording of the message in the Garda station.

McMahon took more and more sick days. The marriage was in serious trouble as both partners indulged in chronic alcohol abuse. It was obvious that the children were suffering. Typically when parents neglect their children they try to over-compensate later and this family was no exception. The boys received the very best of television and electrical equipment. On other occasions they were to witness the troubled and physical abuse their parents inflicted on each other.

The McMahons were not settled in Letterkenny and they put their home on the market during 1998. It would prove to be a long and difficult sale, which was eventually sealed much later.

Karen was extremely worried about the constant persecution of her sister by the McMahons and strongly advised her to end all communication with them. She started to write a diary of their involvement with the McMahons at that stage.

In December 1998 Adrienne received a call from Sheenagh who was crying hysterically. She went out to their house and found McMahon savagely beating his wife in front of their children. The youngest child had stepped in to wipe blood from his mother's lip. The Gardaí were called. The children were understandably very upset and Adrienne bundled all three of them into her car and took them to her home. It was less than ten days to Christmas and while most children were excitedly looking forward to Santa and presents, these children were in the depths of despair.

Karen, a friend and her mother were sitting watching television when the children came in. They were shocked when they saw how upset the children were. Adrienne took them to the cinema in an effort to temporarily erase the images of the physical and emotional abuse that had become the scourge of their family life.

A knock came to the door a couple of days later. Karen opened it and found Sheenagh McMahon in a very drunken state. It was obvious from her appearancethat she had been drinking for quite a long period and she appeared so dishevelled that at first she was unrecognisable. In a slurred voice she demanded to speak to Adrienne while she leaned on the door to remain upright. Karen refused to allow her in. It was 11 a.m. The McMahon's problems were slowly eroding the normal life Adrienne had endeavoured to rebuild.

By the end of January 1999, the McMahons' marriage had disintegrated to the extent that they decided to separate once again. Social workers from the North Western Health Board had become involved in the welfare of the children and the children returned to Buncrana to live with Sheenagh's sister until their mother recovered from the desperate situation she had found herself in.

There was a barrage of phone calls between the McMahons and Adrienne after this. Demands were made on her to come to the house at a moment's notice and McMahon would be found drunk and babbling about Lennon or Leheny or his wife.

McMahon went to Ennis to visit his family. Anonymous calls to Adrienne's mobile phone continued and McMahon even engaged in a process of slow torture, calling Adrienne non-stop all day at her home, at the business and on her mobile. She instructed staff to tell him she was not in but he became rude and abusive to them, demanding they tell him where she was.

Sheenagh McMahon was also calling her. She wanted to know what her husband was saying, where he was and when he was returning. Adrienne was in the path of the McMahons' turbulent marital problems and it was going to destroy her life forever. She was suffocating under the relentless demands being made of her, and the anxiety and stress which this was placing on her was becoming increasingly obvious to her family.

In the strange world of a victim of years of blackmail, fear and coercion at the hands of the members of Gardaí, Adrienne felt that she was unable to confide to her family the living nightmare she was enduring.

14

Guards Investigating Guards

It was the day Adrienne had dreaded. Superintendent Kevin Lennon came to the shop when Adrienne was there and told her that Sheenagh McMahon was 'mouthing' around Buncrana. He told her to go to Sheenagh and tell her that she had been arrested by the IRA the previous day and held for eleven hours. She was to tell Sheenagh that by openly talking around Buncrana she was putting Adrienne's life at risk, and that Adrienne could end up with an IRA bullet in her head. It was March 1999.

Lennon was furious with Sheenagh McMahon. He left after five minutes, telling Adrienne to contact him after she had seen her. The closed circuit television cameras in the shop recorded his visit.

Left to ponder her predicament, Adrienne wished that the McMahons would resolve their differences so that she could put the past behind her. She had been planning to go on holiday within a few weeks for a well-earned break.

Adrienne decided to ask one of the girls in the shop who was going off duty to accompany her to Buncrana in search of

Sheenagh McMahon. They were at the ESB offices when she spotted her car. Adrienne crossed over to Sheenagh's car and told her what Lennon had instructed her to say.

Sheenagh McMahon reassured Adrienne that her name was not going to be mentioned. Adrienne told her that there was more at stake than Sheenagh was even aware of, uncertain of what information she had in her possession. She explained to Sheenagh that she didn't know what she was getting into, begging her to leave it alone. She pleaded with her to drop whatever mission she was on, that she had herself and the children to think of. She had to move on and get her life back together the way it was before when she was so happy with Noel and the children together.

Sheenagh told Adrienne that they had another row and that McMahon was in Ennis with his sister. Adrienne had her mobile phone, and Sheenagh asked her to call McMahon. After giving a message and being told that McMahon would ring back, they sat and waited. When the phone rang, Sheenagh sat with her ear to the phone listening as Adrienne complained to the detective about his wife talking around Buncrana. Sheenagh walked Adrienne back to her car and engaged in a light-hearted conversation with the staff member who had been friendly with Sheenagh's son when he worked in the shop. Adrienne had brought bags of sweets for the McMahon children, which she gave to Sheenagh. They parted company on good terms. Adrienne hoped that the furore would soon die down and that Sheenagh would leave her out of the troubles between herself and her husband.

Much evidence was given by Sheenagh McMahon in relation to the conversation she alleged they had. She gave numerous interviews to the press in the intervening years and always referred to herself and her children as being threatened. The allegation was repeated in the Court of Criminal Appeal and became the subject of much interest in the local press in Donegal. Finally, when under cross-examination by Paul Murray at the Tribunal, Sheenagh made the following admissions:

Paul Murray: It is a fairly simple question, Mrs McMahon, the conversation lasted some considerable period of time?

McMahon: That is the best answer I can give you.

Paul Murray: Let me just go through the sequence of events. Do you agree with me that she was in her car on a street in Buncrana and she saw you in another car?

McMahon: Yes, she was parked over at the ESB office and she crossed the road over to me and she had a friend of hers sitting in the car across the road.

Paul Murray: She got into your car?

McMahon: She walked across and got into my car.

Paul Murray: You had the conversation?

McMahon: Yes.

Paul Murray: Do you recall getting out of your car after that and going over to her car?

McMahon: No, I have no recollection of it.

Paul Murray: And having a further conversation with not only Ms McGlinchey in the vicinity of her car, but also with the girl who was in the car with her?

McMahon: I have no recollection of it.

Paul Murray: Do you remember the girl being with Ms McGlinchey in the car?

McMahon: I have no recollection of it.

Paul Murray: Well, can I ask you to look at page 336, if we could have that up on the screen. Sorry, if I could have that up on the screen with the name blanked out.

McMahon: I do remember now, I do, sorry.

Paul Murray: You do remember that now?

McMahon: Yes, sorry, I am having difficulty, I am tired. It is a long day. The girl that works in the shop with her, Anne-Marie, that is right, I do remember that now. I walked over with her.

Paul Murray: Do you remember at that stage, was your son still working in the shop?

McMahon: No, no, we had moved back to Buncrana, we were living back in Buncrana so Keith was back with me, over in Buncrana with me.

Paul Murray: Was there any chitchat about your son and the daughter working in the same shop and both being known people?

McMahon: I can't recall the conversation that I had with that girl at all.

Paul Murray: Could that have happened? That is Ms McGlinchey's recollection, that there was a conversation between the three of you in relation to the fact that your son either had been working in the shop or was still working in the shop and this other girl, much the same age, and who knows what could happen?

McMahon: I wouldn't disagree with her.

Paul Murray: That did happen?

McMahon: I can't recall it, I have no recollection of it but I do remember the girl being there all right.

Paul Murray: Could that have happened in Ms McGlinchey's car rather than your car?

McMahon: No, that was at Ms McGlinchey's car, yes.

Paul Murray: This was after this alleged threat was made to you?

McMahon: Yes.

Paul Murray: You felt comfortable enough to walk over to Ms McGlinchey's car and have a conversation?

McMahon: Yes, you see, following on from that, Adrienne made another allegation, she said that I was as bad as them on the phone, so there was a combination of things there.

Some days later, Noel McMahon called Karen. He told her that there was another nasty greeting on Adrienne's mobile telephone and that he was trying to alert her but her telephone was switched off.

This greeting was of a sexually offensive nature and was so shocking that one could only conclude that the person responsible had a sick and depraved mind. It became apparent to Karen later that evening that access to the message minder was gained because the factory setting on the telephone had never been changed by Adrienne and the standard personal identification number issued with the telephone was still in use. Anyone could access her phone by keying the factory programmed security code from a remote handset. Karen quickly changed the code thereby saving the message. Then the greeting was recorded on to a number of tapes from the telephone.

A conversation between two men was also recorded on the answer machine. It was obvious that one of the voices was that of Noel McMahon talking with someone. Adrienne arranged to meet Sheenagh to see if she could identify the person with whom Noel McMahon was having a conversation. They talked about money and that 'they were digging deep'. Sheenagh listened to the message and immediately knew that it was the voice of Noel McMahon's brother-in-law.

McMahon called Adrienne later that evening and told Adrienne to wipe the message from the phone, but she insisted she had saved the message and the greeting on the phone. McMahon took the first bus the following morning to Letterkenny but by the time he arrived the sisters had realised the telephone greetings on the phone were uncannily like the voice of Noel McMahon.

Sheenagh McMahon was back on the phone to Adrienne telling her 'they were all dirty'. She said she was going to her solicitor. Adrienne's world was coming in around her and she told Sheenagh to leave her out of her troubles between herself and her husband and not to call her again. Adrienne terminated the call.

Easter fell early in 1999 and as Karen was leaving the shop she met McMahon approaching it with a box. He asked if Adrienne would deliver the parcel of Easter eggs to his sons in Buncrana.

She arranged to have someone deliver them to the home of Sheenagh's sister, where the children were living. As planned, Adrienne went on holidays after Easter. She was glad to leave the McMahons, Lennon and their problems behind. Prior to going on her trip, Adrienne spoke openly at home about the difficulties in the McMahon marriage and the visit of Kevin Lennon to the shop. She told her family about Lennon's fear of Sheenagh McMahon and of perjury committed by Noel McMahon. She had some closed circuit television tape recordings from the shop and she told Karen to make sure she did not mix them up with other tapes, as she did not want the tapes to be mislaid or taped over.

The Garda investigation team under Assistant Commissioner Kevin Carty arrived in Donegal to investigate allegations of Garda corruption. On 16 April 1999 local newspapers reported that

Superintendent Kevin Lennon had transferred at his own request to another station to allow the investigation to be conducted in a transparent and independent manner. Adrienne learned of Lennon's transfer during a phone call home from America.

On Monday 19 April 1999, Eircom were repairing a faulty line which had been reported by Karen. Later that morning, Detective Noel McMahon and his partner Matt Tolan knocked on the door of the McGlinchey home. They said that they were investigating an arson attack on a nearby building under construction. Karen brought them in and made coffee and along with her mother exchanged pleasantries. During the course of their conversation McMahon became interested in the caller ID unit which was attached to the phone. It was not a commonly used device and McMahon became engrossed in the call records it retained.

Karen noticed McMahon furtively gesturing at her, indicating that he wanted to speak with her. Karen was standing as a candidate in the local elections and McMahon remarked that he wanted to check his name on the electoral register to ensure that he was registered. They left the room, leaving her mother and Tolan chatting. As she closed the door of the study, Karen asked McMahon what it was he really wanted. He began by pacing about the room in a dramatic fashion and saying that there was trouble with Sheenagh. He said she was going to make trouble for Adrienne.

The pieces were starting to fall into place for Karen. Adrienne had been so troubled before going on holidays and he was now confirming that it involved himself and Sheenagh. He said that Sheenagh was doing a lot of talking around Buncrana and that she had removed items from his home. He said that he had explosives and weapons stored there, which he should have thrown in the river years ago.

Amazed at such an admission, Karen wondered aloud why he had these items at his home, but he repeatedly said that he should have got rid of them. The next and obvious question was where and from whom he acquired the items. Perplexed as to how anything he had said so far could have caused the remotest trouble for Adrienne, it came like a jolt of lightning to Karen when he alleged that he got the weapons from Adrienne when she was doing runs for the IRA. He said that he stopped her in her car and took the items from her.

Angry, and calling his bluff, Karen told him that she was aware of what went on in Buncrana, and over the years had recorded what Adrienne told her and filed it with her solicitor in Dublin. McMahon was stunned and suddenly pushed Karen against the wall.

She later told the Morris Tribunal, 'The next thing, he just — I had my back to the wall and the next thing, he pushed me up against the wall. First of all he said if everybody stays quiet it would be okay, he said he liked Adrienne, he said he would go to jail before her. I was asking him, what do you mean you're going to go to jail before her. It wasn't making sense to me that this Guard was standing in my room saying to me that he was going to go to jail before her, that he had stopped her with explosives and guns and now he was saying he was going to go to jail before her and that he liked her. It wasn't making any kind of a logical sense to me.'

Karen added, 'Well, I lost my temper, I got really, really angry. He pushed me up against the wall, he said — he put his arm across my chest, he put his face right up to mine, I could smell the drink off his breath and he actually had turned into this vicious — I can hardly explain, his face was an inch from me, and he said, you know, you better tell her to effing zip it or he would zip it for her, that nobody could hear her, she'd be six foot under, he was going to keep it quiet — or, he would zip it for her permanently. I was asking him, what do you mean, who's going to hear her six foot under. My heart nearly stopped, you know, I'm standing in my own house.'

Karen told Peter Charleton that, 'I was shaken, I was very frightened, I was agitated. Ten minutes later, in fact, Noel McMahon had also asked me to ring him, and he had written down his number, I wouldn't have known his number, on a wee yellow sticky thing that was in the study. About 10 minutes after he left I was to go to lunch with a friend of mine. He arrived into the house, I was standing in the kitchen and I was roaring and crying, I was so upset. Mom was up in the sitting room and she didn't know what was going on. I went up into the sitting room. I told the two of them what had happened. Five minutes later after that Noel McMahon rang me on the phone and he was trying to say, you know, don't do anything rash you know like just keep it quiet, if everybody stays quiet it's okay. He told me that the Carty investigation, or rather the investigation into the death of Richie Barron was only a cover for this investigation and to the hoax explosives.'

Detective Tolan's evidence to the Morris Tribunal when asked if Karen was upset in any way was: 'It struck me that the discussion must have been a serious one.'

Karen's evidence has been accepted by the Morris Tribunal.

Karen's immediate thought after she shut the door was one of relief that Adrienne was out of the country. After some time the telephone rang and McMahon was apologising for his behaviour and pleading with her not to tell anyone and to get Adrienne to call him from America.

Eircom were apparently still working on the telephone repairs. The phone was dead within an hour of McMahon leaving the

187

house and the engineer who met Karen later that afternoon was amazed when she asked when the phone would be reconnected. He told her the repairs had been completed. Climbing the pole again, the engineer could not explain how the wire had been cut.

By late afternoon, Adrienne called from America and once again Karen went to a telephone box and told her sister about the visit of McMahon, vowing that on her return they would seek legal help.

Ten days remained of Adrienne's holiday and so much was about to happen.

On 24 April 1999, the shop was robbed as Karen, unaware of what was happening, stood at the front door and then stood aside, allowing the perpetrator to make his escape. The follow up investigation was the most remarkable response to any robbery they previously had. Within minutes, detectives had arrived. Karen was asked for the CCTV tapes from the shop. A detective took a number away with him. Later the following day the tapes were returned but the raider was never apprehended. All the tapes had been examined, but not the tapes containing Lennon's visit. They remained hidden.

It sounded like a banshee's wail. As Karen woke from a night of tossing and turning, she realised that the cry came from her mother Liz in the kitchen.

It was the headline story in the *Sunday Business Post*. A story by Frank Connolly told of hoax explosives finds, and the involvement of two Gardaí and a daughter of a well-known business family. Unaware that Adrienne's involvement with McMahon and Lennon had been so extensive, mother and daughter clutched each other in despair. That Sunday evening Karen sent a fax for the urgent attention of her solicitor, Brian Gallagher, to his office in Dublin. It is summarised as follows:

> Re: a story in the Sunday Business Post 25 April 1999, front page, Garda Investigation in Letterkenny. Adrienne has vital information relating to this, but is in America on holidays at the moment. She is returning on Thursday morning. There are two assistant commissioners waiting here to talk to her, as well as a number of others who want to talk to her first.
>
> I believe the information she has could well have serious repercussions for the Gardaí and further afield. I believe there is a good possibility that my phones are being tapped.
>
> Her information would be detrimental to the careers of several Gardaí, detectives, the Superintendent and I believe possibly the chief superintendent in Letterkenny.
>
> I have been approached by one of these involved, last week, advising 'strongly' that she stays quiet. I will call your office today.

It was clear from her eyes that Adrienne had not had the relaxing break she planned. By 9 a.m., after arriving from New York, they were sitting in the office of their long-time family solicitor, Brian Gallagher. For the first time, Adrienne felt that she had people on her side. The fear of losing her family had overwhelmed her for years, making her vulnerable to Noel McMahon's demands. The puppet was about to cut the strings.

It was a waiting game. Noel McMahon made contact a couple of times but she shunned him. He tried to threaten, intimidate and issue warnings about jail, but they were the same old, tired warnings she had succumbed to over the years. Adrienne had a new-found confidence, she was fighting back, the days of bowing to threats and blackmail were over.

McMahon would not give up. He told her she could not win. Senior management at Bridgend had witnessed her making the drop of fertiliser. It had been in her flat. He had her fingerprints. There were files. She was in Ardchicken and Rossnowlagh. All the evidence was there to convict her. All she had to do was maintain that she was an IRA informer and the inquiry would be cut dead in its tracks, he told her.

Weeks passed and there was nothing. In the early hours of a Sunday morning in mid-May a man was disturbed trying to enter the study window of the family home. The same study where Karen had indicated to McMahon weeks earlier that she had stored the record of Adrienne's involvement with him on her computer. Gardaí were unable to locate him after conducting a thorough search of the grounds.

It was the end of May before the Carty team approached Adrienne for the first time. Out of the blue, they walked into the shop. They introduced themselves as Detective Inspector Hugh Coll and Superintendent Jackie O'Connor. With masterful understatement, they said Adrienne's name had come up in an inquiry and they would be grateful if she would accompany them to the station for about an hour to assist them with their inquiries. Adrienne asked them to wait until she contacted her sister. Karen arrived promptly and told the detectives that Adrienne was quite prepared to speak with them in the presence of her solicitor. The detectives agreed and chatted about the forthcoming election before leaving.

Adrienne, Karen and Liz McGlinchey sat together and discussed the interview that was to take place with the Carty Team. Adrienne told them of the option that McMahon was urging: to claim to be an IRA informer. Rather than breach informer privilege, the investigators would have to drop the case. Karen and Liz were appalled at the grip Noel McMahon and Kevin Lennon still held over Adrienne. They argued that the only way she would end the torment was to admit to whatever activities she was involved in. They pledged their support whatever decision she took, but were happy that she would make the right decision.

Adrienne was nervous, but it was enough for her to know that her family would support her. They agreed that Adrienne would meet with the solicitor and Guards. There was no need for major preparation about what to say. At the meeting she could break the stranglehold Noel McMahon and Kevin Lennon held.

The Carty team said that they were on a fact-finding mission. If necessary, different investigators would be appointed to follow up their findings. Allegations had been made, and the Commissioner had appointed the inquiry team to check the claims and report back. They were sitting in the office of Brian Gallagher. The solicitor asked about immunity from prosecution in return for Adrienne's assistance in the investigation.

Adrienne sat quietly, weighing her options. She realised the enormity of the illegal activities of Lennon and McMahon. She realised that she might go to jail.

For years, Noel McMahon had planted in her the fear that she would be culpable for their activities in the manufacturing and planting of the hoax bombs. She had witnessed the top management in Donegal falling for the corrupt practices of Lennon and McMahon. She knew their ability to persuade. She felt that she had nowhere to turn. An Garda Síochána would always protect its own. She would be the fall guy.

Even with the legal advice available to her for the first time in many years, the manipulation of McMahon and Lennon still held her. Noel McMahon had told her to claim informer privilege. Admit she was in the IRA, admit she was an informer and that would be the end of it. It was the easy way out, and she took it.

Adrienne told her solicitor that she was an IRA informer and she was afraid for her personal safety if that fact was ever made public. The Carty team asked for a statement and arrangements were made to meet later. Her early statements and interviews would reflect her false claim of informer status.

In the following days, Chief Superintendent Austin McNally spoke with Brian Gallagher. There was no question of Adrienne being charged with any offence, the Chief said. On 6 July 1999, McNally told Brian Gallagher that he had spoken to the Director of Public Prosecutions and that there was no question of prosecution. He was pleased with Adrienne's co-operation. He promised her that statements would not enter the public arena. Adrienne would not be called to give evidence in any court or Tribunal and if McMahon interfered with her, appropriate action would be taken.

The guarantees and privilege given by the Guards on behalf of the DPP enabled the investigation team to continue interviews outside the presence of her solicitor. The trudge to Sligo Garda station began. Detective Inspector Hugh Coll told the Court of Criminal Appeal they went to Sligo because Adrienne did not want to be interviewed in Letterkenny. By the time he gave evidence to the Morris Tribunal he said that it was because 'the stations in Donegal would not be suitable because a lot of the allegations were in relation to members based in Donegal.'

Documentation to support the Garda discussions with the DPP in relation to Adrienne's immunity was requested by the Court of Criminal Appeal. These were never produced. Only the sworn testimony of Superintendent Hugh Coll, which supported Chief Superintendent McNally's discussion with the director, is on record. The Chief Superintendent would not have had the authority to guarantee immunity without the direct permission of the DPP. No one could have foreseen the extent to which confidence would be breached.

The Carty team came to hear about Adrienne because of a chain of events that began on 15 March 1999, when solicitor Moya Jane O'Doherty, Sheenagh McMahon's sister, made a report to Buncrana Garda station. Noel McMahon had left a message on Sheenagh's answering machine relating to access to his children, which she took to be threatening.

Superintendent Tom Long sent Detective Sergeant Jim Leheny to investigate. When Leheny reported back, Long interviewed Sheenagh McMahon himself. Sheenagh told Long that Adrienne, Kevin Lennon and her husband had mixed explosives which they later transported to places around Donegal and Northern Ireland.

'I interviewed her at a lengthy period,' Tom Long said later. 'Having said that, she was in a distressed state. I found it hard to gain her confidence.' In fact, Sheenagh told Long that she was so distrustful of the Gardaí that she wanted to go to Martin McGuinness of Sinn Féin.

Sheenagh McMahon refused to let Long take notes of his interview, and was adamant that if he did take notes she was going to Martin McGuinness. He said that it was as a result of that that the senior police in Donegal began to get involved in the inquiry. The sisters — one a solicitor, the other the wife of a detective Garda — had more faith in the vigilante investigative techniques of Sinn Féin than in Guards investigating guards.

15

Forty Days and
Forty Nights

The Carty team had a simple approach. They wanted Adrienne to tell them everything she knew. She was not to worry about what she believed or didn't believe. They were the professionals and they would investigate everything. Their job was to carry out a fact-finding mission. It wasn't necessary to name civilians who were caught up in what had happened. All Adrienne had to do was repeat everything Noel McMahon and Kevin Lennon had told her over the years.

The interviews took more than forty days, spread over four months. The questioners were Detective Inspector Hugh Coll and Detective Sergeant George Kyne. The Carty team told the McGlincheys that they didn't know who they could trust among the Letterkenny Guards. Four days a week, they picked her up in Letterkenny and drove to Sligo. She was told to lie down in the back seat of the car until they had left Letterkenny. It didn't inspire confidence in the ability of the Carty team to control the local Guards.

As always, Adrienne suffered from travel sickness, and took Dramamine. The resulting drowsiness did little to help her concentration during the exceptionally long ten- to twelve-hour interrogations with Coll and Kyne.

Despite the precautions, word got out that the Carty team was interviewing Adrienne. It didn't help that members of the Carty team took to dropping in to the sweet shop while she was working for 'a quick chat' to clarify a point. Before long, her involvement was leaked to the local media. It led to what the family called 'eye-balling'. Some off-duty Guards took to glaring at Adrienne when they saw her in pubs or restaurants.

The weekly routine was taking its toll. Friday, Saturday and Sunday were spent working from 10 a.m. to 4 a.m. On Monday morning, she was collected and taken to Sligo. Back in Letterkenny in the evenings she worked another few hours in the shop. Shattered by the punishing schedule and the side effects of Dramamine, she did her best to remember eight years of her conversations and events involving McMahon and Lennon.

It was a stress-filled summer. Early on, Adrienne got back from a Sligo session and was given a message to meet a friend who worried that his name would be given to the Carty team. The note said he would be waiting for her at Rathmullen beach. The Carty team had told her there was no need to name civilians tangential to the affair, and after work Adrienne drove the ten miles to Rathmullen to reassure him.

Adrienne approached the beach and parked near a potato store. Within seconds, a car pulled up and Noel McMahon emerged. There were two men in the car with him. Years earlier, McMahon had introduced them as Cyril and Alistair, members of the RUC. They bundled her into the car, threatening to put her through the windscreen of her car and drive it over the pier into Lough Swilly.

In the distance, Adrienne saw two more cars. McMahon told her they contained members of the Letterkenny detective unit.

He warned her to withdraw her statement. The watching cars accelerated and passed, horns blowing as they raced up the main road. She recognised one as an unmarked Letterkenny branch car.

Adrienne bolted. She ran across the beach back to Rathmullen. Breathless, she glanced behind to see if she was followed, expecting McMahon to pounce on her at any moment. Her hands shook as she struggled to get her car keys into the ignition. Tears blinded her eyes as she made the journey home. She was furious with herself. She had fallen for the most obvious of hoaxes.

The Carty team had told Adrienne that there was no need to name tangential civilians, so in her first report to the Carty team she didn't tell them she had received a message to go to Rathmullen. Instead, she offered various reasons as to why she was on the beach in the early hours of the morning. It was futile. She had been well and truly set up. McMahon had given her the names of the supposed Letterkenny detectives in the two cars, correctly anticipating what she would do. She named the officers to the Carty team without having established their identities herself.

Through his counsel to the Tribunal, McMahon said that he had only been in Rathmullen with Adrienne in 1992. He did not elaborate except to say they met in the boathouse. As everyone from the area knows, the building that appears to be a boathouse from outside is, in fact, a potato store.

The terms of reference for the Morris Tribunal focus on 'hoax explosives and bomb-making equipment finds'. Perhaps because of this, Mr Justice Morris makes no finding on the Rathmullen incident in his report. The Tribunal heard evidence from Adrienne, summed up above, and a denial from Noel McMahon through his lawyer. There were no witnesses to the event except the two men in the car with McMahon, who may or may not have been genuine RUC officers, and whoever was in the other cars Adrienne saw. Whoever they were, none of them came forward to give evidence. The judge makes no finding as to what happened.

Eleanor McDermott worked in the sweet shop. One night after Karen dropped her off from work, a man approached and said he had a message for Adrienne.

'This will go into her mouth if she doesn't keep quiet,' he hissed as he removed a handgun from his pocket. As quickly as he had approached, he disappeared into the shadows.

Eleanor was terrified. She sat alone in her room through the night. In the morning, she went to work on automatic pilot. She went through the day like a robot, carrying out mundane tasks without emotion or thought. When Karen arrived at work, she noticed her pallor and sent her home. She had still not told anyone of her experience of the previous night.

As she walked home, Eleanor broke down. She phoned Adrienne on her mobile phone, telling her through her sobs what had happened. She felt oddly detached, as if she was another person looking at herself. She got home in a daze, and lay on her bed, crying uncontrollably. Adrienne drove from Sligo to see Eleanor, but to Eleanor it seemed as if she arrived within minutes.

Adrienne asked what had happened and then asked if she could tell some Guards who were outside. She relayed the story to Coll and Kyne. At the suggestion of the Carty team, Adrienne told Eleanor the incident was related to an affair with a married man who was a Guard. The Carty team decided not to approach Karen, who was the last person to see Eleanor, to see if she had seen anyone in the vicinity.

As with the Rathmullen incident, this threat to Adrienne

through Eleanor was not part of the Morris Tribunal terms of reference. The Tribunal made no finding of fact about what happened.

Adrienne had not had a break since May. There were sleepless nights, too many to count. Rushed meals before dashing out to fill orders for the shop or lodge cash at the bank, before another journey to Sligo. By early September there was still no end in sight. Karen approached the team and suggested a week off. They agreed to a break to allow Adrienne to relax.

On 6 September 1999, Adrienne, Karen and their mother Liz were in the Courtyard shopping centre in Letterkenny enjoying a coffee. Adrienne left first. As she neared her car, Noel McMahon approached her. He kept calling to her to talk to him but she refused. He was drunk and was pleading that he had nothing to do with the incident involving Eleanor. He told her that next time he would 'not be able to stop them'. Adrienne managed to get into her car and lock the door while McMahon swore at her. She pressed hard on the horn and he roared that she would have to drive over him. From nowhere a man approached asking Adrienne if she was okay. McMahon asked her if she knew the stranger and swore at him also. He jumped the bonnet of her car as the man pulled him away. She drove forward but McMahon threw himself in front of her. The stranger again intervened. Adrienne was not to know that he was a member of the Garda Emergency Response Unit, but McMahon recognised him from his Dublin days in the Special Detective Unit.

Karen and Liz drove home about fifteen minutes later. There they found Adrienne talking to George Kyne. McMahon had threatened Karen at her home months before, but she had dismissed it as drunken bluster. Hearing what had just happened to

Adrienne, she told Kyne her own story, and agreed to make a statement the following day. Later that evening the members of the ERU were introduced to the family.

Assistant Commissioner Kevin Carty and Detective Inspector Coll met Karen to discuss the threats. Carty said it was regrettable that Adrienne had to be protected by Gardaí from other Gardaí. They discussed her statement, and Carty asked Karen to use her influence on Adrienne to drop the guarantees of immunity from the DPP. She was a State witness, and it would look better if she gave her statement without any inducement. Carty told Karen that Adrienne had not broken any laws and had no need for any immunity. But Karen was concerned, and immediately informed her solicitor of the conversation.

The following day, 8 September 1999, Karen made a full statement to Coll and Kyne. On foot of this statement, Detective Garda Noel McMahon was suspended from the Garda Síochána after a search warrant was issued for his house and members found explosive black powder, bullets and other items in his basement.

The Carty team originally told Adrienne to tell them everything McMahon had ever told her. McMahon liked to invent and boast and told the most fantastic stories to impress anyone who cared to listen. His wife Sheenagh described him as someone who liked to think of himself as a bit of a Starsky and Hutch character. Every tale McMahon had told her, Adrienne repeated to the Carty team as they instructed.

The Carty team were obsessed with the name of the young man whose name had been the bait to get her to go to Rathmullen. The Assistant Commissioner had brought her to his office in Sligo demanding information. Adrienne felt as though she had been through a wringer, washed out and was now being hung out to dry. She just wanted to be left alone, rid of the Carty team and the conspicuous ERU protection. Journalists had already asked Karen for confirmation of a surveillance operation.

On 20 September, in a moment of madness, Adrienne smashed the windscreen of her car. Her half-formed plan was to tell the Guards that the ERU was attracting attention, and they should withdraw. By the following day, she told the Carty team she had committed the act herself. She just wanted to be left alone. Some Gardaí in Letterkenny were being openly hostile and verbally abusive.

Matt Tolan was Noel McMahon's partner in the Letterkenny detective unit. His movements appeared unusual and came to the attention of the ERU. At 11 p.m. on 8 October they recorded that he drove 'up Ramelton Road and past her shop. This vehicle continued up Main Street and did a lap of the town, returning to station roundabout. The vehicle then pulled in on Ramelton Road between the roundabout and the Four Lanterns where it remained for a few minutes before driving up past the shop again. He drove into the Grill car park and out immediately before doing another lap of the town and returning to station roundabout and pulling in at the same location until 11:28 p.m. He then drove up past the shop again. Our subject was this time standing outside the shop and appeared to see him as she immediately went inside. The patrol car then did another lap of the town and returned to Ramelton Road where this time he turned on his lights and parked between the shop and the Four Lanterns. He waited a few minutes before driving up past the shop again and into the Grill car park where we had parked our vehicle. As he went back out on to Ramelton Road Ms McGlinchey drove past in her vehicle. He followed her up to the lights where he stopped beside her. When the lights went green she turned left while he went straight ahead. He returned to the Garda station at 12:01.'

At the Morris Tribunal, Tolan said this was 'a normal patrol on a weekend on the Port Road in relation to public order. I've done that on numerous occasions.' The detective denied that he had sought to intimidate Adrienne McGlinchey. Mr Justice Morris made no finding about the incident in his interim report.

Karen met with Detective Hugh Coll and Assistant Commissioner Kevin Carty on 14 October. They wanted to know if Karen had located tapes Adrienne had given her in 1995 of conversations with McMahon and Lennon. Karen declined to hand over the tapes to them and said she would put them in the custody of her solicitor on her next visit to Dublin.

The investigators asked Karen what she knew about what happened at Rathmullen beach. One of the Guards that McMahon had told Adrienne was in a watching car that night had an alibi, provided by his wife.

Karen had been furious with Adrienne for allowing herself to be placed in such a dangerous position at Rathmullen. In an effort to put her sister's mind at rest, Adrienne had reassured her by telling her that a member of staff had accompanied her there and had waited in the car until she came back. Adrienne asked Eleanor McDermott to verify the story to Karen. At the meeting, Karen told the assistant commissioner that there was a witness, Eleanor McDermott, who could back up Adrienne's account of what had happened.

Ten days after her meeting with the Carty team, on 24 October, a break-in occurred at Karen McGlinchey's home. She saw the intruders approach the house and dialled 999. She gave her name and address and some detail of the intruders, who seemed to be wearing balaclavas. One intruder entered the house and assaulted her, while the others disappeared around the side of the house. They didn't stay long and didn't ask for money or jewellery, in fact they asked for nothing at all. There was no Garda response to the 999 call and Karen went to the shop for Adrienne. She was bleeding from her lip and her mouth hurt where the intruder had grabbed her. Karen told Adrienne not to tell Eleanor McDermott, who was working in the shop, about the intruder, as she had already had one upset when a stranger had shown her a gun as a threat to Adrienne.

Adrienne took her sister to Letterkenny hospital. She was X-rayed and told by the doctor that she had a tiny fracture of her jaw. He recorded his diagnosis on the casualty card and told her she would have to wait for the radiologist's report to see if further treatment was required. Back home, Karen could see nothing missing at her first cursory look. The following day, the Carty team investigated the non-response of Letterkenny Gardaí to the emergency call.

Jo McGlinchey owned a B & B next door to Adrienne and Karen. She is Bernard McGlinchey's sister and aunt to Karen and Adrienne. The detectives from Letterkenny interviewed her. Certain comments she made to the Carty team were put to Karen while in the witness box at the Morris Tribunal. The following is an extract from the direct evidence of Karen being questioned by Mr Peter Charleton SC:

Charleton: Can I just ask you a number of things? You have an aunt called Jo; isn't that right?

Karen: I have, yes.

Charleton: One of the things that she said to the Carty team was to be careful as to whether this happened at all. It may be that she is a lady who, I mean no disrespect, shoots her mouth off or it may be that she was sceptical about emergency reports being made. Again does that assist the chairman in any way?

Karen: No, actually I would have no reason why she would say that because she herself has been the subject of quite a number of break-ins also.

Karen's evidence was accepted by the Morris Tribunal.

It would be three months before Karen discovered that the tapes Adrienne had made of Lennon and McMahon were missing. It was a further three years before she would discover that photo negatives taken during a family holiday with her mother, which had also been in her study, were found in the locker of Superintendent Kevin Lennon in December 2002 by the Carty team.

By October 1999 the Carty team had their statements and allegations in writing, albeit as yet unsigned. On 15 November 1999 Eleanor McDermott was arrested and taken to Manorhamilton Garda station. She was questioned in relation to firearms offences by the Carty team, who wanted to know about the stranger who had shown her a handgun and told her 'this is for Adrienne'.

At the Morris Tribunal, Eleanor McDermott testified that she was told by the Carty team of a plan devised between Karen and Adrienne to fabricate a false break-in to their home so that Adrienne would gain credibility with the Carty team.

After two days in custody, Eleanor retracted her statement. 'I was ready for the knacker's yard at that stage and I was just ready for going home, and if they had said to me sign this confession to murder I would have signed it just to get home,' she told the Morris Tribunal. 'I didn't care. They said to me sign something to say you apologise to the Gardaí; I signed it. They said you two were friends, that's the way it was, you sign that, and I signed it.

'It was the only way to get home and I was afraid, what's the phrase, to upset the apple cart. I was afraid if I disagreed again at this point I would be kept longer. I had already been threatened before that I would be kept another week, they told me if I gave in to what they wanted I would be out in an hour. I said, okay fine. If you say it didn't happen I'll sign it. Those statements were not my words.'

Since it did not concern the events in the terms of reference, the Tribunal made no findings of fact concerning Eleanor McDermott. Mr Justice Morris noted that the Tribunal 'found nothing to suggest misbehaviour on the part of the Carty investigation team'.

In March 2000, Adrienne agreed to meet with the Carty team and sign her statements. They took her to Brockagh Garda station where they argued and Adrienne walked out of the station. Because it was in a remote area, service to her mobile phone was not available.

Despite the stress of her interview process, Adrienne's statement to the Carty team concludes with the following: 'I would like to apologise to any members of this investigation team that if they felt that I have confused them in certain aspects, it was never my intention but due to pressure from others this may have happened. I would like to state that I have the utmost respect for Commissioner Carty, Austin McNally, Hugh Coll and George Kyne to which I have found to be very understanding and treated me with respect at all times.'

The Carty team would not be left open to any accusations of mistreatment of a witness whom they had interviewed for over forty days during the summer months of 1999.

Within weeks, certain people of known republican backgrounds were taking notice of Adrienne's car outside the shop and made a deliberate note of her registration in her presence. An article in a national paper written by an ex-Garda described her as one of 'two local women being used as so-called IRA informers by members of the Gardaí'. Adrienne wrote to Garda Commissioner Pat Byrne to complain.

The letter, dated 12 July 2000, read as follows:

A half page feature in Saturday's *Irish Times* 8 July 2000 in which an ex-Garda, whom I assume is retired, referred to me as one of 'two local women being used as so-called IRA informers by members of the Gardaí'.

Last night, a senior member of the Provos here in Donegal along with two others made a point of taking the registration of my vehicle outside my business premises. Their demeanour was threatening and sinister. As you know, unlike Gardaí, when the Provos want to make a point they don't need to hide behind a balaclava and wave a gun in a person's face. I have been derided by senior officers of the investigation team for expressing any apprehension about the response of the Provos to my participation in these events. I have never been a member of any organisation in my life, least of all the IRA. To have been an informer for that organisation, one would have had to infiltrate their ranks. The Garda Síochána have now placed me in a situation where there is now widespread erroneous speculation that I was an IRA informer.

For a number of years, I have been blackmailed by Kevin Lennon and Noel McMahon and in more recent years the latter was extorting money from me. For their own personal gains they had portrayed me as a top IRA informer and activist which was unquestioned by the senior ranks.

It is distressing for me that current and former Garda officers are free to put my personal and my family's well-being at risk by continuing to selectively drip-feed the media with information that could only come from statements that I have made or from internal false records maintained on Garda files about me. When I first met with members of your investigation team in my solicitor's office, I was given certain assurances by them. I was told the investigation would be carried out by Gardaí from outside this county. I was told any and all statements made by me would remain confidential. Not only has this confidence been breached by this investigation and not only have I been subjected to the most horrendous harassment, intimidation and personal threats against me and my sister by Gardaí under investigation and other unidentified persons, I have to read on an almost weekly basis in the national media distorted facts and innuendo relating to me.

What I find deeply disturbing is that other witnesses in this investigation are informing me of what local Gardaí are telling them about my role in this investigation. I am also gravely concerned that Gardaí who have been named in my statement have been given full access to that statement to read.

The Commissioner appointed Detective Inspector Coll to investigate the issues raised in Adrienne's letter. No action was taken.

Attempts were made to generate a love triangle scenario. Security correspondents were happy to quote Garda sources who said that Adrienne and Noel McMahon were having an affair. It would have suited Garda authorities if this had been the case. The alternative for the Garda authorities was too awful to contemplate.

To date, despite the findings in the Carty report, the evidence presented to the Morris Tribunal and the findings of Justice Morris, the Garda Commissioner has refused to acknowledge or admit publicly that Adrienne was never an IRA informer or a member of that organisation.

16

Wrong Arm of the Law

The summons was served just before the bank holiday weekend. Adrienne could not think what she could offer in evidence to Frank Shortt's appeal against his conviction for knowingly allowing drugs to be sold in his nightclub in the early 1990s. Shortt's defence team had successfully applied to the courts for discovery of all the allegations in the possession of An Garda Síochána relating to Detective Garda Noel McMahon during certain dates, which effectively referred to the Point Inn case.

Adrienne knew there was nothing in her statement about the Point Inn. She would tell the court that Noel McMahon had said he committed perjury against Shortt during a drink-fuelled gripe against Lennon, but it would be her word against his. She was in no position to prove it. Besides, the assurance of immunity from the Director of Public Prosecutions was supposed to mean that she would never have to appear in court or have her statement brought into the public arena.

She managed to contact her solicitor Brian Gallagher and told him of the summons. Brian engaged Paul Murray BL to make an application to the court on her behalf. Brian told the sisters to wait across from the Four Courts until he came for them. Late in the morning, he joined them in the Legal Eagle bar and told them that the court insisted that Adrienne appear as a witness.

The pub seemed to be a popular bolthole. A familiar face dropped in for a quick shot of brandy before the serious business of justice could begin. Watching Noel McMahon swig the brandy and smack his lips, then wash it down with a cool beer, she wondered how someone could take an oath before God and the court under the effects of alcohol.

Adrienne's nervousness was palpable as the registrar went through the formalities of swearing her in. Drained and pale, she had waited all morning drinking tea. That seemed light years away now. She felt afraid and vulnerable. Three senior judges waited for the truth, the whole truth and nothing but the truth. Senior and junior counsel for both sides faced her.

She thought there would be rows of seats, and maybe even a balcony, somewhere that the masses would have observed proceedings and interjected with the necessary heckling, when the occasion arose. But just a few rows of hard benches sufficed. The Shortt family had taken the only two available benches in the centre of the room, so she had the pick of the side pews.

Along the back of the courtroom sat the Guards. Like a brass band waiting for a conductor, their buttons shone and sparkled. Epaulettes denoting just about every rank sat proudly on shoulders. Present and correct, the players were in place.

No one from the Carty team had told her she would be called as a witness. No one had told her that her involvement with Gardaí in Donegal would be the focus of the court. Sitting at the back, it was easy to read the smugness behind the eyes of the Gardaí. She was going to be exposed in the most dramatic fashion. There would be no protection from the court, from the legal fraternity, and least of all from the Gardaí. She would be examined by the defence team of Frank Shortt and cross-examined by counsel for the State. Gardaí would have the protection of the counsel for the State. Paul Murray, her own barrister, had unsuccessfully applied for anonymity for Adrienne. There had been widespread reporting in the media surrounding the corruption in Donegal and an alleged IRA informer.

Sheenagh McMahon had given a television interview to Frank Connolly on the TV3 20:20 programme on 30 July 2000. The interview was replayed for the Morris Tribunal. Introducing the interview, Connolly said that the identity of a Garda's wife 'had been concealed for her own safety'. During the course of the interview she described how her husband 'had got involved with a girl who I believed at that time was an IRA informant, who was helping him and his senior officer with his work. ... They said she would have been telling them where there was IRA finds and dumps. I believed she was an informant for the Guards of the IRA. ... He would have told me that she was going to show him where there was an IRA dump. ... When myself and my husband separated, the girl they were involved with came over from another town and told me there was an awful lot of loose talk about what went on in my house and I assured her I was not talking because I was concerned for her safety, because I felt if I ever mentioned her name, that she could get shot.'

As Adrienne began her evidence, Eoin McGonigle SC read memos and interviews to her. He appeared to doubt her inability to recall certain dates and interviews. Adrienne was shocked at the inaccuracies in the unsigned memos taken by the Carty team, which until then she had not seen. Detective Inspector Hugh Coll told the court that she had refused to allow anything relating to the Point Inn to be put into her statement and refused to allow notes to be taken when she was talking about the Point Inn. His sworn evidence was that he had managed to 'surreptitiously' take down key words as he sat at a table with her and another detective. At the bottom of the last statement she signed, it said she agreed with everything in her memos relating to the Point Inn.

Frank Shortt was returned for trial to the Circuit Court on 6 January 1994, which was also the night of the party in the McMahon house to celebrate the success of the Ardchicken mission and days before the display at Bridgend on 11 January 1994, which McMahon and Lennon laid on for border Superintendent Fitzpatrick and Superintendent JP O'Connor. Adrienne had her own troubles at the time, and was unaware that Shortt had received a three-year jail sentence. The case had been heard in Dublin after she had left Buncrana and was living in Letterkenny.

Shortt owned a nightclub in the quiet border village of Quigley's Point. It was a family operated business. In 1992, after completing extensive renovations, he had advertised 'Raves in the Cave' nights. Raves were just becoming popular, and were associated with the drug culture. Other prominent nightclubs in Donegal were also hosting raves.

Noel McMahon worked undercover in the Point Inn to detect drug deals at the same time as he was instructing Adrienne to have rockets and tripods made.

Kevin Lennon was appointed an inspector in 1992 and the operation at the Point was his baby. He christened it 'Operation Spider'. Towards the end of April or in mid-May 1992, Noel McMahon brought Adrienne to Kevin Lennon's office in Buncrana Garda station. It was the first time she met Lennon. His office was on the top floor. Lennon asked her if she ever went to the Point Inn, if she would go with some friends and see if there were drugs being dealt. Adrienne had never been to the Point Inn.

She didn't socialise with the girls from Jay Bees, though she knew that many of the staff went there.

McMahon told Adrienne the identity of a girl who was allegedly supplying drugs, and asked her to buy some drugs for him. He gave her £80 to make the buy. Adrienne told the girl she was having a party in her flat, but the girl was suspicious. Adrienne had never shown any interest in drugs before, and was not the type she normally supplied. She told Adrienne she would have to wait. With the £80 still in her pocket, Adrienne and Yvonne went on a spending spree in the pub. The girl later told her she couldn't get the drugs and Adrienne had to work overtime to repay McMahon the £80 she had spent.

McMahon was desperate to get drugs. He was getting overtime every week, and needed results to justify his undercover role. Drug dealers in the nightclub had recognised him, he told Adrienne, and he was finding it difficult to make buys. He needed his own supply to make his work more convincing. Each Sunday night he was on duty in the Point Inn, dressed as Mr Cool, wearing tracksuits and sneakers in an attempt to merge with the rave set. Sheenagh McMahon said she could not understand why he was undercover in the first place, he was so well known he would be recognised immediately.

McMahon told Adrienne he could get drugs himself. Instead he told her he wanted her to go to the Point Inn and plant drugs he would supply. He showed her a map of the interior layout, and told her when she had placed the drugs, she was to immediately leave the premises and get away from the area.

The raid was planned for the August bank holiday weekend. McMahon told her to go to Lifford and to be certain of being seen. The weekend before the raid on the Point Inn, Adrienne and Yvonne were in Lifford. Adrienne had to collect a tripod. They had gone to a pub and were arrested as they left by a Lifford Guard. They had been hysterically laughing and taken to Letterkenny and later released without questioning the following morning. McMahon told her to go back to Lifford and be seen the following weekend. This would be her alibi in the event that she was recognised in the Point Inn, he told her. Adrienne agreed, but was terrified of the idea of going into the nightclub and planting drugs. Getting steel tubes manufactured, or generally doing McMahon's bidding had never implicated innocent people as far as she was concerned. When he sent her to buy drugs, he said it was to show senior officers. There had been no mention of planting them. On the night of the raid, she was to ring him once she had her alibi in Lifford. He would collect her and take her to Quigley's Point, she would drop the drugs, then leave the area in his car. She opted to stay in the pub and managed to drink so much that she was unable to call him.

It was years later when she heard that Frank Shortt was convicted on Noel McMahon's evidence, and not until she appeared at the Court of Criminal Appeal did she hear that he had served three years in jail. Shortt was also fined £10,000. Three weeks after he was convicted, his premises were burned down in an arson attack. The culprits are still at large.

Adrienne sought the protection of the court to avoid self-incrimination in the manufacturing and planting of homemade explosives. She requested anonymity because of a fear for her personal safety, but this was also rejected. The court decided that it was not satisfied that 'any risk of the sort she mentions has in fact been established'.

Leaving the courtroom, Karen saw a posse of media and television camera crews in the main foyer. She assumed there was a high profile case being heard that day and someone of notoriety would feature on the evening news. There are two exits from the Four Courts, the main and a side exit. As they had come in through the side exit, they made to leave by it. A pleasant young man approached and identified himself as a cameraman from TV3. He told them that the media were waiting to see which exit they would use. The girls were stunned. They had not expected this much interest.

The cameraman offered them some friendly advice. Stand and allow the photographs to be taken. The photographers will get their shot no matter what, and if the sisters tried to evade them it would look worse on television, as if they had something to hide. It would all be over in ten seconds.

Lights. Camera. Action. The ten seconds turned into a walk down the steps and across the road, as drivers in passing cars called out asking if they had they won the lottery. The pub, which had served them tea earlier in that morning, was open and they grate-fully stepped into it out of the glare of the cameras. They ordered a large gin and tonic for Karen and a cup of tea for Adrienne.

In the morning, the media lined up on one side of the small courtroom. They were all there. RTÉ, TV3, the national papers. Everyone was waiting for the next instalment of the story.

By mid-morning Adrienne was explaining to the court that the money she received was for buying fertiliser and icing sugar. In the course of her evidence she had to make way for her sister Karen to take the stand. The following day, Karen made way for Hugh Coll.

The judges questioned Inspector Coll about the guarantees given to Adrienne's solicitor. He told the court that there was a consultation between Chief Superintendent McNally and the office of the DPP. He said that as far as he was aware, the guarantees were by phone. Chief McNally would have contacted Adrienne's solicitor after consulting with the DPP. When Coll was asked if he could recall what the guarantees were, he said there was something about Adrienne not being prosecuted, or that she wouldn't have to tender evidence in relation to an inquiry. He was not exactly certain. He told Justice Hardiman that they had a copy of the guarantee.

Justice Hardiman addressed the counsel for the State, noting that the document would appear relevant as Adrienne had claimed privilege on her first day in court. He said that if she had been given guarantees along the lines Inspector Coll described, it seemed difficult to see why the court wasn't informed at that stage. He asked that the document be produced before the end of the afternoon. Hardiman hammered his point home, saying he could see no reason why a letter in the possession of the Garda Síochána could not be produced in court. It should have been mentioned or produced at the time when the privilege was claimed. The judge expressed his displeasure that the court seemed to be getting information in a piecemeal fashion.

Mr Eoin McGonigle SC read into the public record the agreement reached between Adrienne's solicitor and the Gardaí, recorded in a communication between Chief Superintendent McNally and Brian Gallagher. The note, kept by Brian Gallagher, recorded McNally's assurances from the DPP that there would be no prosecutions or publication of her statements.

The State lawyers seemed confused as to what was agreed with the DPP, and didn't think assurances about non-prosecution had been given. Hardiman sought clarification from Coll to make certain that he had not mistaken his evidence, repeating back to him that McNally had a consultation with the DPP, following which he gave Adrienne the assurances through her solicitor. Coll assured him that was correct.

The appeal was a hearing for an application by Frank Shortt for a certificate of miscarriage of justice. Anything other than issues relative to that application were peripheral. The court had allowed Adrienne's counsel to make applications on her behalf, but there was no provision for her counsel to cross-examine witnesses on her behalf. Adrienne had tried to explain to the court the circumstances in which interviews were held, and that much of what was recorded was taken out of context or incorrectly. She always maintained that the Carty team had discussions for weeks before anything was written down. Coll confirmed that memos were not recorded for every meeting the Carty team had with Adrienne.

By the time it came to the cross examination of Adrienne by counsel for the DPP, the State had adopted the position of exposing Adrienne as a Garda informer, putting it to her that she had provided information on certain matters to Gardaí. Mr Justice O'Donovan enquired of Adrienne if she knew the meaning of the phrase 'informer'. After replying yes, he again asked if she had heard of the phrase a 'Garda informer' to which she replied that she had, but wouldn't consider herself a Garda informer.

When Lennon took the stand he painted a dramatic picture of Adrienne as an alleged IRA informer. Lennon gave details of C77s which outlined, according to him, associations she had with individuals suspected of being on the run from Northern Ireland. He explained that the C77s were secret internal Garda intelligence bulletins. He said he personally did not fill out C77s because he would not hijack another man's information, but he would have discussed it with his senior officers as part of security policy. The court was informed that her 'Garda handlers' Detectives Smith and Tolan were present and available to give evidence. The proposition now seems odd, since the Carty Report found she was not an informer and was available to the Court of Criminal Appeal and counsel for the State.

The informer label was tagged onto Adrienne until the Morris Tribunal found that she was never an informer or a member of the IRA, and cleared her name in 2004.

Sheenagh McMahon gave considerable evidence against her husband. There were very few seats available in the small court-room and the three women — Adrienne, Karen and Sheenagh — found themselves sharing a bench. Small talk passed between them until eventually Sheenagh was invited to join the sisters for lunch. They were amazed when she agreed to lunch on condition that they were out of sight of the court. They were somewhat bemused as they walked along one side of the quays and Sheenagh along the other. On the way back, the charade had to be main-tained as Sheenagh entered by the front door and the girls the side door. As they were leaving to go home for the weekend, Sheenagh asked for a lift to Donegal. Once again, a cloak and dagger operation took place while Sheenagh sneaked into the car for the journey to Donegal.

Noel McMahon's notebook was thoroughly examined by the court. In the middle of the notes were the all-important references to the Point Inn, which the court was particularly interested in. The court also looked at a draft statement he had prepared in the original prosecution of Frank Shortt.

On 31 July 2002, the judgement in the case of Frank Shortt v DPP, delivered by Mr Justice Hardiman, found that there had been a miscarriage of justice in the conviction of Frank Shortt on 28 February 1995. 'Some of these are substantive and some relate to the credibility of those principally involved. Cumulatively, however, they leave the court in no doubt that a miscarriage of justice occurred,' he wrote. The judgement also stated that 'had Ms McGlinchey not said what she did the process which led to the discovery of other, unquestionably significant, facts relating to this conviction would not have started.'

17

Getting to the Truth

Adrienne's aunt had given her a very special cross. It had been blessed by the Pope and was much cherished for its spiritual powers. Padre Pio medals and numerous Mass cards adorned her bedroom. Faith in the system was what was needed, but her fate lay in God's hands.

The Carty report had never been made public. The Garda Commissioner forwarded it to the Minister for Justice in 2000. On 26 July 2000, Commissioner Pat Byrne made a dramatic announcement of personnel transfers. Chief Superintendent Denis Fitzpatrick, the head of the Donegal division, was transferred to Dublin, heading up the National Traffic Bureau. Some saw the move as a demotion. Superintendent Kevin Lennon was transferred to duties in Garda headquarters in the Phoenix Park. Three other senior Donegal officers not involved in the explosives module of the Morris Tribunal were also transferred. The transfers, and reports that Gardaí involved in other aspects of the investigation had objected to transfers, raised further questions and fuelled speculation as to what was contained in the report.

Two years later, the media fall-out from the Shortt miscarriage application further fanned the flames. Frank Shortt had served three years in prison for allowing drugs to be sold in his nightclub, and his premises were burned in an arson attack. Noel McMahon had been the principal prosecution witness at his trial. Along with Kevin Lennon, he was severely criticised in the Court of Criminal Appeal. Following the judgement, the Commissioner suspended Lennon and Garda Tina Fowley, who had also worked on the Shortt case. Noel McMahon had already been suspended since Carty investigators searched his house in September 1999.

The Tribunal of Inquiry into Complaints Concerning Some Gardaí in the Donegal Division was created by a resolution passed by the Dáil and Seanad Éireann on 28 March 2002. Former President of the High Court Mr Justice Frederick Morris was appointed as the Sole Member. Justice Morris assembled a team of high profile barristers to assist his work. Peter Charleton, best known as a prosecuting barrister, and Paul McDermott, a well-known defence barrister, were the senior counsels. They were joined by junior counsel Mr Anthony Barr, son of Mr Justice Robert Barr, head of the inquiry into the shooting dead of John Carty at Abbeylara.

Former Garda Superintendent Michael Finn and Brian Steel Garvie of the Royal Canadian Mounted Police were appointed as Tribunal investigators. Another Canadian, retired Mountie Patrick Cummins, later relieved Mr Garvie when he returned to Canada.

The terms of reference for Adrienne's module required the Tribunal to investigate whether 'some Gardaí in County Donegal may have been involved in hoax explosives and bomb-making equipment finds (in particular discoveries on 11 September 1993, 19 November 1993, 11 January 1994, 14 March 1994, 4 June

1994, 13 June 1994 and 18 July, 1994) and a review of the management and investigation of these issues.'

Although the Tribunal operated from Clonskeagh in Dublin, the opening statement was delivered in Donegal town. Between the Dáil resolution and the opening statement the following November, Adrienne had become a public figure at the Shortt hearing, and evidence and statements that were attributable to her were made available to the court upon discovery. To these were added selections drawn from statements in the Carty report read into the public record by Peter Charleton.

The McGlinchey family felt that the opening statement — read into the record by Peter Charleton — could leave an impression that Adrienne was an IRA informer. This caused them concern about Adrienne's personal safety. Among a number of quotes from Garda statements to the Carty inquiry was one from Sergeant Michael Murray, the scene-of-crime examiner stationed at Buncrana, who described Adrienne McGlinchey and Yvonne Devine as 'known active members of the Provisional IRA'.

Peter Charleton said that Detective Garda Danny Kelly made a statement in August 1999 in which he said that he found Adrienne with bullets, and 'in a later statement' called her 'a Walter Mitty-type person'. In fact the 'later statement', made in September 1999, is, with the exception of a single line, identical to the first report he sent to Superintendent Jackie O'Connor of the Carty team on 15 May 1999. This first report from Kelly makes no mention of the bullets Adrienne gave to him. His August 1999 admission about the bullets came only after Adrienne herself told the Carty team about the incident. It would be months before the public hearings began and she had an opportunity to give her evidence before the Tribunal.

In the interest of natural justice, when an allegation was made, any response or denial was also referred to. Charleton noted in his opening remarks that 'every time an allegation is made, we will indicate the detail of what is alleged. We will indicate the reply or explanation given by the party against whom it is made, in equal detail.' Adrienne's allegations about what really happened at each of the finds to be investigated were accompanied by the denials of Noel McMahon and Kevin Lennon. Adrienne felt that the same cautions were missing in repeated statements concerning her. For instance, when Charleton mentioned Eleanor McDermott's arrest and detention in Manorhamilton, he said she 'told Gardaí that the report of the burglary at Karen McGlinchey's house was a false report, and that Adrienne McGlinchey had told her so'. Charleton did mention the denials from Adrienne or Karen. It would be almost two years before the Tribunal would say it accepted Karen's evidence.

The family took great exception to the commentary that counsel gave in relation to the failed attempt by Det Sgt Tom Sreenan to get a search warrant when fertiliser was thrown out of the Crescent flat in September 1993. Adrienne's behaviour was described as 'ostentatious'. Counsel opined that it was hard to imagine that it was anything other than a deliberate attempt by her to draw attention to herself. Adrienne's evidence, that she wanted rid of the fertiliser in case it was discovered by the Guards, got no mention. Instead, Charleton referred to the 'firing' of fertiliser out of the window of the flat, 'in full view of the public'. No members of the public were present during this incident, only Tom Sreenan and other Guards, who had to leave when O'Connor refused a search warrant. The family's understanding was that the finding of facts was a matter for the Tribunal and they did not therefore believe that it was appropriate for Counsel to describe the incident in such florid terms. Adrienne's solicitor objected in this regard on her behalf because, of course, the reality of the situation at the time was that Gardaí surrounded the flat, which contained a substantial amount of fertiliser. Noel McMahon or Kevin Lennon did not feature among their number, and it was hardly surprising in those circumstances that she made an attempt to get rid of the fertiliser.

It was obvious to Adrienne that she faced an uphill battle to clear her name. She knew that she was never in the IRA and that she was not an informer. The Tribunal was set up after allegations from two opposition TDs that the Carty inquiry might have been compromised. Despite this, the Tribunal had relied heavily on the Carty report in its opening statement, giving the impression that they intended to use Carty as the template for their inquiry.

Near the close of his statement, Peter Charleton noted that 'the Carty investigation team were able to interview a number of persons who flatly stated to them that Adrienne McGlinchey never had any connection with Sinn Féin or the IRA.' It seemed that the statement fell on deaf ears. The damage had already been done. For almost two years, the media would refer to Adrienne as the 'alleged IRA informer'. Adrienne feared that many people would discount the word 'alleged'. Throw enough mud and some of it will stick.

Getting to the truth of matters in Donegal was not going to be easy, but Charleton was anxious to point out that 'this Tribunal will be over very quickly if people tell the truth'. Recognising that 'witnesses who tell the truth may well contradict themselves and may well be confused. Witnesses who have all been part of the same event may see what has occurred to them differently from each other' probably gave hope to some people, particularly Adrienne who had been questioned at length by the Carty team without benefit of records, notes or diaries, and had been through

the ordeal of the Court of Criminal Appeal. One of the most difficult tasks facing the Tribunal was the obdurate position adopted by
some people, and counsel warned, 'we do not believe that it is to
the benefit of An Garda Síochána that people, when confronted
about their duties by superior officers, are apparently allowed to
remain silent.'

One of the greatest difficulties facing the Carty inquiry was that
they were dealing with persons who had certain rights conferred
on them by the fact that they were Guards. The protection of
their organisations would stifle any meaningful investigations into
the unlawful activities of some Gardaí and contributed to the
stalemate. None of the Gardaí ever envisaged the setting up of a
public Tribunal into their conduct. Some of them were convinced
that they were the law, and as such were above the law and
beyond reproach. Statements taken by Carty were part of an internal fact-finding mission, which would go nowhere. Any internal
inquiry would not be held in public. The Commissioner, Pat
Byrne, tried to downplay the allegations in the media, intimating
that it was a minute number of officers involved.

Just before Christmas 2002, the Tribunal delivered boxes of files to
Adrienne with a request for a statement of response by early
January. It seemed an almost impossible task and the girls spent
the Christmas poring over statements and documents.

The Garda Commissioner had claimed privilege over some
documents on national security grounds. In particular, privilege
was claimed over C77 forms. During the Point Inn hearing,
Lennon had said that the 'cloak of informer privilege was
removed' and counsel for the DPP repeatedly referred to the

so-called Garda handlers and, of course, the C77 forms. Now the Tribunal was faced with a quandary. In Ireland, there is a privilege against an informer having to reveal his or her identity. This privilege extends to Garda records of information from informers. Garda policy is to always claim privilege over C77 forms.

The situation was bizarre. Adrienne denied she was an informer. The Carty report sent to the Commissioner found she was not an informer. Yet the Commissioner insisted that privilege still extended to the C77s. Adrienne had no idea what might be recorded about her in the Garda vaults. In an effort to break the logjam, she waived any informer privilege, since she knew she was not an informer anyway. She wanted all the evidence heard in public. Her lawyers wrote to the Tribunal to say they were 'firmly instructed that our client has no objection whatever to waiving whatever privilege might be attributed to her in relation to the "Lennon locker" documentation and the C77 documentation'.

Discussions between the legal teams continued. Finally, the Privileged Documents Protocol was produced. Nothing in a C77 form could be reported. The Commissioner's legal team had effectively gagged anyone who had sight of the intelligence bulletins.

Karen and Adrienne were summoned to appear before the Tribunal on 3 March 2003 and following days. Cheques for €150 were enclosed with the summons. The Tribunal had supplied a list of bed and breakfast accommodation in a pack detailing bus times and the location of the Tribunal. Lunch and evening meal vouchers would be supplied, they were told. In the event, they managed to make a deal with one of the nearby hotels, the Montrose, which would include breakfast and evening meal.

They had been shown around the hearing room during a visit in February, and Adrienne had the opportunity of taking the seat in the witness box and getting a 'feel' for the place. The hearings took place in a specially converted building in Belfield Office Park. Compared to the tiny Donegal courthouse where Peter Charleton had read the opening statement, it was state-of-the-art. Large plasma screens dropped from the ceilings, allowing the public and media to watch witnesses up close. They could see at close range each witness, the blemishes on a face, the sheen of a bald pate, the untreated roots, and most important of all, their reaction to questions. Each of the large desks supplied for the legal teams featured banks of electrical switches and a mini screen. Live transcripts were fed through to the legal teams.

In the first weeks there was considerable media interest, but the ordinary public didn't seem to care. The Tribunal did not affect the ordinary Dubliners, who saw it as a side show conducted by Gardaí in Donegal. On RTÉ, Vincent Browne highlighted the proceedings regularly, barely hiding his amusement as the events unfolded. The girls tried to put themselves into the position of those who did not know the story. For them, the story of a life used and abused by An Garda Síochána was less amusing.

Adrienne took the stand during the third week of hearings. Giving evidence to the Tribunal was less intimidating than the Court of Criminal Appeal — this time she had her own legal representation. Her barrister and solicitor could cross-examine the Guards who for years made statements about her alleged status as an IRA member and informer. Counter-allegations which to date had been unchallenged would be examined in detail. Despite the fact that she had made allegations of Gardaí being involved in the manufacturing and transporting of homemade explosives for finding later, others who had less involvement, but had turned blind eyes to the activities of their colleagues, seemed intent on doing as much damage to her reputation and credibility in a misguided attempt to remain loyal to their corrupt friends. In his report, Justice Morris criticised seventeen named serving and former Gardaí for corruption, negligence, lying and withholding information. He was scathing in his criticism of the culture of silence within An Garda Síochána, and the phenomenon of 'Garda speak', where witnesses fenced verbally with counsel to avoid answering difficult questions.

Every day on the stand, Adrienne clutched the cross her aunt gave her as she gave evidence. Swearing the oath on the Bible was not simply a legal ritual for her. She called on God as her witness throughout the entire delivery of her testimony.

Of course, there were contradictions from what she had told Carty. Had she gone first to the shed or the house in Rossnowlagh? Could she have been in the house at all? Was she there once, twice or three times? By the time Carty, the Court of Criminal Appeal and the Tribunal were finished with her, she couldn't remember how many houses and sheds she had been to and if she was there once, twice, three times or at all. She told the Tribunal about stops for alcohol on the journey to Rossnowlagh, which she explained caused her difficulty and confusion surrounding that particular night. In his report, Justice Morris found that she had consumed alcohol on the excursion.

Adrienne got through her testimony hour by hour rather than day by day. She looked on it as finally clocking out from the 1990s. Peter Charleton took her through the evidence, challenging every utterance. Often he wanted a simple yes or no, but for Adrienne it was not so simple. There was background to each event. What went before gave meaning to what she had been through. Individual incidents, bags tossed over walls or runs through the convent grounds seemed ridiculous on their own. History gave them context. At times it was unbearable for Karen to hear her sister give such heart-rending evidence about the turmoil she tried to fight before being so exposed. She had been directed to do certain things. Lennon and McMahon had used her for their own ends, but the fear and dread of her family knowing the truth about her years in Buncrana was simply overwhelming.

She explained her feelings to Peter Charleton when Lennon told her that Sheenagh McMahon was talking about her around Buncrana: 'I am sitting at home, back with my family, running a business, I have used my home, our lands, our sheds, I have used my flat, I have gone and put stuff down with Guards. Maybe I was being selfish but that is the way it was and I was thinking to myself, I had used the business, I had used the attic, I had used the sheds, I had sat in our sitting room, I had ground fertiliser in our sitting room and here was two people, that were drinking very heavy, and didn't care and I am sorry, but that is the way it was. Then Kevin Lennon was sending me down and she was telling me to ring Noel and Noel was telling me to wind up Lennon. You know, I will say that 1998 and 1999, between them all they had me wound into everything and I was very selfish because I was thinking of myself, to protect myself for my family.'

Her memory wasn't perfect. Adrienne remembered the envelope left at the door for Noel Jones, she remembered the bullets in the envelope, remembered Jones taking the envelope, remembered him returning it. She remembered later filling a lunchbox with the bullets and going into Strabane with it. But Charleton still demanded to know who put the bullets in the envelope. Adrienne didn't remember. She told him she could have put them in the envelope herself for all she could remember, but she had no memory of how they got there. It might have been her; it might have been Noel McMahon or Kevin Lennon. Six times she told him she could not remember, until Charleton eventually accused her of playing silly games and wasting his time.

Adrienne told Charleton a further six times that she couldn't remember, before he suggested that she did not want to remember because she didn't want to take responsibility for a ridiculous note included with the bullets. Adrienne could only wonder. She took responsibility for being involved in all the finds, in the manufacture of homemade explosives, transportation and planting and later finding, and yet he could suggest she had problems with a silly note.

Evenings after the hearings were spent walking along the pier at Dún Laoghaire. It was the only place to clear heads and minds. The girls didn't analyse evidence given or about to be given. They took it day by day, knowing that at some point it would be over.

Back on the stand, Adrienne was cross-examined by lawyers for the Gardaí on the basis she was either a member of, or informer against the IRA. It received widespread publicity. Official documents always give weight to the appearance of truth. Contemporaneous documents speak louder than words. The reputations and careers of the authors of the Garda reports were at stake and they would use these reports to prove the authenticity of her IRA status. Her status as a member of a well-known family had been the most attractive part of promoting her so-called subversive stature. It received widespread publicity. Finally, the last question was asked.

As Adrienne reached the end of her evidence, the Tribunal rest day changed from Monday to Wednesday. On the rest day the Tribunal did not hear evidence, allowing lawyers to catch up with the documentation needed to question each witness. For the witnesses travelling from Donegal, it meant an extra day spent in Dublin unless they made the midweek 250-mile round trip. Travelling by car from the south Dublin location to Donegal took in the region of five hours. There was no early finish on a Friday to facilitate rush hour traffic out of the city. Spent and exhausted, the girls arrived home for the weekend break late on a Friday night before returning to Dublin on Sunday. Travel sickness was a significant factor for Adrienne and they decided to leave their car in Dublin at weekends and do as other witnesses did and take the flight from Dublin to Derry.

Many of the civilian witnesses who attended the Tribunal stayed in the Montrose Hotel. Sheenagh McMahon, who had been staying in a different Dublin hotel, moved to the Montrose and spent her evenings having dinner with Karen and Adrienne, or the threesome would drive to Dún Laoghaire and go to the cinema. After breakfasting together the three ladies would drive to the Tribunal, but once in the environs of the building, Sheenagh would resort to the cloak and dagger charade adopted years before at the Frank Shortt hearing, of getting dropped off before the entrance, fearful of a waiting photographer who might capture the moment forever on camera. In the hearing room, she remained aloof and detached from the girls, choosing to take a seat behind and away from them. By evening, they were laughing together at the cinema in Dún Laoghaire, putting the events of the day behind them.

In the early stages of the hearings the various parties melted into cliques of their own. Lennon and McMahon and the legal teams of the Garda Representative Association took the nook outside the front door where they could smoke and presumably plan strategies. It became the smokers' corner. There was very little interaction between the parties. As time went on and the media left, polite comments passed between them.

There were very few days when there wasn't an attack on Adrienne. The sillier Gardaí made her look, the more their testimony was reported in Donegal. One local radio station delighted in reporting the Garda who said that Adrienne and Yvonne were code-named K and P, after a popular brand of nuts. It was not surprising that the findings of the Morris Tribunal came as a shock to many people in Donegal.

There were good days and bad. When a Guard corroborated something Adrienne said, faith was restored in An Garda Síochána. The most memorable phrase came from Garda Christy Galligan, who described an atmosphere of 'gay frivolity' when Adrienne was held in Burnfoot Garda station. The evidence was not unexpected. His statement had been circulated throughout the Tribunal, but often in the case of previous witnesses their evidence was disappointing when it was finally delivered. Adrienne's legal team were busy recording notes at the table, listening but not looking, preparing for the cross-examination. It is difficult to describe the sight of a lawyer almost rising out of his seat as the words fell from Christy's mouth. 'Gay frivolity' and Brian Gallagher leaped up straight. He tried to look at the witness and gauge the chairman's reaction at the same time. Swivelling in his seat he turned to smile at the sisters who were equally pleased but afraid to breathe in case someone somewhere was going to put a stop to the notion that at last someone in the Garda Síochána was telling it how it was. Brian couldn't hide his glee, but there was no stopping Christy. He was on a roll and he was telling the chairman about the charade that had taken place in his station all those years ago. By all accounts Brian was going to have a seizure such was his excitement, staring at the witness, his new hero and his faith restored. It marked some form of relief for the sisters as the prospect of an actual award of costs became real. Galligan's evidence supported Adrienne's contention that the entire search and arrest that followed a report by her landlord was a charade. The evidence of Christy Galligan marked a turning point in the

Tribunal. Karen and Adrienne sensed that Christy's evidence had caused the first major chink in the case of Lennon, McMahon and their co-conspirators.

The bad days got pretty awful. Many of the Garda witnesses called her an 'attention seeker'. Many said she was a known member of the IRA, or a suspected member, or an associate, but when questioned none had ever seen her in any IRA house or associating with known IRA members. Most said that they had heard she was involved with the IRA, but when pressed none could remember where they heard this. Yet they remained committed to hearing all the evidence up to the end.

With hindsight, there were comical moments. The sisters had become so involved in the working of the Tribunal, the evidence of the various witnesses and the contrasts between their previous statements and their evidence on the stand, that at times they forgot they were in full view of the chairman. While all the legal teams had their backs to them, the chairman faced them all day. The girls got into an animated discussion between themselves about a particular ruling he had made when they came to the attention of the chairman. Looking directly at them he noted their displeasure and alerted Paul Murray to the fact that they were consulting each other. He asked their barrister to explain the legal intricacies of the ruling. Thankfully all the legal teams present did the decent thing. Not one of them turned to look at them.

The Tribunal was very poorly attended. After Adrienne's evidence was completed, most of the media left. The cameras were gone. All but two of the journalists were gone. A trickle of public interest remained. Gardaí called to give evidence took one of the two hundred seats available. With the exception of the sisters who remained for the entire module, there were less than a handful of other people at any one time. On the days of the attendance of former Ministers for Justice, members of the staff in the Tribunal building expressed huge interest and the attendance in the public gallery swelled in numbers for the hearing of their evidence in particular.

On 21 May 2003, Sergeant Mick Murray, the scene-of-crime officer from Buncrana was giving evidence for the second day. He asked to address the Tribunal about 'a matter of concern'. He told the chairman that two weeks earlier he had seen 'the McGlinchey sisters engaged in behaviour which I considered to be unethical'.

Bill Shipsey, a senior barrister representing Adrienne, immediately rose to ask that Sergeant Murray put any complaint in writing so that he could investigate it. The chairman told him that if the sergeant wanted to say something he thought relevant he would hear it, and Mr Shipsey would have an opportunity to consider what he said, and answer if it was appropriate.

Sergeant Murray went on to say he saw Karen McGlinchey reading Ciara McLaughlin's statement, and 'specifically heard her saying, you'll remember that, you'll remember that'. He was with two other Guards, and they went quiet to try and hear what was being said, and Karen McGlinchey said 'hear the silence of the lambs.'

Tribunal lawyer Paul McDermott then asked Sergeant Murray to make a statement to his own lawyers outlining his allegation.

The sisters were stunned and left the Tribunal with their legal team to prepare a response. Karen recalled the incident vividly. She had spoken to Ciara while Tribunal investigator Michael Finn was present. Ciara had signed a form for the Tribunal waiving any 'informer privilege' she might have had when she gave Noel Jones information years before. Ciara had then sought Karen's advice, as she had no independent legal advice and wasn't clear exactly what she had signed up to. Karen knew she had never said 'you'll remember this' or 'hear the silence of the lambs.'

The next morning, the headlines boomed 'Sisters engaged in unethical behaviour' and 'Garda sergeant tells Tribunal of "unethical behaviour"'. However, Mick Murray's promised statement never materialised. In November an exasperated Karen wrote to the chairman outlining how Ciara had approached her with the waiver documents, and gave the names of several lawyers and journalists who were present at the time, as well as the investigator Michael Finn. She pointed out that after waiting six months they still had no statement from Sergeant Murray. She told the chairman, 'If at any stage during a hearing assertions are made or evidence is sought to be addressed which might damage the reputation or good name of any individual but of which the Tribunal had not notice then procedures will be put in place either by an adjournment of the hearing or otherwise to deal with this situation, so as to ensure that fair procedures are observed. 15 July 2002. I am quoting these words with the greatest respect to you Sir, as they are your own. I feel that in the interests of fair procedure, I have been denied the opportunity of placing before you, my version of the event as alleged by Sergeant Michael Murray on 21 May 2003, Day 37.'

Outlining her case she told the chairman that, 'Sergeant Murray went further than that, by falsely asserting under oath to you chairman that I was making certain remarks, and those remarks were following from my reading of her "statement or memo", which, if you have read the document, you will know that such utterances, as he alleges, make no sense.'

'This false and mischievous allegation, which he made, garnered media interest, particularly in Donegal and the allegation was given separate prominence.' She added that, 'I have waited patiently since the 21st May 2003 for the promised statement, which Sergeant Murray told you he was going to submit.'

The chairman replied the next day to tell her that if he had to make any determination on the issue he would extend her legal representation so that Bill Shipsey could question the sergeant.

In his report, the judge found that when it came to the search of Adrienne's flat 'Sergeant Murray was anxious to present himself to the Tribunal as both a truthful witness and as a member of An Garda Síochána who carried out his duties in a conscientious manner. The Tribunal is satisfied that he was neither.' But while his evidence about the search of the flat was discounted, his allegation that Karen coached a witness was never addressed. Mick Murray continues to serve in Inishowen. To Karen, the affair contrasted with the handling of Superintendent Fitzgerald, who when he made allegations against Kevin Lennon on the stand was told to commit them to writing overnight to allow Lennon to cross-examine.

Murray was not the only Garda criticised by the judge. Both he and retired Detective Sergeant Des Walsh were found to have 'withheld vital information' about the search from the Tribunal out of misguided loyalty to their friends Noel McMahon and Kevin Lennon.

Tom Rattigan was the detective that landlord John Mackey first contacted after finding what seemed to be rockets under the bath in Adrienne's flat. He was criticised for 'an appalling dereliction of duty' in failing to preserve the scene and notify the Garda authorities, and 'behaved disgracefully' in only contacting Noel McMahon about the discovery.

Chief Superintendent John McLoughlin was border super-intendent in Donegal before Denis Fitzpatrick. He gave evidence that Adrienne was a 'Grade A informer'. The Tribunal found that there was 'no rational basis on which such a view could be held' and rejected his evidence.

Superintendent Denis Fitzpatrick succeeded McLoughlin as border superintendent. He went on to become Chief Superintendent, the most senior Garda in Donegal. Along with Superintendent John P O'Connor he was found to be negligent by the Tribunal. In the weeks after the judge published his report, both men retired on full pensions from An Garda Síochána. Retired Chief Superintendent Sean Ginty was also negligent in failing to investigate incidents properly.

In total, seventeen serving and former Guards were criticised for negligence, gross negligence, giving incomplete or untruthful evidence, and failing to perform their duty.

Adrienne was labelled a mischievous attention seeker. Notwithstanding that, the allegations she made which formed the basis for the terms of reference were all corroborated in the findings of the Tribunal and that 'in respect of the matters central to its inquiry Adrienne McGlinchey had told the truth.' The huge finds at Ardchicken and Rossnowlagh were found to be hoaxes. The trips to Strabane and Bridgend were orchestrated by Kevin Lennon to demonstrate his abilities to the RUC. The search of her flat in the Crescent, Buncrana and her subsequent arrest were a charade designed to stop a real investigation of what was going on. What Justice Morris found difficult to pinpoint was when exactly the manipulation of her by Lennon and McMahon began, but suggests that it was slowly, subtly and over time.

Few people come out of a Tribunal with their reputations entirely intact. The Gardaí are still reeling from the words of Chairman Morris, none more than Kevin Lennon and Noel McMahon. Lennon had told the Court of Criminal Appeal and the Tribunal that he did not know Adrienne until late 1993 when he was a detective inspector, but the judge found that 'while a uniformed Inspector, [he] had an involvement with, and an interest in protecting, Adrienne McGlinchey. That interest could only have arisen from some determination of his own to illicitly use her for his own self-interest.'

Lennon and McMahon 'were joint conspirators in the enterprise of using Adrienne McGlinchey as a tool to promote their interests. Ultimately, further facts allow the conclusion to be drawn that this took the form of using her as an informer credited with leading them to serious finds of subversive material.' McMahon offered his resignation within weeks of the Morris report in July 2004. Lennon was fired by the government in October 2004.

Records from the 'Lennon locker', which were discovered in December 2002, were found by Justice Morris to be 'notes as to the corrupt practice in which he and Detective Garda McMahon were engaged'.

Day 80 of the Morris Tribunal:

> Garda Martin Leonard: When an examination or an investigation is done like this inside in the Garda Síochána there was no Tribunal following on. It is the nature of the Gardaí, we don't name the names — we don't want to get anybody into trouble in the Garda Síochána internal matters. There was no public inquiry.
>
> Mr Peter Charleton SC: So you block any names coming out in any of your statements?
>
> Garda Martin Leonard: We try our best to make sure — we are not going to be hanging our people.

Without fundamental reforms to eradicate the Martin Leonard philosophy, there will continue to be scandals in An Garda Síochána.

18

The Gimp

I hope Bill Shipsey will forgive me for quoting his advice to Adrienne before she took the stand. It was meant in the best possible way and not designed to insult any member of the bar. 'Barristers,' he said, 'are basically odd. They find it difficult to function in normal situations, but what they are exceptionally good at is thinking on their feet.

'People who are familiar with the court system,' he told her, 'are able to anticipate where a barrister is leading with a question and this comes to people in time.' Admittedly, it was after about thirteen months attending the hearings when the pattern became clear for the girls.

Among other documents, numerous photographs and negatives were found in what has become known as the 'Lennon locker'. Some of those photographs have been reproduced in this book.

It is difficult to give the full flavour of the Tribunal or indeed to record every detail of every piece of testimony. Some of it was delivered in that special Donegal way such as the night one witness was told it was his bedtime. 'When I was about halfway over I met someone who I took to be a Guard and I says to him, it's a right kind of a night, he says, it is but it's time everybody was in bed. I took great exception to that on my own street, as a resident of the place, and the way I viewed it was, if it was a Guard it was wrong, and it was time to go to bed. If it wasn't a Guard, it was certainly time to go to bed, you know. If I had felt it wasn't a Guard I would have had phoned the Guards. So, as I say in Buncrana, I sort of knew by the gimp it was a Guard.'

Then there was the witness who tried to explain to the chairman the extent of a cannabis and drinking habit. It is hoped that the following extracts from the Tribunal record in this chapter will give a sense of the ludicrous extremes:

Q. What does it involve, being on cannabis?
   A. Smoking it.
   Q. How often?
   A. 24 hours a day.
Drink was apparently consumed as follows:
   Q. What was the extent of your alcohol intake?
   A. Whatever I could hold just.
Later the witness explained the phenomenon of being high:
   Q. You said you were as high as a kite?
   A. Yes.
   Q. What did you mean by that?
   A. As high as a kite.
The testimony continued:
   Q. How long were you in Burnfoot Garda station?
   A. A few hours. I was there several times.
   Q. How were you [on] each occasion?
   A. Stoned out of my mind.

Tribunal counsel, back on the subject of being high, wanted a description from the witness of how it felt to be stoned:

Q. Explain to me, what do you mean not good, were you just tired or were you hallucinating or what were you?

A. Stoned, I told you.

Q. But would you explain stoned, I don't understand the word stoned?

A. High as a kite.

Q. Does stoned mean you are asleep?

A. High as a kite.

Q. Does it mean you are hallucinating?

A. High as a kite.

Q. Are you hallucinating?

A. No.

Q. Explain to me the sensation you experience when you are as high as a kite?

A. You could be laughing, you could be away in la-la land.

Q. Away where?

A. La-la land, did you ever hear that?

Q. I didn't, you might explain that to me?

A. Did you ever hear of away with the fairies.

Q. Not really, I don't know or understand what you mean by away in la-la land or away with the fairies, explain that to me.

A. Well, you wouldn't be in the right state of mind.

Q. Pardon?

A. You wouldn't be in a right state of mind, would you like me to get you a doctor's report.

Q. No, I want you to tell me person to person and explain to the Tribunal and the chairman, what you mean by away in la-la land and away with the fairies, because it is important we understand what your state of mind was when you made your three statements to the Carty team back in 1999. So would you tell us what you mean by away with the fairies? Tell us what is going through your mind when you are away with the fairies?

A. It could be anything going through your mind.

Q. Give us an example.

A. I'm not really sure myself now, I'm only off it recently.

Q. Recently?

A. Yes.

Peter Charleton SC is one of the leading barristers involved with the Tribunal. His quick-witted remarks, dripping in sarcasm, often caught witnesses by surprise. It is impossible to try and give a summary of his examination of Kevin Lennon when dealing with the photographs found in the 'Lennon locker'. Peter Charleton probably does not realise his spontaneous remarks often translated into some of the more hilarious and farcical testimony Lennon gave.

Peter Charleton: You know the photographs that have been produced before the Tribunal?

Kevin Lennon: Yes, sir.

Peter Charleton: Which are good quality photographs that don't seem to me to be done on a twopenny ha'penny camera that you buy on holidays and throw away having had developed?

Kevin Lennon: Yes, sir, they were taken on a disposable camera sir, yes.

Peter Charleton: What were?

Kevin Lennon: Those photographs.

Peter Charleton: Of the flat?

Kevin Lennon: Yes.

Peter Charleton: You say they were photographs handed to you, maybe you will tell us about what photographs were handed to you?

Kevin Lennon: I was looking for proofs of intelligence matters.

Peter Charleton: Yes?

Kevin Lennon: That was coming to me and I couldn't get the proofs advanced so I bought disposable cameras and I gave them to Ms McGlinchey to prove to me that there was some materials in situ wherever they may be and I might be able to follow it on.

Peter Charleton: When was this? Before or after 14 March 1994?

Kevin Lennon: Oh, before. I think it was before that, yes. It was before that.

Peter Charleton: So she gave you — you gave her disposable cameras?

Kevin Lennon: Yes.

Peter Charleton: A very, very good quality disposable camera it would seem?

Kevin Lennon: Yes.

Peter Charleton: She went and she took photographs of materials in situ?

Kevin Lennon: Yes, sir.

Peter Charleton: In a bedroom with a sink?

Kevin Lennon: Yes, sir.

Peter Charleton: In a wardrobe?

Kevin Lennon: That's what the photographs reflected, yes.

Peter Charleton: Yeah. And did you ask her about them?

Kevin Lennon: I asked her about them, yes, and she said that she wouldn't — she knew where the location was, she'd tell me where it was.

Peter Charleton: Yeah?

Kevin Lennon: She would tell me where these materials would be eventually but she wouldn't tell me where they were at the time.

Peter Charleton: Yeah?

Kevin Lennon: So the photographs were produced to me and I couldn't establish anything from them.

Peter Charleton: Of course you couldn't establish anything from them, but you could establish that they were in somebody's bedroom?

Kevin Lennon: Yes.

Peter Charleton: There was explosives beside the bed, beside the sink, in the cupboard, in the airing cupboard?

Kevin Lennon: I think it was somewhere around December of ...(INTERJECTION)

Peter Charleton: Did you ask who is this crazy person keeping explosives in her flat, in his or her flat?

Kevin Lennon: No, in a house.

Peter Charleton: In a house?

Kevin Lennon: Yes, I did.

Peter Charleton: With loads of bottles of shampoo?

Kevin Lennon: Yes, sir.

Peter Charleton: Well, men don't usually have lots of bottles of shampoo in their bedroom, do they?

Kevin Lennon: I didn't notice that part of it. I think it was in December of 1993 and I couldn't get to the bottom of it.

Peter Charleton: Here she is, she is handing you photographs. She is saying here are all these bombs in preparation, in situ, but I'm not going to tell you where they are?

Kevin Lennon: Yeah.

Peter Charleton: Ah come on, do you really expect anybody to believe that?

Kevin Lennon: That's my position.

Peter Charleton: Did you believe it?

Kevin Lennon: I believed that there was materials out there somewhere.

Peter Charleton: Why not arrest her because from December through to March those could have been put into a bomb and blown the limbs off people across the border?

Kevin Lennon: Because she said that nothing would get out of control, that she would tell Detective McMahon if there was anything happening and he would tell me.

Peter Charleton: But are you placing your faith then in the IRA?

Kevin Lennon: I am placing my faith in an informer, sir, who was a proven informer and I placed my faith in that.

Peter Charleton: Look, did somebody take photographs of the scene of the 14th March, either on the 14th, 15th, 16th or any day after the 14th March, Garda photographs and present them to you?

Kevin Lennon: No, sir.

Peter Charleton: They didn't?

Kevin Lennon: No, sir.

Peter Charleton: How do we account for these photographs then apart from this extraordinary story of you buying disposable cameras for Adrienne McGlinchey and her coming back with this story that somewhere in the county of Donegal there are these things in preparation but she is not prepared to tell you anything else?

Kevin Lennon: I think the albums actually show that they were done in December of 1993.

Peter Charleton: How do you mean 'the albums show they are done in December 1993?' Can we look at the photographs?

Kevin Lennon: No, sir, the albums, I think, show a date on the front of them.

Peter Charleton: We don't have to believe that do we. Anybody can print any date on the front of a photograph. On the other hand, if the camera is recording automatically on the interior the date the photograph is taken on, there may be some validity in that. This photograph is the one I'm referring to. I think you can see there?

Kevin Lennon: Yes, sir.

Peter Charleton: Sir, I can call them up on the screen but it takes a long time. Then here is a photograph showing a sink with a great deal of shampoo and other lotions?

Kevin Lennon: Yes.

Peter Charleton: Radox, Silvikrin, Silvikrin, some form of deodorant, soap, what looks like bubble bath and a large green tube of material. Does that look like a lady's sink? I know I am not supposed to be sexist in any respect, but let's face reality, women spend a great deal more time on their hair than men?

Kevin Lennon: Yes, sir. But the point is that that wouldn't stick out in your mind if you just looked at a photograph.

Peter Charleton: It sticks out in my mind. I'm looking at that and I see two bottles of Silvikrin, a bottle of bubble bath, Radox, some form of spray deodorant, a big bar of green soap, a second bar of green soap and big large green jar of some kind of lotion?

Kevin Lennon: Yes, sir.

Peter Charleton: That is a ladies accoutrements; isn't it?

Kevin Lennon: That didn't reflect in my head anyway.

Peter Charleton: And bizarrely enough the lady has a big, big bag of Two Sward beside her wardrobe?

Kevin Lennon: Yes, I see that.

Peter Charleton: Well when Adrienne McGlinchey handed you this photograph as you say in December 1993, didn't you say to yourself, ah, McGlinchey's bedroom?

Kevin Lennon: No, I didn't.

Peter Charleton: When you saw the next photograph with, again, cosmetic accoutrements, apparently this time on top of the wardrobe, did you say that to yourself?

Kevin Lennon: No I didn't take any countenance of the accoutrements in the bath.

Peter Charleton: You are a trained observer, I mean you are a detective, I'm not. Why not?

Kevin Lennon: I am not a trained detective but I am a reasonable detective.

Peter Charleton: Here is another photograph of the two sward taken from another angle?

Kevin Lennon: Yes.

Peter Charleton: And on top of that you have a bottle of Buccaneer which I think is something to do with shoes and you have what looks like Johnson's baby lotion and you have various other bottles of cosmetic type preparations.

Now I don't think that a member of IRA dressed in black or combat gear or otherwise who is a man would have these, together with Two Sward in his bedroom, do you?

Kevin Lennon: I don't know whose bedroom it is, I just don't know.

Peter Charleton: Did you ask her whose bedroom it was?

Kevin Lennon: I asked and I was told you'll get the information when it comes to fruition.

Peter Charleton: Did you ask why are the volunteers spending so much time on their hair and their bath preparations?

Kevin Lennon: No I didn't, sir, I wasn't interested in that part of it. I was only interested in what was going on.

Peter Charleton: Well do you regard those observations I have made as being particularly sharp or informed observations or do you think they are the kind of observations that any reasonable person or any reasonable policeman might have made having been handed these photographs by Ms McGlinchey?

Kevin Lennon: They are sharp on you studying them very closely, but I was only interested in the other, I wasn't interested in that aspect of it.

Peter Charleton: How closely do you need to study them? I held them up there, they are visible to the chairman, they are visible to you and you are two to three metres away from me?

Kevin Lennon: I wasn't told it was in Ms McGlinchey's bedroom or flat.

Peter Charleton: Look, aren't these scene-of-crime photographs taken on the 14th March by somebody in the Gardaí?

Kevin Lennon: I wouldn't think so, no.

Peter Charleton: You wouldn't think so?

Kevin Lennon: No.

Peter Charleton: No?

Kevin Lennon: No.

Peter Charleton: You think those photographs with that detail whereby you can read labels at a distance were taken with a disposable throw-away camera?

Kevin Lennon: All I can say to you is this, sir, that any photographs I got were taken by a throw-away disposable camera.

Peter Charleton: Just tell us, what follow up did you do in relation to these photographs when you got them in December '93?

Kevin Lennon: I went to Detective McMahon and I asked him about it, could he get a location, pinpoint a location about it and he said he'll try but he couldn't, he couldn't come across it.

Peter Charleton: How is he supposed to pinpoint a location? We know it's a woman?

Kevin Lennon: Through Ms McGlinchey.

Peter Charleton: Would you agree it's a woman? It has to be a woman who is keeping that two sward and those various bags of perhaps ground-up material or for all we know other military paraphernalia?

Kevin Lennon: I agree now from what you say to me now.

Peter Charleton: Superintendent, you are a highly intelligent man, you must have known at the time this was a lady's bedroom that you were looking at?

Kevin Lennon: To be honest with you, sir, I didn't even consider it.

Peter Charleton: You didn't consider it?

Kevin Lennon: No, because I didn't look at that aspect so closely and unfortunately I didn't.

Peter Charleton: Aren't these photographs that prove that somebody took photographs of this material in place in the bedroom, not in the bathroom, thereby exploding the myth that these materials were confined to the bathroom on the official Garda search on the night of 14 March 1994?

Kevin Lennon: Well, first of all, photographs weren't taken that I know of on the 14th March 1994, but them photographs were taken which do show materials in a bedroom, yes.

Peter Charleton: Did you figure it was a bedroom?

Kevin Lennon: It's quite clear it's a bedroom, yes.

Peter Charleton: But it's not quite clear that whoever uses the bedroom spends a great deal of time lathering their body and doing their hair?

Kevin Lennon: Well that wasn't a consideration that I looked at at the time.

Peter Charleton: Why weren't headquarters informed then?

Kevin Lennon: Well, it wasn't by any deliberate neglectful position, I was just waiting to see would anything develop out of all this.

Peter Charleton: So headquarters weren't informed about the rocket, they weren't informed about the vial of HME, ground-down fertiliser, and they weren't informed of the photographs emanating from McGlinchey?

Kevin Lennon: No, sir.

Peter Charleton: But you had the photographs?

Kevin Lennon: Yeah.

Peter Charleton: You couldn't say it was up to somebody else to report them, you had them and you put them in your locker?

Kevin Lennon: I had some photographs but there were other photographs produced to me, I just want to clarify that, by the Carty Team that were in a press that didn't belong to me at all. In any event, them ones, yes, I accept them, yeah.

Peter Charleton: Why not send up photographs such as that to Garda headquarters, indicating the source of same in terms of the information that you give them and asking them for directions, someone's bedroom stuffed full of explosive in the course of preparation. Would you think it would be of no interest to them?

Kevin Lennon: I was of the view they couldn't do much about it because they was only photographs at the end of the day, but at the same time perhaps I should have done it and I didn't do it, but for no deliberate reason I didn't do it.

Peter Charleton: Do you think these photographs were taken with a disposable camera?

Kevin Lennon: That's what I was told, sir, yeah.

Peter Charleton: I am not entitled to give evidence and I am not entitled to contradict that, but do you not think they are very high quality photographs in terms of one's ability to read writing on bottles, to look at patterns of wallpaper?

Kevin Lennon: Yeah, I agree they are quite high quality, but I haven't a clue about photography, sir, to be honest, I'm not into photography and I don't know anything about it.

Peter Charleton: Those photographs I showed you are marked APP 55?

Kevin Lennon: I don't know anything about photography or the quality of photographs in terms of that position.

Peter Charleton: Did you ever get photographs that Ms McGlinchey took where she is photographed in her car and she looks like a blur?

Kevin Lennon: Yeah.

Peter Charleton: In the darkness?

Kevin Lennon: Yes, sir. I don't know what those photographs are about and I don't know where they came about.

Peter Charleton: What other photographs did you get?

Kevin Lennon: I got some photographs, let's see, what other ones I got? I got them anyway and I don't know if I got the ones about the car. I got a number of photographs off her and I did get, a what do you call it, you know the thing that develops after developing the photographs? What is it? A negative at one stage and I got them developed, it happened to be a family album.

Peter Charleton: Would you look at this, it's called 272? There, for example, is a photograph of Ms McGlinchey in her car?

Kevin Lennon: Yes, sir.

Peter Charleton: You can just about make out her shape and the fact that she has an eye and an nose and nothing else?

Kevin Lennon: Yeah.

Peter Charleton: Was this in your possession ever?

Kevin Lennon: Yeah, that was in the room or in the locker or in the room or...(INTERJECTION)

Peter Charleton: I know, that has been proven, but I am asking you, did you ever have it in your possession or is it a mistake that someone found it among your other personal effects that we have been going through?

Kevin Lennon: No, I'm not saying that is — I presume that is one of the albums, yes.

Peter Charleton: So you did have this in your possession?

Kevin Lennon: Yeah, I'll accept I had that, yes.

Peter Charleton: What explanation was given to you when she was showing you this photograph of herself in the car, this extraordinarily bad quality, grey photograph?

Kevin Lennon: She didn't tell me who took it or anything and I couldn't put a position on it. I think it was with Detective McMahon I discussed it.

Peter Charleton: What is this next thing, which is a whole load of bags of white material sitting up, apparently in an attic?

Kevin Lennon: That photograph was given to me all right.

Peter Charleton: And?

Kevin Lennon: And I couldn't identify the location in it.

Peter Charleton: So now you have two locations, you have somebody's bedroom with shampoo and lotions?

Kevin Lennon: Yes, sir.

Peter Charleton: And you have what is obviously an attic from the quantity of pipes?

Kevin Lennon: Yes.

Peter Charleton: And the fact that there is roof-type struts going up with felt material between the roof struts?

Kevin Lennon: Yes, and I asked Detective McMahon about them, could we develop it out to see where that place was, with Ms McGlinchey. He said that was a long time ago, that stuff was gone, sure I couldn't put it any further.

Peter Charleton: Here is clearly someone's domestic situation, it's a stairs?

Kevin Lennon: Yes.

Peter Charleton: And there is a huge bag of fertiliser sitting at the bottom of the stairs, which is not the ordinary thing you find in someone's home or flat?

Kevin Lennon: Yes, sir.

Peter Charleton: You got this as well?

Kevin Lennon: I got that as well, yeah.

Peter Charleton: It's all part of the same album?

Kevin Lennon: Yes, it is, yes. That was given to me in a disposable camera, yes.

Peter Charleton: Who is EM?

Kevin Lennon: It must be someone in headquarters, I'd say.

Peter Charleton: It says photographer and it's marked EM?

Kevin Lennon: Earl Maher, the late Earl Maher.

Peter Charleton: He is a deceased member of the Garda photographic section who developed it?

Kevin Lennon: Yes.

Peter Charleton: Did you actually go up to headquarters to give them to him to develop them?

Kevin Lennon: I sent them up, sir, I think.

Peter Charleton: By post?

Kevin Lennon: As far as I remember now.

Peter Charleton: What was your problem then getting these photographs and sending them back to Garda headquarters by post?

Kevin Lennon: Ah, there was done, I didn't do it.

Peter Charleton: Can I ask you to look at this, the last photograph in this album, which is a quantity, perhaps amounting to a ton, I don't know, I can only estimate?

Kevin Lennon: Yes.

Peter Charleton: A number of bags, perhaps freezer bags, one on top of the other, in the corner of an attic, perhaps beside a cistern?

Kevin Lennon: Yes, sir, I see that.

Peter Charleton: Yeah. Well, if there is sugar added into that and you put it into an item that will confine it, such as a beer keg?

Kevin Lennon: Yes.

Peter Charleton: And you add a detonator charge, you have a very powerful explosion?

Kevin Lennon: Yes, sir.

Peter Charleton: Well, are Garda headquarters not entitled to know about that?

Kevin Lennon: Yeah, I suppose they are but I didn't — I put my hands up, I didn't send it up to them.

Peter Charleton: Well, I'm not so much asking you to put your hands up as asking you to consider the following proposition: That the reason Garda headquarters weren't told about these matters is because these were never going to be items of paraphernalia used for the purpose of terrorism, because they were McGlinchey items and you didn't send them up because you knew they were McGlinchey items and you knew of her lack of involvement with a terrorist organisation?

Kevin Lennon: No.

Peter Charleton: I am just putting that proposition to

you, a reasonable man might so conclude, to give you a chance to deal with it?

Kevin Lennon: Yeah, and I accept that could be the position but that is not my mindset or my position on the matter.

Peter Charleton: Did you get this set of photographs then, which I am going on to now, which is APP 54?

Kevin Lennon: Yes, sir.

Peter Charleton: Which mainly consists of photographs of rifles or a rifle?

Kevin Lennon: Yes, sir.

Peter Charleton: For the purpose of the note, it's 252 on the computer, sir, but APP 54 in terms of the hard copy. So, when did McGlinchey give you these?

Kevin Lennon: I got them from Detective McMahon and I got them developed.

Peter Charleton: Right?

Kevin Lennon: Yes, sir.

Peter Charleton: That shows a rifle with a magazine underneath it?

Kevin Lennon: Yes, sir.

Peter Charleton: And if one looks towards the centre of the screen, there is what I presume is a clip-in magazine enabling that rifle to discharge?

Kevin Lennon: Yes.

Peter Charleton: However many bullets are contained within the clip?

Kevin Lennon: Yes. That's a .22 rifle from my estimation of it.

Peter Charleton: Does a .22 rifle often have a clip on it?

Kevin Lennon: Yes, sir.

Peter Charleton: An ammunition clip?

Kevin Lennon: Yes, sir, they can have.

Peter Charleton: That is a training weapon for the IRA?

Kevin Lennon: That is what it was represented to me to be.

Peter Charleton: And then if one goes on three more photographs, one sees a man's foot?

Kevin Lennon: Yes, sir.

Peter Charleton: One side of it?

Kevin Lennon: I seen that, yes.

Peter Charleton: Yeah. Why weren't Garda headquarters told about this rifle?

Kevin Lennon: Well, that was a rifle I was told that we would get in time, that it was a training weapon for the IRA for target practice and that we would get it.

Peter Charleton: You'd get it from whom?

Kevin Lennon: Through Ms McGlinchey, it would be presented to us when the opportunity was right.

Peter Charleton: Can I move on again? This is a different rifle because it has a telescopic sight?

Kevin Lennon: Yes, sir.

Peter Charleton: And I am holding that up on the basis that it will come on the screen shortly?

Kevin Lennon: Yeah.

Peter Charleton: There is a foot beside it?

Kevin Lennon: That's right, sir, yes.

Peter Charleton: There is an addition a flower pot, whereas I suppose people's doorsteps may look somewhat similar, they may also look somewhat dissimilar. Now, did you get these from Adrienne McGlinchey?

Kevin Lennon: Yeah, through Garda McMahon, yes.

Peter Charleton: Who is this second rifle supposed to be belong to?

Kevin Lennon: I thought the two of them were together when they arrived in two separate photographs but anyway, they were two training weapons, supposed to be, for the IRA.

Peter Charleton: They are different from each other, aren't they?

Kevin Lennon: Yes, they appear different, yes.

Peter Charleton: Well?

Kevin Lennon: I don't kow if that's a rifle or a shotgun, I'm not sure of that one there.

Peter Charleton: I don't think shotguns have telescopic sights?

Kevin Lennon: You could put one on one, yes.

Peter Charleton: With what purpose, one might wonder, given the purpose of shot is to spread out endlessly, it's not a precision weapon?

Kevin Lennon: Maybe it's a rifle, I stand to be corrected but it looks like to me a single barrel shotgun.

Peter Charleton: It may look that way to you, I don't see any point at which it breaks. But in any event, let's not worry about that?

Kevin Lennon: Yes, sir.

Peter Charleton: The question is, you got this?

Kevin Lennon: Yeah.

Peter Charleton: It was in the context of Adrienne McGlinchey, again being able to take photographs of train-ing weapons?

Kevin Lennon: Yes, sir.

Peter Charleton: In what circumstances was she able to take photographs of IRA training weapons, to go around with a disposable camera in her bag and apparently whip it out and flash off a few photographs where the IRA are, I don't know, out asleep, having coffee, but certainly not paying any attention to her?

Kevin Lennon: I was told that they were supposed to be in a hide and that she was able to know where they were kept for training purposes and that she was afraid to hand them over because if she did, they'd know she'd come across them.

Peter Charleton: If she was to even lend them to Detective Garda McMahon or to yourself, she might never get them back. Why weren't Garda headquarters told about that?

Kevin Lennon: The reason being that I was intent that we would get them in terms of what their usage was and then you could do something about them.

Peter Charleton: What would you do about them?

Kevin Lennon: You'd several options, sir, about them. You could bug them.

Peter Charleton: You could what?

Kevin Lennon: Bug them, sir, put a device in them.

Peter Charleton: Bug them, yes, I am sorry, I just didn't catch that?

Kevin Lennon: Yes, and track them.

Peter Charleton: Yes?

Kevin Lennon: So that was my intention, that we would do that if we got them.

Peter Charleton: Did you have bugs in Donegal or did you have to call in assistance from Garda headquarters in that respect?

Kevin Lennon: I could have got them very easily, yes.

Peter Charleton: From headquarters?

Kevin Lennon: Yes.

Peter Charleton: Yeah.

Kevin Lennon: And that would be the intention to do that. I think that would lead you to whoever was using them.

Peter Charleton: Did you ask Adrienne McGlinchey, could you please lend me your rifle?

Kevin Lennon: Yeah.

Peter Charleton: You bug them by what, by drilling into the stock?

Kevin Lennon: No, you take the stock off, sir, and put the tracking device in them.

Peter Charleton: Underneath the barrel?

Kevin Lennon: In behind the...(INTERJECTION)

Peter Charleton: The mechanism?

Kevin Lennon: Yes, the stock.

Peter Charleton: Yes?

Kevin Lennon: Yes, sir.

Peter Charleton: But she wasn't forthcoming with the rifles?

Kevin Lennon: No, sir, but I didn't tell her what I was going to do with them if I got them.

Peter Charleton: She might have presumed that you were going to keep them and not give them back to her?

Kevin Lennon: Well, no, that wasn't my intention anyway.

Peter Charleton: And then what about these photograph here of a radio or walkie-talkie type device sitting on a large white plastic bag, the markings on which I can't read?

Kevin Lennon: Yeah, well I never seen her with a radio and I don't know what that is about to be honest with you but that was one of the photographs presented.

Peter Charleton: You see, could I ask you this: In detective work you look for distinctive things and here's a distinctive bag and here is an item, which perhaps could be identified by an expert in headquarters, you have the combination of the two things, if you found the bag was sold, would it be possible to find out perhaps the kind of customers who would go into that place and maybe narrow down the search even a little bit further?

Kevin Lennon: Yes, but I don't think you could enhance that bag to read the writing on it, that was my view of it.

Peter Charleton: But you didn't send it to headquarters?

Kevin Lennon: No, sir, I didn't, no.

Peter Charleton: Again I have to put the proposition to you that a reasonable man might conclude, given the lack of communication in the ordinary way with headquarters about matters that were coming specifically to you, that this indicates a determination not to let headquarters know about something because you have a guilty conscience about it?

Kevin Lennon: No, sir, I have no guilty conscience about anything.

Peter Charleton: All right?

Kevin Lennon: I done it that way, sir. I hoped that I would be led to the sources of these things and I bona fide believed that and I believe that the source was good and that down the road that it would develop into a process where all these things would be achieved and found and possibly people with them.

Peter Charleton: And then did you get this set of photographs, which is APP 68, small photographs of extra-ordinarily poor quality, showing a landscape and a river, which I assume is the Finn River but I don't know?

Kevin Lennon: I can't see them from here.

Peter Charleton: Can I ask Mr Fogarty to pass them to you. I think Mr Maguire will try and get them on the screen. It's book 252, appendix 68.

Kevin Lennon: No, sir, they aren't my photographs.

Peter Charleton: Did you ever see those before?

Kevin Lennon: No, sir, and I'll tell you why. I think they were found in the press in room 207 and they are not my photographs. They were there before my time. I understand that Ms McGlinchey did give to Detective Garda Kelly and Detective Garda McMahon some photographs of military installations and that they sent in some intelligence docu-ments on them, attaching them. But they were not mine, sir, them.

Peter Charleton: Now, can I ask you about what you knew of the interior of the flat of 14th March?

Kevin Lennon: I didn't know anything about it, sir.

Peter Charleton: Nothing?

Kevin Lennon: No, sir.

Peter Charleton: So if the chairman finds, which with all respect to the chairman, he is probably obliged to find that there is a conflict of evidence in relation to this matter, vis-a-vis the first visitors to the flat seeing rockets underneath the bath and underneath the bed, by which I don't know mean a huge amount of rockets, I mean obvi-ously one underneath each or perhaps one in the shadows and one obvious in either location, and they not being found by the Gardaí later on, can you offer any explanation in relation to that?

Kevin Lennon: No, sir, I can't, because I wasn't there and I wasn't a party to the whole day down there, so I mean, I don't know where they went to and I didn't see them. The only rocket-type things I saw was those two ESH 2 and 3's I think they are.

Peter Charleton: Yes. Could I have 1104 on the screen please, and 1104-1 thereafter. This is the telex sent to Garda headquarters. Could I ask you to identify who authorised this sending of this telex to Garda headquarters?

Kevin Lennon: I presume it was — oh, Inspector McMorrow sent that up, that's the authorisation for sending the telex.

Peter Charleton: It says: 'In the course of searching one of the bedrooms in the flat, Gardaí located some plastic bags concealed in a wardrobe.' That accords with our photographs, doesn't it?

Kevin Lennon: It does, sir, yes.

Peter Charleton: 'The following items were located: 37 X 5 pounds plastic bags, containing a white substance believed to be a mixture of fertiliser and icing sugar. 2 X 1 hundred weight of Maxi Sward fertiliser.'

19

Quis Custodiet Ipsos Custodes?

The security of the State and the national interest are phrases bandied about by civil service mandarins who serve to protect the nation. Within the Garda Síochána, a select group of Gardaí operate from Crime & Security, working to maintain our security and national welfare. Many Garda Commissioners since the 1970s have had associations with Crime & Security. Noel Conroy, Pat Byrne, Eugene Crowley, Lawrence Wren and Ned Garvey all came from this background. Crime & Security was the way to get noticed.

Items of so-called intelligence submitted by Gardaí to Crime & Security have been deemed to be so secretive that the contents of these were never divulged in public at the Morris Tribunal. Occasionally, when a Garda witness tried to back up his story he referred to the submission of his C77. Protocols were established to ensure the disclosure of C77s in private session, but the public have been sheltered from the revelations of 'intelligence' gathered by law enforcers across the country. The only hint of what went on behind closed doors comes in the final report, when Justice Morris called for an independent audit of Crime & Security.

These so-called elite members of the closed shop are often referred to as the 'spooks' in fiction thrillers. By all accounts their arrival at the Tribunal was spooky at times.

One could tell they were not of ordinary Garda standing. In Garda-speak, their mechanically propelled vehicles ground to a stationary halt outside the main door as they unloaded the State secrets, which they guardedly carried, casting furtive glances at all suspects in their peripheral vision, most of them barristers unravelling Garda corruption. Dapper and smart in clean cut suits with matching clean cut close shaves, they had the appearance of men who had studied the mannerisms of agents in the hallowed halls of Quantico. In the initial stages of the Tribunal, as they waited for public sessions to end, their briefcases containing the top secrets of An Garda Síochána remained chained and locked to their wrists. The threat posed to the State was taken very seriously.

For most of the time at the Tribunal, Karen and Adrienne were the only people in the public gallery with the exception at times of a witness waiting to be called. Crime & Security would take no chances that the thick piles of reports about the PIRA activist, bomb manufacturer and informer might fall into the hands of 'Shorty' the phantom Provo.

Justice Morris in his conclusion found that Adrienne had never been a member of the IRA or a genuine informer, which raises the question about what exactly was going on in private session that the Gardaí did not want the public to know. For her part, Adrienne repeatedly said she had nothing to hide and wanted all evidence heard in public. The extent of the involvement of foreign agencies in the New York trip was never made public. The extent of the involvement of Crime & Security was never made public. For the most part the evidence about the American trip was heard in closed private session. Leprechauns in

New York selling bags and making a few quid would hardly constitute a breach of State security. Or would it?

The political animal will wait to see how the wind is blowing before making public pronouncements. During the course of the Tribunal, Karen and Adrienne met Dr James McDaid, the Letterkenny-based TD and then junior minister in the Department of Transport at the airport on their way home one weekend. Dr McDaid was on his way to a meeting. Pleasant as always, he made small talk but when invited by the girls to come to the Tribunal, he shuddered at the thought. He declined their invitation to visit the Tribunal inquiring into the conduct of the Gardaí in his constituency.

Most people were surprised to see Dr McDaid posing happily with Kevin Lennon while the superintendent was giving his evidence to the Tribunal. The two were spotted at a GAA function in Donegal, and the picture made the front page of the *Donegal Democrat*.

More surprising was the junior minister's public response to the Morris report, when he asserted that only a small number of Gardaí were involved in corruption and lies. Seventeen Gardaí — including two former heads of the Donegal division and senior superintendents — were found to have been either negligent or lying or corrupt. McDaid's statement stood in stark contrast to Minister for Justice Michael McDowell's worries that there could be 'worse to come'.

Justice Morris concluded that 'it is certain that as corruption in the form of deceit, the abuse of investigations through inventions against suspected criminals and bribery have arisen in other police forces, they will also occur within An Garda Síochána.'

There will always be ambitious Guards who want to move on to bigger and better prospects. An Garda Síochána have vast powers, and with them comes the danger of using and abusing citizens. As long as Gardaí can submit anonymous secret bulletins to be filed away on C77 forms at Crime & Security Branch, there is always the possibility of creating another 'Donegal', another phantom terrorist threat. If the Tribunal showed nothing else, it demonstrated that what passes for intelligence gathering within An Garda Síochána is often derived from little more than gossip and rumour.

Gardaí have perfected the art of manipulating people and the unfortunate circumstances of their families over many decades. The high profile of the McGlinchey family and their well-publicised marital separation was consistently used by various Gardaí to peddle to one side of the family or the other the lies orchestrated by Lennon, McMahon and other members. Reports to headquarters generally included background such as 'Adrienne McGlinchey is a daughter of Bernard McGlinchey who operates the Golden Grill, a well known place of entertainment in Letterkenny. He is also a Fianna Fáil County and Urban District Councillor for that area.' The brief biographical details added nothing to the reports, but the aura of a businessman and senator's name acted subliminally to impress readers and give authority to the profile of the suspect.

In an effort to save their skins several Gardaí gave remarkable evidence. Kevin Lennon memorably gave evidence to the effect that he was willing to see Adrienne executed by the IRA if it meant taking large caches of explosives out of commission. Noel McMahon's view that 'an informer anywhere along the border is regarded as probably the lowest form of life, even lower than a drug pusher' may not come from Garda manuals but it remains immersed in our long and deep-seated national history.

Files relating to the explosives module were submitted to the Director of Public Prosecutions. Before Justice Morris published his report, he asked An Garda Síochána what prosecutions were planned, in case the report might prejudice criminal proceedings. They replied with a summary of investigations. No one will be prosecuted as a result of any of the bogus explosives finds the Tribunal investigated. Noel McMahon will not be prosecuted over alleged assaults the Tribunal heard about, or for possession of the cannabis, explosive powder and ammunition found when the Carty inquiry team searched his home. A direction is still awaited from the DPP on whether Kevin Lennon will be prosecuted over alleged misappropriation of funds resulting from materials found in the 'Lennon locker'. As of July 2004 a file was still being prepared as a result of issues arising out of the Shortt Miscarriage of Justice case in 2002.

During the course of her evidence, Adrienne gave some insight into the level of knowledge Gardaí in Buncrana had during her years of involvement with Lennon and McMahon.

> Charleton: Can I suggest this to you: A reasonable person might conclude from all of this, that you can do something at the behest of Noel McMahon once, twice, maybe ten times, but when it comes to fifty times of running around with electrical components, finding yourselves arrested, doing all the things that you have told about angle grinders, welding machines, pinning up black plastic bags over the windows of your flat, a reasonable person might conclude, this woman was simply being mischievous and drawing attention to herself, in other words she was playing with the Gardaí, making fun of them. What have you got to say about that?
>
> Adrienne: Well, if I was a Guard I would probably say the same thing. But they did not know at the beginning,

because I know, half of Buncrana Garda station knew exactly what was going on and they knew all them times, them finds, that Noel McMahon and Kevin Lennon and I were doing it. Will one of them sit up here and say that now?

Chairman: How do you mean that, half?

Adrienne: They all knew.

Chairman: All knew what?

Adrienne: They all knew we were planting the stuff. They all knew what was going on. They have come to me afterwards. In 1997 I was stopped by a Guard: 'Oh, you got Lennon promoted. You and Lennon, McMahon, all planting the fertiliser. Every one of them knew.'

Chairman: I just want you to clarify something for me. When you say everybody in the Garda station knew what was going on or half the people in the Garda station knew what was going on, what is it that you say they knew?

Adrienne: They knew that my flat was being used by Kevin Lennon and Noel McMahon. At the beginning they did not know, I do not know what they knew, but I know when that fertiliser and that icing sugar was being ground in my flat, half of them Guards knew. That is what I am saying.

Chairman: Knew that your flat was being used?

Adrienne: That we were making the stuff and that we were making it up in Noel McMahon's house. They all knew. Everybody knew what was going on. Tom Long sat up here the last day and he was, if I remember rightly, he was questioned, why did he say something to Sheenagh McMahon. Why did he write down? Because they all knew, everybody knew and they did not care what was going on.

Everybody turned their back and everybody is saying: 'Oh, we couldn't do nothing.' Well, they were Guards too, they should have stopped them doing what they were doing to people like me. I am sorry.

Chairman: How would they have known? How do you think they would have known?

Adrienne: We were right on the street, Noel McMahon was carrying bags of fertiliser into my flat. They were carrying stuff, we were making it in the flat. It was going off all day, he could do what he wanted in the Garda station. He would tell me to get arrested, get back out again in a half an hour. They all knew, everybody knew. Somebody can sit here and form an opinion about something, why don't they say they knew? Just one person say they knew. That is my opinion, sorry.

Mr Charleton: Who do you think knew? It is all very well to say half the Gardaí in Donegal. For example, you are giving testimony and the chairman is very happy to receive the testimony I am sure but you have said something there, like a Guard stopped you in 1997 and said: Ah, you are the woman who got Kevin Lennon promoted to Superintendent.

Adrienne: Yes. He made a lot of money out of you, to be specific in what he said. They used you for their own gains. Detective Sergeant Tom Sreenan outside the ESB in Letterkenny, and I contacted Noel McMahon and I said to Noel, how many of them knew? And Noel McMahon said to me, now I must be specific, 1997, 1998, his answer was: 'We will get his pension taken off him.' All I am saying here, it is embarrassing for me to say what I done, I ground fertiliser and I did all these things. But they were the law and they sat back and they didn't care. Yes, there was Guards, there was Tom Sreenan and Noel Jones, who went up to Ballyliffin, they all knew, they knew that we were using a surveillance van, they knew there was Garda cars being used. They were up in my shed, different Guards, there was 20 bags of fertiliser sitting in the shed, why has nobody wrote a statement about that?'

The full cost of the Carty Inquiry and Morris Tribunal is not yet known. Without reform, the unsatisfactory situation of Guards investigating Guards will continue behind closed doors. Internal Garda inquiries will be held where members are the judge and jury of their colleagues. If Gardaí continue to cover for their corrupt colleagues, and continue to tell lies, more money will end up in inquiries. The Kerry Babies Tribunal looked at Garda activities a generation ago. The Morris and Barr Tribunals are looking at them today. Without reform, there will be more expensive Tribunals.

In the USA, high profile Senate Committees can compel witnesses to appear. The Irish public purse will be drained of much needed resources until Dáil committees are given the power to carry out similarly unimpeded inquiries.

The mission statement of An Garda Síochána is 'To achieve the highest level of Personal Protection, Community Commitment and State Security'. But as long as Gardaí believe in closing ranks to protect their colleagues, corruption will continue to flourish in An Garda Síochána.

Adrienne has moved on. There is no point in bitterness. She gave her evidence, and freed herself from the past. In the end, she had a simple story to tell. It was a story of one woman's mistake, which led to her being exploited by rogue members of An Garda Síochána. For their own self-interest they persecuted and blackmailed her for over eight years. It was a story of charades. It was a story of being in the wrong place at the wrong time, of being passed off as a highly-placed informer, courier, bomb manufacturer and the lover of senior IRA operatives. It was a story of abuse of the Secret Service funds for personal Garda use. It was the story of long nights preparing tons of homemade explosives at the behest of the Superintendent Kevin Lennon and Detective Garda Noel McMahon.

It was a story of cover up. It was a story of lies by Guards who swore to uphold the law and to tell the truth, the whole truth and nothing but the truth.

It was a story of how senior Garda management failed to follow basic procedures, allowing the charade to continue. It was a story of the extension of the charade to involve the police force of Northern Ireland and the FBI in America.

It was the story of how a blind eye was turned to the illegal activities of Guards in Donegal, and a story of the bullying and fear that was prevalent among the force at the time. It was the story of the rise of Kevin Lennon from traffic corps sergeant in 1992 to Superintendent in 1996. It was the story of alcoholism and brutality, beatings and misery perpetrated by Detective Garda Noel McMahon on Adrienne McGlinchey.

This was the story of Adrienne McGlinchey, who faced her accusers and told the truth. She faced the State and said 'Yes, I did it, but I did it with Superintendent Kevin Lennon and Detective Garda Noel McMahon.'

In the end, she was vindicated.